PELICAN BOOKS

THE ANCIENT KINGDOMS OF MEXICO

Nigel Davies was born in 1920 and educated at Eton. He was Conservative M.P. for Epping from 1951, where he succeeded to part of Winston Churchill's wartime constituency. In 1962 he settled in Mexico City, where he studied at the National University of Mexico, and he took his doctorate in archaeology at London University. He now devotes himself to writing and lecturing on ancient America, and is the author of *The Aztecs* (1973), *The Toltecs* (1977), *The Toltec Heritage* (1979), *Voyagers of the New World: Fact and Fantasy* (1979) and *Human Sacrifice* (1981).

In 1980 the President of Mexico awarded Nigel Davies the prestigious Order of the Aztec Eagle for his contribution to Mexican culture.

D1006985

NIGEL DAVIES

THE
ANCIENT KINGDOMS
OF
MEXICO

PENGUIN BOOKS

Penguin Books Ltd, Harmondsworth, Middlesex, England
Viking Penguin Inc., 40 West 23rd Street, New York, New York 10010, U.S.A.
Penguin Books Australia Ltd, Ringwood, Victoria, Australia
Penguin Books Canada Ltd, 2801 John Street, Markham, Ontario, Canada L3R 1B4
Penguin Books (N.Z.) Ltd, 182–190 Wairau Road, Auckland 10, New Zealand

First published by Allen Lane 1982
Published in Pelican Books 1983
Reprinted 1985

Copyright © Nigel Davies, 1982
All rights reserved

Printed and bound in Great Britain by
Cox & Wyman Ltd, Reading
Set in Linotron Palatino

CONTENTS

LIST OF PLATES

PREFACE

In my book *The Aztecs* and in two volumes on the Toltecs, I covered the limited period for which we have written data on Ancient Mexico in the form of codices and chronicles.

I felt an obvious urge at this point to go back further and complete the picture by providing for the general reader a synthesis of pre-Hispanic Mexico's history and culture from the birth of higher civilization in about 1500 B.C. until its destruction soon after A.D. 1500.

Many books have been written on the final era, dominated by the Aztecs, and a few on the first, initiated by the Olmecs. My previous study of the Toltecs was on a more technical level and little has been written in plainer language of the intermediate centuries from A.D. 0 to 1300, during which first Teotihuacan, and then Tula, the Toltec capital, played a paramount role.

To relate the story, and to make a continuous narrative, I have concentrated on these four ecumenical cultures, whose traces are found all over Mexico and in some cases beyond: Olmecs, Teotihuacan, Tula and Aztecs. A basic knowledge of their achievements may serve as a backcloth, against which Ancient Mexico as a whole can be seen in clearer perspective. They were not all 'kingdoms' in the strictest sense of the word, but I preferred to use this term in my title rather than 'empires', which would be more apt to mislead.

Other important peoples, whose impact was more regional than universal, clearly have to be taken into account. However, if I had tried to do them full justice in a single volume, the result would have been disjointed and lengthy. In the short bibliography for each period, a few works are given that deal in more detail with certain regional cultures, such as that of Oaxaca.

Equally, while the Mayas are frequently mentioned in the context of their relations with the rest of Mexico, they are not themselves the subject of this book. Several admirable general accounts of the Maya land exist. And while its civilization is interlocked with that of Central Mexico, it none the less remains a theme requiring separate treatment.

My book is a history in the broadest sense, in so far as it follows a chronological order. However, in conformity with modern trends, it is not just a tale of kings and princes, but also offers a summary of what is known of each community as a whole, describing, where possible, peoples' beliefs, art, houses, food and general way of life; special attention has been paid to economic and other changes that took place from one era to the next.

In dealing with Nahuatl texts, I was once more helped by the late Thelma Sullivan; I am also grateful to Evelyn Rattray and other colleagues who read parts of the manuscript.

COMPARATIVE CHRONOLOGY

Based on chart in *America's First Civilization* by Michael Coe

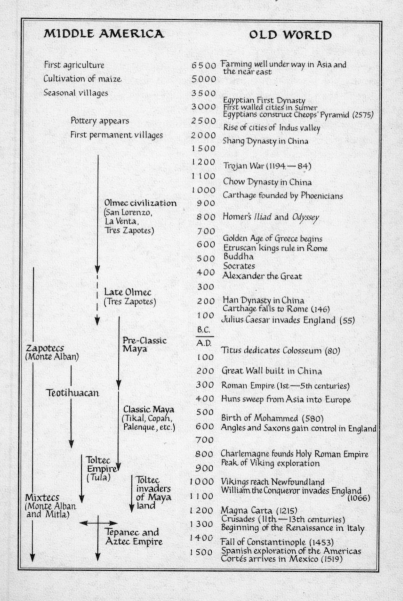

MIDDLE AMERICA		OLD WORLD
First agriculture	6500	Farming well under way in Asia and the near east
Cultivation of maize	5000	
Seasonal villages	3500	
	3000	Egyptian First Dynasty / First walled cities in Sumer
Pottery appears	2500	Egyptians construct Cheops' Pyramid (2575)
First permanent villages	2000	Rise of cities of Indus valley
	1500	Shang Dynasty in China
	1200	Trojan War (1194 — 84)
	1100	Chow Dynasty in China
	1000	Carthage founded by Phoenicians
Olmec civilization (San Lorenzo, La Venta, Tres Zapotes)	900	
	800	Homer's *Iliad* and *Odyssey*
	700	Golden Age of Greece begins
	600	Etruscan kings rule in Rome
	500	Buddha
	400	Socrates / Alexander the Great
Late Olmec (Tres Zapotes)	300	
	200	Han Dynasty in China / Carthage falls to Rome (146)
	100	Julius Caesar invades England (55)
	B.C.	
Zapotecs (Monte Alban) — Pre-Classic Maya	A.D.	
	100	Titus dedicates Colosseum (80)
	200	Great Wall built in China
Teotihuacan	300	Roman Empire (1st — 5th centuries)
	400	Huns sweep from Asia into Europe
Classic Maya (Tikal, Copan, Palenque, etc.)	500	Birth of Mohammed (580)
	600	Angles and Saxons gain control in England
	700	
Toltec Empire (Tula)	800	Charlemagne founds Holy Roman Empire
	900	Peak of Viking exploration
Toltec invaders of Maya land	1000	Vikings reach Newfoundland
	1100	William the Conqueror invades England (1066)
Mixtecs (Monte Alban and Mitla)	1200	Magna Carta (1215)
	1300	Crusades (11th — 13th centuries) / Beginning of the Renaissance in Italy
Tepanec and Aztec Empire	1400	Fall of Constantinople (1453)
	1500	Spanish exploration of the Americas / Cortés arrives in Mexico (1519)

1

BEGINNINGS

To the south of the Bering Strait, the smooth ocean floor is covered by shallow waters. For much of the past seventy thousand years, until the end of the Fourth Ice Age, the sea level fell, at times more than 100 metres, and uncovered a flat sub-continent, joining north-east Asia to north-west America. About twelve thousand years ago, as the ice melted, this land bridge sank beneath the waves for the last time, and will not re-emerge unless the world enters a fifth ice age. It was over this landmass that Man entered America; since climatic conditions were harsh, he probably followed its southern shore, at a latitude more or less corresponding to the present-day Aleutian and Kurule Islands.

The original home of the first migrants is likely to have been in north China, where some of the earliest human remains have been found. None the less, American Man is not a typical Mongol, and his skin is coppery rather than yellow; clearly his ancestors included men of other races, also present in east Asia; some of these were dark-skinned Negroids, while others were the fairer and more hairy Caucasoids. Descendants of such Negroids are still to be found in the remoter parts of several countries bordering the Indian Ocean, while the Ainus of northern Japan and certain east Siberian tribes are basically Caucasian. A medley of physical types thus existed in America, though a Mongoloid veneer overlays the majority with their straight black locks, smooth hairless bodies and high cheekbones.

Prehistoric sites rival each other as to which can produce the earliest radiocarbon date for Man in the New World, though one day a more definitive answer to the question will surely be given. Among the oldest authenticated dates are those of Old Crow in the Yukon Territory of north-west Canada, where the most recent tests yield a figure in excess of forty thousand years before the present, but this is not likely to be the final solution; comparable dating of human remains also comes from Santa Rosa Island, lying off the west coast of Southern California.

The first Americans consisted of tiny bands of hunters, who came in successive waves over the course of fifty thousand years. The journey was less a migration than an overspill across the subcontinent of Beringia, which offered few obstacles to their passage. They simply followed the animals that had moved into America aeons before them, and their prey included reindeer, moose and horse, together with the giants of the animal kingdom, the mammoth, mastodon and bison. As they trekked onwards, little did these arctic hunters know that they would one day reach the tropics, whence their Asian forbears had moved northwards many thousands of years before.

No one knows exactly when these early migrants first reached Mexico, though their presence in 21,000 B.C. in Tlapacoya, near Mexico City, is indicated by radiocarbon test. In this region Man found a rich variety of plant life at his disposal, and he was able to obtain a much more varied diet than he had enjoyed farther north. But while more vegetable food was available, many of the larger beasts, including the mammoth, horse and camel, eventually became extinct; however, others such as dogs, cats, deer and hares survived and helped to enrich his fare, together with rodents and grubs, of which large quantities were eaten.

Mexico, where so many migrants into the New World were to make their home, was far from being a homogeneous territory like, say, Spain or Italy, divided from its neighbours by mountains and enjoying a uniform climate, with only gradual changes as one moved from north to south.

In contrast, the many ranges of Mexico tend to split the country into countless smaller valleys, each of which forms a world of its own. Such mountain barriers do not act as a frontier, like the Pyrenees or the Alps, and do not therefore serve to shield the more civilized south and centre from the great dry plains of the north that stretch from the 22nd parallel to the U.S. border and beyond. This was a key factor in the history of Ancient Mexico, whose central highlands were never free from pressure by nomads who roamed the arid north-west and whose way of life when the Spaniards came still recalled those early hunters who had crossed over from Asia.

Mexico moreover differed from most of the Old World in that, like much of South America, its geography is three-dimensional: climate depends less on whether one travels north or south than on the altitude of a given place, and conditions can vary greatly over short distances. Today, for instance, on the road to Veracruz from Mexico City it takes less than an hour to drive from bleak highland to lush lowland scenery; at Christmas-time people from Mexico City may leave artificially heated homes and after a thirty-minute flight reach Acapulco, where their hotel has to be air-conditioned. These climatic contrasts are also basic to Mexican history; the marked difference between temperate highlands and tropical coast acted as a spur, first to trade, and later to conquest. Higher civilization, as we shall see, probably first flourished on the coast; great cultures later emerged in the highlands, but much of their religion rested on tropical traditions and its observance required a whole array of coastal products, such as gaudy feathers and jaguar skins. Therefore those who lived in the Central Plateau, themselves under pressure from the arid north-west, felt a constant urge to penetrate the coastal tropics.

Another feature of the land was the profusion of edible plants, as compared with the meagre choice of animals that could be domesticated. The domestic dog and turkey added little to the average diet and the lack of major sources of animal protein, such as the cow and the pig of the Old World, would affect the economy of the cities that arose in the New. An even greater handicap was the absence of the horse, which could both carry Man himself and serve him as a beast of burden. Hence in a land where the motivation to move from place to place was strong, the means to achieve this end were restricted, and Man had to proceed on his own feet and carry his goods on his own back.

This fragmentation into countless mountain valleys, each with its own mini-ecology, had another effect: these geographical units tended to develop their own languages, and a babel of tongues was spoken, most but not all of which belong to a few major linguistic groups. These languages survived until the Conquest and some are still spoken today. One product of Mexican civilization was a system of glyphic signs for people and places that were common to many regions but were enunciated quite differently in each, in conformity with the local tongue.

Of these many valleys, the large central basin has played the leading role in Mexico in the past and continues to do so, as the seat of today's vast capital city. Known as the Valley of Mexico, it stands at an altitude of 2,200 metres, and is poised midway between the two oceans. Measuring 100 kilometres from north to south and 60 kilometres from east to west, the flat basin is ringed by a great horseshoe of mountains, of which the most spectacular are the snow-capped volcanoes to the east, called the Sierra Nevada. Beyond this Sierra lies the Valley of Puebla, second only in importance to the Valley of Mexico itself. Throughout history, whoever controlled these two basins was well placed to dominate the whole country. Nowadays the countryside in the Valley of Mexico is rather dry and denuded, and that of the Valley of Toluca to the west, 300 metres higher in altitude, is even more so. But when the first settlers arrived both were lush and wooded, and the Valley of Mexico was partly covered by a lagoon until Conquest times.

Even before the large mammals became extinct, the earlier hunters seldom gorged themselves on mammoth stew or barbecued bison. To obtain such fare was a major venture and Man came to rely for his protein-intake more on humbler animals, such as gophers, squirrels and rabbits; the mouse loomed larger in his daily fare than the mastodon. Remnants of mice, charred but complete with bones, show that people swallowed them whole, fur and all.

Much of their food came from plant-gathering, and it was often less trouble to pick fruit and berries than to course endlessly after an antelope. However, plant food had a major snag: supplies were seasonal and the small bands of hunter-gatherers had to be always on the move in order to obtain enough calories to keep alive. This problem was less pressing in the well-watered central valleys, with their abundance of fish and fowl, but it was acute for the people of the Valley of Tehuacán, lying some 200 kilometres south-east of Mexico City towards the Gulf Coast. Nowhere is the contrast more stark than between the luxuriant vegetation of the nearby coastal tropics and the aridity of this valley; nowadays it is covered by cactus and scrub, its tawny surface quilted with patches of vivid green wherever sugar-cane can be grown with the help of irrigation.

Here in these rather forlorn surroundings a forgotten genius made an epoch-making discovery when he learned that by dropping back into the soil some of the seeds he had gathered to eat, he could make a plant grow. This took place in about 6000 B.C. and marked the beginning of a new era in the history of American Man. The avocado pear and some kind of squash were the first to be cultivated, while other staple foods such as maize, chilli and beans still grew wild. Progress was gradual but between 5000 and 3500 B.C. maize and beans were also domesticated, though such crops still formed only about ten per cent of the total diet.

This progress from hunter to farmer has been meticulously charted by Richard McNeish in the course of many gruelling years of work in the dry dusty caves and caverns of the Tehuacán Valley, aided by a formidable team of experts. To obtain clear sequences, over a hundred samples were taken for radiocarbon dating. McNeish and his team were able to identify these first farmers and to make a concise study of their way of life. Not only could their diet be reconstructed from skeletal remains, but the paraphernalia which they left behind shows how they made their tools and even how they cooked their food.

Their day began early: sometimes the men went hunting and might spend a whole week away from their families in pursuit of a large beast. Before departing, the hunters would check the traps set for smaller animals, such as rabbits and mice; a number of specimens of traps have been found by archaeologists; very probably children also were sent from time to time to inspect them, as happens in the country today; children, unencumbered by school lessons, were always a major addition to the labour force.

The women were not expected to walk long distances like the hunters, and one of their main tasks was to tend the crops. Quite often the men also stayed at home to do other important work, such as toolmaking, which was time-consuming. The women naturally did the cooking, and primitive ovens have been found; food was demonstrably on the plain side, though Mexican food in such remote times was already heavily spiced with chilli. Evidence also exists of stomach ailments, and sanitary conditions were far from ideal.

The invention of agriculture had enabled groups to settle in one place, and the first villages date from about 3000 B.C. By this time cotton was also being planted and people were already growing the basic triad of plants, maize, beans and squash that have ever since been the staple foods of the country population. The first maize cobs were only the size of a strawberry; the bean developed somewhat later and made a vital contribution to the diet, as it contains more protein than maize and other plants. Some time after 2500 B.C. the first pottery of Central Mexico appeared; cotton began to be woven into fairly complex designs, though more common weaving materials were strands of yuca or agave plants.

These earlier textiles and ceramics were already used in primitive versions of those rites that were to become so basic to Mexican culture. Even in the older burials in Tehuacán many funerary objects were found, suggestive of quite an elaborate ritual. Some bodies were charred in a way that indicated cannibalism rather than cremation, while their severed heads had been arranged in baskets; from one of these heads the flesh had been scraped and the skull cracked open before being roasted, perhaps in order to cook the brains. Evidence thus exists of early forms of human sacrifice which, like many Middle American rites, has a long history.

As villages grew in size, these spiritual urges gathered force and led to the building of the first temple mounds, another enduring feature of Mexican culture, and to the making of innumerable clay figurines. The second millennium B.C. heralded the initial phase of Mexican civilization, generally called the Pre-Classic. Its other name, the Formative, is apter, since during the period certain enduring patterns were set and the basis laid of that unique creation of human genius in the region usually termed Mesoamerica or Middle America; it shares a complex of definable traits, such as ceremonial centres, human sacrifice, painted codices, a special religious calendar and the ritual ball-game. Though I shall employ more often the term 'Mexican' than 'Middle American', the latter is a better definition. Middle American culture does not follow the limits of modern Mexico; it was not present in its entirety in the arid north; on the other hand, to the south-east it embraces Guatemala and El Salvador, and stretches as far as the frontier between Nicaragua and Costa Rica, where Andean influences from South America predominate.

It was not until 1913 that the leading American anthropologist of his time, Franz Boas, working with the Mexican scholar Manuel Gamio, first identified the three main horizons of Middle America, usually called the Pre-Classic, the Classic and the Post-Classic. The Pre-Classic covers the last two millennia B.C., while the great cultures of the first millennium A.D. belong to the Classic, followed in its turn by the militaristic, or Post-Classic, age that ended with the Conquest.

Boas drew excellent sketches of the many Formative figures that he unearthed, but systematic excavation of this archaic period only began in 1928, when George C. Vaillant made his first dig at Zacatenco, situated just off the highway that leads out of Mexico City to the north; he later worked at Ticomán in the same area.

Vaillant laid the foundation of Formative studies by dividing into types the countless figurines that he found. Both pottery and figurines were mainly found in burials, which included a number of children who had been killed, indicating once more the early presence of human sacrifice.

An outstanding trait of the Formative is its universality, and its

typical figurines reappear all over Middle America. These clay statu-
ettes, mostly female, can still be found in the ground in many places.
Though naked, they have impressive coiffures and headdresses,
often in the form of turbans. We do not know their exact purpose,
though they were certainly linked in some way with fertility and with
the crop cycle.

During this Formative phase small villages grew up on the shores of
the lagoon which then covered much of the Valley of Mexico, and
whose waters still served as a shield to the Aztec capital when the
Spaniards arrived. Such villages imply the presence of more people,
needing more food, and their appearance coincides with a rapid
improvement in the size of maize cobs. The Valley of Mexico was at
that time as blessed by nature as any other region of the New World;
the climate was temperate and the soil rich; its marshes abounded in
water fowl and the wooded hills were well stocked with deer and
other animals. It was ideally suited for the part which it was to play in
Mexican history.

This preponderance evolved only gradually; the Formative remains
of the Valley of Mexico, though better known, were no more
advanced than those of other regions. The role of this central basin,
however, will serve as a connecting link throughout our story, whose
main theme consists of those four successive cultures whose impact
was not regional but universal. Of these, the last three were based
upon the Valley of Mexico, where traces of the first are also plentiful.
By telling their story, as far as it is known, the saga of Ancient Mexico
can be presented as a continuum, rather than as a jumbled assembly
of data.

Of the four cultures which are our principal, but not only, topic, the
first, the Olmec, began some time before 1200 B.C. and grew to
maturity on the distant Caribbean Coast, whence it spread to other
parts of Mexico, including the central valleys. Their role was henceforth pivotal and the second culture, the Classic, that arose in the
early centuries of the Christian era, was dominated by Teotihuacan,
situated on the eastern fringe of the Valley of Mexico. Teotihuacan
influences have been found throughout Mexico and even beyond, in
Guatemala.

Teotihuacan fell in about A.D. 750 and the third people to claim a
certain universality were the Toltecs of Tula, which lay a little to the
north-west of the Valley of Mexico. This Toltec Empire, that
flourished during the eleventh and twelfth centuries of our era, was
centred not only upon Tula, but also upon Culhuacán, situated in the

central valley. Tula had declined by A.D. 1175, but Culhuacán survived and provided a link with the Aztecs, whose rulers claimed to be descended from those of Tula and Culhuacán. Their capital, Tenochtitlan, lay in the very heart of the Valley of Mexico.

The fourth contender for power, the Aztec Empire, came into being in 1428, after all rivals had been defeated, and only lasted until 1521. The lands which the Aztecs were to conquer by force largely coincided with those where Olmec and Teotihuacan influences, more cultural and commercial than military, had been most strongly felt. Archaeologists in recent decades have mapped the traces of these universal cultures in many regions, such as Oaxaca to the south-east, or on the Pacific Coast; the latest studies have also yielded more data on the influences which the Central Plateau brought to bear on the Maya land.

To seek an understanding of these four cultures, one must first study the core region, or heartland, where they first arose. It was here that each evolved, in terms of modern archaeology, its own system, or pattern of life, that differed in a number of ways from that of its forerunners.

The influence of these successive cultures, or systems, varied greatly in intensity from one part of Middle America to another, as we shall see. The degree of intensity did not necessarily depend on distance from the heartland; for instance, the Teotihuacan presence is far more marked in Kaminaljuyu, near Guatemala City, than in the intermediate region of Oaxaca. Hence we are concerned with something more complicated than diffusion in its simplest form, whereby waves of culture are transmitted evenly on all sides, their force merely fading as the distance becomes greater, like the ripples caused by a stone dropped into a pond.

Therefore, two important questions will constantly arise throughout this study: first, the causes which led these key cultures to expand, and to expand more in some directions than in others; second, the reasons for their decline and the underlying changes which accompanied the rise of their successor. These are among the key problems which today face students of Middle America.

2

THE OLMEC ERA

THE DISCOVERY

Notwithstanding the progress made in the arts of weaving and pottery, people throughout Mexico still lived in small villages whose headman was little more than a big fish in a tiny pond, not unlike the mayor of a small town today. In his style of living and his manner of dress, this headman differed little from the rest of the community. Similar social patterns survive in remote corners of Guatemala and Mexico, where things change little from one generation to the next, and ceremonial, ordered by local elders, is all-important.

But towards the end of the second millennium B.C., an epoch-making step was taken; from the midst of those rustic hamlets arose the first ceremonial centres, adorned with pyramids and palaces, built round plazas tiled with mosaics. Where petty chiefs had claimed obedience, kings now held sway, attended by richly clad warriors and courtiers; fine sculpture and painting took the place of cottage crafts; instead of mere shamanism, elaborate rituals called forth a hierarchy of priests, who became Middle America's first intelligentsia; they recorded the motion of the stars, studied the mysteries of time and space, gaining an esoteric knowledge that raised them above their fellow men. This dramatic advance from tribe to state is comparable to what occurred in the Old World nearly two thousand years earlier, when the first city-states arose in Mesopotamia and the first pharaohs ruled in Egypt. In both instances, in the Old World and the New, about five thousand years had then elapsed since Man first learned to till the soil.

The people who thus transformed the social fabric of Mexico lived in a coastal region which roughly corresponds to the south-east part of the present-day state of Veracruz. In this hot and humid land rubber thrived; hence some fifty years ago its inhabitants were rather arbitrarily named 'Olmecs', which means 'The People of Rubber' in Nahuatl, the language of the Aztecs. The Olmec influence was to spread throughout Mexico and beyond, and their culture is important not only because it was original, but also because it was universal.

The discovery of this pioneer civilization was no sudden or sensational triumph of archaeology. On the contrary, after the first traces of the Olmecs came to light, a long time was to pass before anyone had an inkling of their significance. This is all the more surprising since the first relic to be found was no mere pottery fragment but a colossal stone head, weighing about 20 tonnes.

After the Mayas of the Peten Jungle in Guatemala and of the Yucatán Peninsula in Mexico had been discovered and described by the American explorer John Lloyd Stephens in the 1840s, they reigned supreme for a century as the founders of Mexican civilization. The popular imagination was fired by the finding of city after city buried deep in the Peten and for a hundred years scholars and laymen alike remained convinced that nothing earlier or better could conceivably have existed. Peru is a parallel case: the Chavin civilization is now known to have been roughly contemporary with the Olmec and to have played the same pioneering role. But for a long time after Chavin was first discovered, archaeologists insisted that it could not possibly be the original culture of Peru, because it was so sophisticated.

The first Olmec head was discovered by José María Melgar as early as 1862, a bare twenty years after Stephens published his *magnum opus* on the Maya. However, for a long time the Olmecs were not even given a name, and they only came into their own much later, when their true place in history was finally recognized in the 1940s. In drawing attention to the stone head, whose Negroid features bore no relation to any known Maya object, Melgar had no thought of revealing a new culture, but merely sought support for theories about Negro voyagers who had visited America. The head was not in fact the first Olmec object to be discovered. A small mask had belonged to the collection of the kings of Bavaria since the mid-eighteenth century, but gold embellishments were added and it was taken to be a Hindu piece.

After Melgar, the Olmecs were once more relegated to oblivion, broken only by a visit by the greatest of all students of Ancient America, the German Eduard Seler, who in 1905 went to inspect this singular head. Seler, with rare intuition, was the first to suggest that such pieces were the product of a more universal culture, rather than a regional peculiarity confined to a small stretch of the Gulf Coast. More Olmec objects had by this time been found, including a stela from Alvarado, but they attracted little comment.

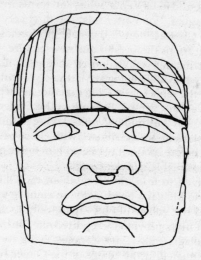

Figure 1. Colossal head from San Lorenzo

La Venta, later to become the most important Olmec site, was first discovered in 1925 by the Danish anthropologist Franz Blom, accompanied by a young American, Oliver La Farge. They unearthed a second colossal head, together with six other large stone objects, including a stela and an altar, all carved in a strange but unmistakable style. Like the earlier discoverers, they tended to underestimate the importance of what they had found, since they too were obsessed with the idea that the Maya was the parent culture of Mexico and that these carvings, therefore, had to be Maya. Notwithstanding its most un-Maya aspect, they still insisted that the large stone altar (known as Altar 4) had 'a strong Maya feeling'. None the less, four years later Marshall H. Saville, director of the Museum of the American Indian in New York, took a more independent view; in a paper published in 1929, he treated these finds as a new culture to which he gave the name 'Olmec', by which it has been known ever since.

Olmec, so far confined to the steamy coast of southern Veracruz, was soon to assume a new dimension. George Vaillant, at that time Curator of the American Museum of Natural History in New York, began in 1928 his study of village sites on the outskirts of Mexico City, and was astonished when he dug up a small jade earring of a crouching beast, half-human and half-jaguar, that exactly recalled what Blom had found in La Venta, whose art forms were imbued with the cult of the jaguar. Soon after this, the discovery of Olmec-type rock carvings at Chalcatzingo in the state of Morelos confirmed the pan-Mexican nature of the mysterious new culture.

The suspicion that this was an entirely distinct civilization was only fully confirmed when archaeologist Matthew W. Stirling entered the field and played the same role in Olmec studies as Stephens had done for the Maya a century before. To work in the Olmec heartland, the Land of Rubber, was a formidable undertaking in those days, before the archaeologist could protect himself with effective insecticides and antibiotics, and before modern roads led him to his goal, set deep in remote and inhospitable surroundings.

Stirling, resolved to find out more about the Olmecs, began his quest by a visit to Melgar's head. After an eight-hour ride on horse-back he reached the village of Hueyapan, only to discover that the carving was not in its previously reported site, but was to be found near another village, called Tres Zapotes, lying to the west of the Tuxtla Range, situated in the centre of the Olmec heartland.

His search for the head had led Stirling to an Olmec site of the utmost importance, containing a number of great earth mounds in which he dug during 1939 and 1940. On 16 January 1939 he made an epoch-making discovery: at the base of the largest of these Tres Zapotes mounds he found a stela (Stela C) with a vertical row of bar-and-dot numbers, apparently giving a date in the method used by the Mayas. But on the opposite side of the stone was a highly stylized jaguar mask, typically Olmec. Stirling was astonished to learn that, according to his reading of the numbers on the stone, they recorded a date some 260 years older than the earliest carved on any monument from a Maya site.

Matters were now brought to a head, once this Olmec-type stela had been found in an Olmec site, situated far to the west of the Maya land, and ostensibly much older than any dated Maya monument. Opposing schools of thought argued the matter, and two leading Mexican scholars were bold enough to espouse the Olmec cause and insist that they, not the Maya, were the 'mother culture' of Mexico. The first of these was Alfonso Caso, famous above all for his excavation of Monte Alban; the second was the art historian Miguel Covarrubias, who by then had amassed his own hoard of Olmec pieces, coming both from the Caribbean Coast and from Highland Mexico. At the same time, however, Maya specialists still maintained that the new finds were nothing but an offshoot of that civilization.

Meanwhile, Stirling had also worked in La Venta, where he made important finds in rapid succession. Following these studies of Tres Zapotes and La Venta, the Mexican Anthropological Society held a round-table conference in 1942 to discuss the whole problem. By now most experts were prepared to agree that the Olmecs were indeed Mexico's first civilization. However, Eric Thompson, the great Mayanist, fought a last-ditch action on behalf of his chosen tribe, and sought to demolish the Olmec case with unfailing skill and erudition. Though in a minority, Thompson's arguments were so cogent that even Stirling was ready to recant and accept a date of between A.D. 500 and 800 for the fall of La Venta; Thompson himself had proposed A.D. 1200.

The Mayanists, supported by other specialists, were therefore still unrepentant. They only yielded in 1957 in face of a new bombshell, when the University of Michigan laboratory produced a whole series of radiocarbon dates for La Venta, ranging from 800 to 400 B.C. After this, the greater antiquity of the Olmecs became an accepted fact; in 1957 a further set of tests gave dates of from 1160 to 580 B.C. for La Venta and since then even earlier figures have been obtained from other sites. Hence radiocarbon dating has proved fundamental to our understanding of Olmec culture in its home base and of its spread to other regions.

Once the Olmec claim to be the first civilization had been widely recognized, the obvious question arose: who were they and where had they come from? Following the discovery of Olmec remains all over Mexico, on the Pacific as well as the Caribbean side and also in the Central Plateau, some argued that they were a specific tribe, while others viewed them less as a people than an art style, based on a common cult, and adopted in various regions. However, styles as well as peoples must originate somewhere; and the question remained: where?

OLMECS AND UNCLE SAMS

Among the smaller Olmec objects which had by then been found all over Mexico, many represent human beings whose noses are snub and jaguar-like and whose mouths are often deformed into a kind of snarl, sometimes displaying jaguar fangs. This Olmec art form has often been called 'were-jaguar', since it portrays beings half-child and half-feline.

Olmec works of art range from such tiny jade figurines to the huge stone heads found only in the coastal region of southern Veracruz. While these heads have no truly feline traits, thick lips and snub noses are common both to them and to the smaller figures. It is therefore not surprising that their so-called Negroid features led to speculation as to the antecedents of people whose traits seemed un-typical of the American Indians, and revived Melgar's speculations on African migrants.

As Olmec civilization came to be better known, matters were further confused by another discovery: while Negroid features were common in Olmec art, it was found that the Olmecs also portrayed people whose appearance was the very opposite. In addition to the were-jaguar baby face, certain reliefs and statues depict an oldish man, with aquiline nose and goatee beard, sometimes referred to as 'Uncle Sam'. A few Olmec statues show people with slit eyes that are more Chinese than African.

To explain the apparent presence of two different races, one with aquiline and the other with Negroid features, it was first proposed that the Negroids were the masters and the Uncle Sams their slaves. Books were even written setting out to prove that the Negroids were slaves in Phoenician boats, who had mutinied against their owners, some of whom they then brought with them to the New World as their servants.

But while in some cases the Uncle Sams are depicted as naked captives cringing before the overweening presence of a thick-lipped warrior, such theories are untenable because the roles are sometimes reversed; for instance, in the Alvarado Stela a flat-nosed personage is shown as subservient to an aquiline warlord. Moreover, the two types occasionally merge, and elements of both the bearded man and the feline child are embodied in the same person, as in the famous statue known as 'The Wrestler' in the Mexican National Museum, which portrays a man with the Negroid lips of the were-jaguar but with a goatee beard typical of the Uncle Sam type.

In so far as Negroid features are depicted in pre-Columbian art, a more logical explanation surely exists that does not depend upon flights of fancy involving African seafarers. Negroid peoples of many kinds are to be found in Asia as well as Africa, and there is no reason why at least a few of them should not have joined those migrant bands who came across the Bering land bridge that joined north-east Asia and north-west America for so many millennia.

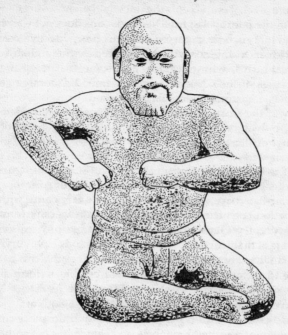

Figure 2. The Wrestler

Small men with Negroid features were the aboriginal inhabitants of many lands facing the Indian Ocean, including India itself, the Malay Peninsula and also the Philippines, where they still exist today. One need go no further than Manila International Airport to find proof of their existence. Nearby stands the Museum of Philippine Traditional Cultures; facing the entrance is a wall covered with photographs of 'unfamiliar faces'. In marked contrast to the typical Mongoloid Filipinos of today, many of these are dark-skinned aboriginals, known as 'Negritos', who now live scattered along the east side of the main island of Luzon; they mostly have thick lips and black skins. The Weddas of Ceylon are another of these Negroid aboriginal groups. It is therefore not in the least surprising that such elements should have joined the ranks of those early migrants who crossed the Bering bridge before it sank beneath the waves; their presence offers a more logical explanation of Negroid features than any other.

Therefore, even if one accepts the uncertain premise that Olmec art is based on the portrayal of true Negroids, this does not warrant the conclusion that such people were Africans. It is perfectly possible to find individuals in Tabasco today who have faces not unlike those of the colossal heads, whose features also somewhat recall the large stone carvings of the Cham culture of Cambodia, another country that still has a Negroid aboriginal population.

Moreover, the smaller Olmec objects represent creatures that are not solely human but part jaguar in varying degrees. Some of these peculiar hybrids have fangs and paws, which are also found in a few of the larger statues. Sometimes an adult Negroid holds in his arms a child that is more markedly jaguar-like than the larger figure. The features of such children are obviously not those of Africans, but of were-jaguars, perhaps inspired by the artist's familiarity with Negroid elements present in Mexico and whose forbears came from Asia.

The apparent presence of the two contrasting physical types in Olmec art is at first sight puzzling and no skeletons have survived in the humid Olmec heartland that might help to clarify this mystery. None the less, the fusion of two different peoples to form a single culture – as we shall see – was a not uncommon feature of Middle American civilization. In what was essentially religious art, the main characteristics of the two types, the aquiline and the more common snub nose, would serve as symbols and therefore tend to be over-emphasized, if not caricatured, just as in later cultures a beard was often used to denote great age, particularly for gods.

Discounting the more romantic notions of an Olmec seaborne migration, doubts persisted as to which part of Mexico was their place of origin, since they were later present in almost every region. The problem has been hotly debated; Miguel Covarrubias became convinced that Olmec civilization first flourished in the state of Guerrero, bordering the Pacific Ocean, but won little support for this view. Others have insisted with equal force that they originally came from Highland Mexico. However, a fairly broad consensus now maintains that their heartland or home territory lay in the rubber land of southern Veracruz and Tabasco.

Not only are the colossal heads confined to the main sites of this region. It is the only place in which Olmec civilization appears in its entirety, and where every one of its characteristic traits is to be found. In view, therefore, of this consensus, before writing of the Olmec

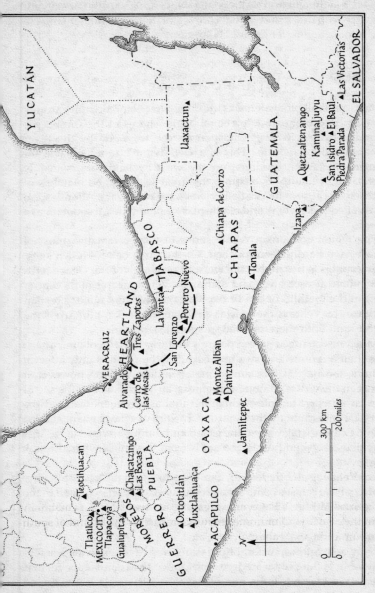

MAP 1. THE OLMEC EXPANSION

presence in other parts of Mexico, La Venta has first to be considered, together with other sites of that core region, which is fundamental to any understanding of Olmec civilization.

THE HOME BASE

What is generally considered as the Olmec heartland occupies an area of about 18,000 square kilometres on the shores of the Caribbean, bounded by the River Papaloapan on the west and by the River Tonala on the east side. This is a well-defined zone, suitable for human habitation, bordered on the west by land that is mainly inundated, while to its east are the great waterlogged marshes of Tabasco. Because of its location between the two rivers, Alfonso Caso once called this New World cradle of civilization the Mesopotamia of Mexico.

The region contains a whole series of Olmec remains, most of which have hardly been touched. Of the three better-known sites, Tres Zapotes is situated at the western extremity of the Olmec territory, while at its eastern end stands La Venta; nearer to its centre, lying at the foothills of the Tuxtla Range, is the third major site, San Lorenzo. La Venta is the most impressive, while San Lorenzo is the oldest, and both therefore have a special significance.

Much has changed since Stirling's first trip to La Venta in 1940. It was then a remote and swampy island, to be reached only after an arduous journey by river launch and on muleback. Now, however, it has been the victim of modern progress; an airstrip bisects the site of Mexico's earliest temples; where her first astronomers watched the stars, oil flares light up the night sky. In Stirling's day jaguars, deified by the Olmecs, still roamed the island and during his first stay a large one killed three hogs only 200 yards from the house where he was living.

La Venta itself, therefore, has little to offer the tourist today. However, he can see some of its greatest works of art exhibited in the La Venta Park at Villahermosa, capital of the state of Tabasco. A number of other Olmec statues were taken to the Archaeological Museum of Jalapa, mainly from San Lorenzo.

Only a small proportion of the ruins were ever excavated before they were bulldozed by modern developers. The Island of La Venta is situated in marshes lying east of the sluggish Tonala River, fifteen kilometres from the coast. It measures about five square kilometres, and is separated from the surrounding country by a series of swamps, in which the level of water rises and falls according to the time of year. The climate remains hostile, and the dry season only lasts from April to May, when torrential monsoon rains begin again. The average annual rainfall exceeds 2,000 millimetres.

Building in La Venta began in about 1100 B.C. according to radiocarbon dating; it reached its climax in 800 B.C. and around 500–400 B.C. construction came to a halt and the centre was ceremonially demolished; the possible reasons for this act of violence will be considered later. Accordingly, while La Venta is somewhat later than San Lorenzo, it predates Tres Zapotes, which basically belongs to a third, or late, Olmec phase, running from about 500 to 100 B.C.

La Venta was built of earth or dried mud and hardly any structures are of stone. The monuments are grouped round a patio surrounded by basalt columns, each weighing nearly a tonne. Studies of La Venta show that it was very carefully planned and that it was built on a central axis, like so many later Mexican sites. This axis is an imaginary line tilted 8° west of north, along which many rich offerings were placed. The plaza is dominated by the principal pyramid, which stands at its southern end. It is thirty metres high and covers a large area, being roughly circular in shape, with a diameter of 128 metres. Unlike the later pyramids of Mexico, it was not covered with a layer of stucco.

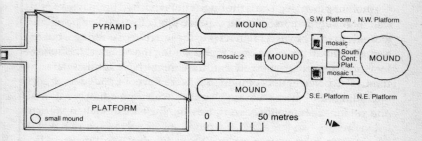

Figure 3. Plan of La Venta ceremonial centre

The most surprising feature of this pyramid was only discovered in 1967, after it had been cleared of its heavy forest cover and its surface could be seen and measured. After Robert F. Heizer's work on the site in 1959, it was still thought to conform to the pattern of later pyramids, with rectangular base and flat sloping sides, rising in tiers to a truncated platform at the top (as in Figure 3). However, once it was fully uncovered, it became obvious that the structure was neither rectangular nor flat-sided; it was found instead to be a kind of fluted cone, its rounded sides consisting of ten alternating ridges with gullies in between. By any standard it is an impressive monument, formed by a mound of piled-up earth with a mass of 100,000 cubic metres.

Notwithstanding the distinctive form of its main pyramid and the lack of stone buildings, La Venta is a true prototype of the Mexican ceremonial centre. The concept of the ceremonial centre is at least present, and the feeling for order and symmetry, together with that mania for ritual, basic to any understanding of Ancient Mexico. Already one finds pyramids and platforms built round a patio, as part of a site based on a recognizable axis.

People of rank were sometimes buried under platforms or in artificial mounds. The most remarkable of these was Tomb A of La Venta, a funerary mound for an important person. In La Venta seven of the typical Olmec 'altars' were found; they consist of a huge stone rectangular block, supporting an even larger table top. The front of the block has a deep niche, usually containing a human figure carved in the round. The site is also notable for its stelae; the most striking is Stela 3. It depicts two Olmec chiefs with towering headdresses who face each other, while chubby dwarfs with were-jaguar features float above them.

Another salient feature is the huge effort lavished upon works of art that were simply buried in the massive pits, of which five have been located. Archaeologists often refer to these as burial offerings, but not a single human bone has been found among the remains, though the treasures are often arranged as if they might have formed part of a tomb. The rich contents of these pits were never intended to be seen and admired by human eye, since they were immediately interred; and yet for sheer quality of workmanship they are unique in Mexico.

One pit was so large that it would have involved the removal of nearly 1,000 cubic metres of clay; it was dug down to a depth of five metres through a mound situated on the north side of the ceremonial plaza. Another even larger offering was buried eight metres deep; at its bottom had been placed over a thousand finely finished slabs of green serpentine. Much of the content of such pits consisted of polished stone axes with incised decoration; one of them contained 258 of these. The siting of such offerings, as well as of several mosaic floors, was strictly related to the central axis, and archaeologists were therefore able to calculate where they were likely to be found.

The purpose of the three mosaic pavements that belong to the final phase of La Venta civilization is also unknown. Two of them were laid on platforms flanking the south side of the main plaza; each consists of 485 oblong blocks of serpentine, set in coloured clays. The mosaics are shaped in such a way as to represent the form of a jaguar. Like the pit offerings, they were covered over and hidden from public view as soon as they were finished.

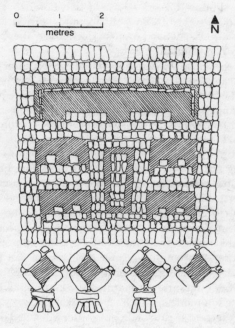

Figure 4. Mosaic floor from La Venta

In addition to La Venta, Tres Zapotes unquestionably ranks among the major Olmec sites, but information is rather fragmentary, owing to the lack of detailed exploration since Stirling's first digging in 1938 and 1939. Tres Zapotes is large; it contains over fifty mounds, grouped in regular patterns. Stirling unearthed a colossal head, but his most vital find was Stela C, already mentioned, with its Maya-type date that provided the earliest clue as to the antiquity of the Olmecs. Like La Venta, Tres Zapotes has nothing to offer the visitor, who will find there little more than a cornfield. Olmec remains in general are more to be sought in museums than on the original sites.

The third great site, San Lorenzo, was also first located by Stirling in 1945, but little was known about it until it was excavated by Michael Coe from 1966 to 1968. The Yale archaeologist was much attracted by its central location within the so-called Olmec heartland. He made his first visit in 1964 after a five-hour journey by river boat from the grimy oil town of Minatitlán. San Lorenzo is really a triple site, consisting of Tenochtitlan (not to be confused with the Aztec capital that flourished nearly three thousand years later), of San Lorenzo proper, three kilometres south-west of Tenochtitlan, and Potrero Nuevo, three kilometres south-east of San Lorenzo. Collectively they are known as San Lorenzo Tenochtitlan.

Coe's first season in 1966 led to a major discovery after he had taken a number of samples of charcoal, so valuable to the archaeologist as a source of radiocarbon dates. The figures obtained were unexpectedly early, and ranged between 1200 and 900 B.C., suggesting that San Lorenzo had reached its zenith several centuries before La Venta.

San Lorenzo had a long and eventful history. According to Coe's detailed reports, the area was first settled well before 1300 B.C. by pottery-using farmers; certain of the structures that he found date from this initial phase, before the true San Lorenzo culture began in 1200 B.C. At this moment, Coe believes that a band of outsiders, belonging to a vastly superior civilization, took over; they in their turn disappeared in about 900 B.C., when the site was occupied by yet another group, though the length of their occupation is not known with precision; a few centuries after their arrival San Lorenzo was deserted and left uninhabited until about A.D. 900, when it was settled by other migrants, who farmed the land, but whose cultural attainments were modest.

Only in his second season of digging, after a detailed map had been made, did Coe realize that what he had at first regarded as natural ravines and ridges were in reality part of a gigantic man-made undertaking. The long flat-topped ridges that flank the site had clearly been artificially constructed, though the underlying purpose of all this drudgery was not clear. Two of these ridges, each about thirty metres long, are mirror images of each other and every feature of the one is identically matched in the other.

On a line running from north to south, the ceremonial centre is over one kilometre long; it has no great pyramid like that of La Venta but contains several hundred earth mounds. These are mostly not monuments but house mounds; to judge by their number, the population might have amounted to about one thousand, though San Lorenzo obviously served as ceremonial centre for a very much larger number of people from the surrounding country.

Some of the most striking stone objects were found at the bottom of the ravines and gullies or on the slopes that led down to them. It was first assumed that they had simply been rolled downhill when the site was first abandoned. But after further studies, Coe discovered that many stone statues had fallen down into the ravine as a result of centuries of erosion; originally they had been interred with meticulous care within the ridges above the ravines, accompanied by serpentine axes and other artifacts.

Figure 5. Altar from Potrero Nuevo

San Lorenzo's architecture is uninspiring, since it can boast of no pyramids, plazas or colonnades. In addition, it has yielded relatively few of those remarkable smaller jade figures found in such profusion in La Venta and in many other parts of Mexico. If such objects ever existed, as they probably did, they have disappeared. The site is outstanding for its larger stone statues. In addition to nine colossal heads found there, its most spectacular works of art are the great carvings often rather confusingly called 'monuments'. Of these the most impressive, known as Monument 34, is headless, having been deliberately decapitated. It represents a kneeling man, slightly larger than life size, who was probably a ball-game player. Perforated discs placed at the shoulders show that the statue was once fitted with movable arms, recalling the much smaller jointed figures of later times. Another great carving, Monument 37, represents the headless and crouching figure of a huge jaguar with walrus-like tusks.

These stone figures had been systematically mutilated and then buried along certain fixed alignments within the ridges, which thus became a graveyard for every carving on which the iconoclasts could lay their hands. Coe believes that hundreds more may one day be uncovered, as part of this peculiar pattern of idol-smashing and reburial.

Coe's reconstruction of events in the earliest known Mexican ceremonial centre are revealing. He senses a pent-up though demonic fury, culminating in the supreme sacrilege in which great works of art were hacked to pieces; where possible, heads were severed from bodies and 'altars' were smashed. There are no signs of any outside invasion. The possible motivation of such destruction, repeated at the fall of a number of great centres of civilization in the course of Ancient Mexican history, will be considered later.

Among the most remarkable achievements of the people of San Lorenzo was the construction of quite an elaborate drainage system, the first form of water control known in the New World. Part of this system was built into a ridge and, when rediscovered, water still gushed forth during heavy rain. The drains were made of U-shaped stones, placed end-to-end and buried in a trench. The principal line of drainage runs from east to west and it is fed by three subsidiary lines. The sophisticated design of the joints between the branch and main drains bears witness to the skill of Olmec engineers.

OLMEC SOCIETY

Art and architecture of the Olmec heartland were clearly the product not of tribes but of kingdoms. This transition from tribe to state may have been fairly brief but the step, once taken, was decisive. No houses either of rich or poor have survived, but all the evidence points to a complex organization and shows that, unlike people of former times, the Olmecs lived in a stratified society; their rulers controlled the surplus labour of their subjects, and commanded the services of skilled craftsmen.

A civilization had emerged that was capable of dragging huge blocks of stone over long distances, and of piling up thousands of tonnes of earth at the ruler's behest. The basalt used for making the colossal heads and the monuments came from the south-eastern slopes of the Tuxtla Mountains, ninety kilometres west of La Venta as the crow flies. The heads weighed up to twenty tonnes and Stela 3 as much as 25 tonnes; therefore to bring the basalt blocks to La Venta was a prodigious undertaking. They first had to be dragged forty kilometres overland to the nearest navigable water; from there they could have been floated down to the sea at Coatzacoalcos on giant rafts, conveyed along a coast often lashed by heavy surf, and finally up the River Tonala to their destination.

The features of the colossal heads are so stereotyped that it is to be doubted that they are stone portraits of individual rulers; they seem more likely to be a series of representations of the same divinized being, perhaps regarded as a universal ancestor or cultural hero, who invented the different arts and skills. In contrast, some of the richly caparisoned figures in reliefs, rock carvings and stelae seem to be real people, probably priest-kings. The objects carried by these stately beings are significant; some bear clubs but on no known monuments or smaller carvings are the spears and spear-throwers of later times to be seen. Occasionally an object that looks like a knuckle-duster is ceremonially held in one hand.

Ignacio Bernal gives a tentative estimate of 350,000 inhabitants for the whole Olmec heartland, stretching from La Venta to Tres Zapotes, based on a figure of twenty people per square kilometre. This population was fairly spread out, and only rulers, priests and their attendants lived within the ceremonial centres; these served as a place of pilgrimage for villagers in the surrounding territory, who would have supported the privileged residents of the sacred precincts by payment of tribute in the form of goods and labour, a pattern that was to endure throughout Middle American history. While members of this ruling élite are depicted in reliefs and murals, these do not tell us whether the heartland was a single kingdom or was divided into petty states, a question to which further reference will be made.

The modern archaeologist no longer confines his attention to the deeds and customs of such exalted beings. In addition, he studies human culture as a whole, based on the relationships between its different classes, and seeks to learn how people lived and worked and what were the techniques at their disposal. In the Olmec territory, apart from certain areas now affected by the oil industry, the way of life of the inhabitants has not changed radically and the study of today's conditions offers many clues as to what their life was like thousands of years ago, and on how they met the severe challenge of their environment, which remains much the same. A generation ago such studies would have been much harder to achieve; to reach conclusions of this type, detailed information is required on local vegetation, soils and land-use patterns and the archaeologist is reinforced by specialists in many fields, such as biologists, botanists and agronomists. His work is also helped by a full use of aerial photography; Coe tells how, in his investigations, aerial maps were used to tie in with the data gathered by his group of experts, who would ply the present-day inhabitants with questions as to how much maize and other food their land could produce, for how long and how often it had to lie fallow, and as to what each household consumed. The lack of skeletal remains in such a climate prevented any modern comparison with the diet of people of Olmec times, through a study of fossilized excreta; however, it is fair to assume that there has been no radical change between the diet of today and that of yesterday.

In general, the Olmec region was not unhealthy; there was probably then no malaria, and in pre-Columbian days the waters would not have been contaminated by domestic animals, a problem that arose from the sixteenth century onwards. Methods of soil cultivation are basic to the Olmec economy and their study gives us an idea of how many people could have lived in the area. Clearly their system of farming was able to provide a surplus amount of food, without which a stratified society of this kind cannot exist. The surplus, however, was not big enough to permit large concentrations of population in small areas.

The basic crop was maize, which still amounts to ninety per cent of the peoples' diet today. The soil is fairly fertile, and can produce two crops per annum of maize, though it soon becomes exhausted. Such deterioration is brought about by the system known as slash and burn, used by tropical peoples in many parts of the world. A patch of forest is felled during the short dry season; just before the heavy rains begin in May, the wood is burned and darkens the sky with a pall of smoke. After the first rains the seed is sown, using a simple digging stick. But after a few harvests the crop yield falls and the ground has to lie fallow for five long years before it can be used again. The drawbacks of the system are obvious: it is most extravagant in land use and therefore provides food for only a limited number of people; though it was used to support both the Olmec and the Maya civilizations during their heyday, its defects have often been cited as one of the causes of the Maya collapse. Certain evidence is at present coming to light that the Mayas also used more intensive methods of cultivation. Nothing is known of the Olmecs in this respect, though traces of such methods dating from later times have now been found in the heartland itself.

In the Olmec region, moreover, the growing of food is complicated by the huge mass of water carried by the rivers, swelled by endless heavy rain. During the wet season much of the low-lying land is flooded and the soil then becomes so heavy in clay and poor in nutriments that it cannot be farmed at all. Above the high-water mark in the hillier zone, soils are better and provide two good annual crops. The best land of all is the strips along the river banks that are covered with a deep layer of silt brought down by the current. Nowadays the richer inhabitants farm these strips, which were probably always owned by the local élite, and thus became a source of power as well as wealth.

Notwithstanding the importance of maize in the diet of the average person, a rich variety of other foods was available. The Olmecs were hunters as well as farmers, and even today, when in many parts of Mexico game is almost extinct, people of that region ride out with their dogs and hunt white-tailed deer and other animals that are also known to have formed part of the Olmec diet. Fish and aquatic birds were plentiful throughout the year. The dog and turkey had already been domesticated and served as another form of food.

We possess good data on hunting practices in San Lorenzo, unlike other sites in the region, owing to a rather lucky accident of bone conservation. Though hunting took place, its scale was apparently limited. Weapons were not very efficient, and few projectile points have been found; to judge from the remains, more dogs were eaten than deer. Most abundant of all are bones of fish and turtle.

If most people worked on the land, Olmec artistic achievement postulates the presence of a class of full-time artisans, though none of their workshops has been found. To make delicate carvings out of hard jade with instruments of stone demanded the utmost skill, involving every imaginable technique, including the use of abrasives, drills and saws, the marks of which are still visible on some objects. Jade was their favourite medium for figurines, but the lapidaries also made tools such as axes and chisels from serpentine, and worked a variety of other stones, including andesite, basalt and quartz. In addition to farming and specialized crafts, building was a third occupation that required a fairly large labour force, also needed to transport heavy materials and to remove huge quantities of earth. Part of this work could have been done by land workers between crops.

On the basis of such data, in an area where not a human habitation or even a human bone survives, only these rather generalized observations can be made on the way of life of the ordinary citizen. Obviously, since the population was relatively spread out, he spent many hours walking from place to place. As a member of a rigid class society, the calls upon his time for the purpose of heaving stones and moving mounds of earth were considerable, though as a fervent worshipper of the jaguar god, he probably performed such tasks with a willing heart. If his diet was simple, he enjoyed a greater variety of food than was later available to the civilizations of the Altiplano. And if his existence was monotonous, the monotony – as was to occur in all Middle American cultures – was relieved by elaborate and colourful ceremonies that were part of that religion which was basic to his whole way of life.

CREATIVE GENIUS

Far from being confined to one region, unmistakable examples of Olmec style are found in many places. Before, however, trying to trace the course of this intellectual expansion, one must consider the basic art forms which were used and the religion of which they were the visual image. These forms have all been found in the heartland, except for mural painting, whose survival the Tabasco climate did not favour.

The Olmecs produced a great assortment of objects, varying in size from the miniature to the colossal and made out of a wide range of materials. They can be roughly divided into those that were monumental and others that were portable; this distinction is important, since giant statues carved *in situ* suggest some physical Olmec presence in the place where they were found, whereas the smaller figures could easily have been traded by intermediaries.

Olmec art is distinguished from that of its successors, particularly from Teotihuacan, by its realism and its lack of geometric abstraction. Another important feature is a certain 'classicism', in contrast to the baroque forms of Maya art. Figures stand free in space, and most statues are fashioned in the round. Central to its iconography is the concept of the man-jaguar, though other animals and birds appear at times. One carving from Potrero Nuevo actually shows a woman copulating with a jaguar and may represent the basic myth of Olmec origins. The typical were-jaguar being has a flat head, often with a peculiar V-shaped cleft in the middle; it is snub-nosed like a child, or a jaguar, and the corners of its mouth are drawn down as if snarling or crying. Some of these statues portray stylized humans with certain jaguar traits, while others are more cat-like and wear jaguar masks. In

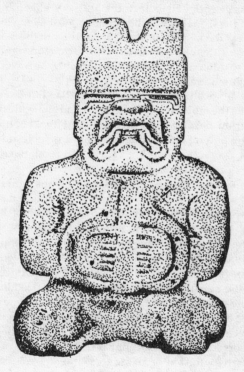

Figure 6. Anthropomorphic jaguar
from San Lorenzo

every case animal and human elements are combined and very few true jaguars, lacking any human traits, are depicted. In addition, jaguar masks are occasionally adorned with bird feathers, and sometimes the felines are shown with serpent tongues. The colossal heads lack the jaguar element; equally the many smaller figurines of dwarfs and hunchbacks have no feline characteristics.

Stone sculpture is the supreme achievement of Olmec art. On the other hand, their pottery is poorly preserved; it is mainly monochrome and was not used for ceremonial purposes. The colossal heads are confined solely to the heartland and a total of sixteen are known, of which four come from La Venta and nine from San Lorenzo. They range from 1.6 to 3 metres in height and are all carved from blocks of basalt rock. Their features are very alike, and only the expression differs; one even smiles, though most have a more solemn aspect; all wear the helmet-like headdress, though the design of each varies slightly. Attempts have been made to categorize the heads and assign them to different periods. More probably, however, they were all made within a limited timespan.

Olmec stelae mostly come from the heartland and are rare elsewhere. Unlike the more stereotyped heads and altars, the stelae differ greatly one from another. They are important for what they tell us of Olmec culture and religion. Among the most notable are Stela 2 and Stela 3 of La Venta, representing figures that recall the richly caparisoned rulers carved on many Maya stelae.

No less remarkable are the very lifelike little stone figures. A few are made of coarser material, but most are of serpentine and jade, and no other people of Mexico ever produced such a wealth of objects made of jade. The latter is a generic term for two stones, jadeite and nephrite. The Olmecs used jadeite, which is the harder of the two; it was never employed by the Chinese until the eighteenth century, when they began to import it from Burma. A few Olmec objects are made from the transparent dark-green jade, so prized in China, but most are blue-green in colour. In these smaller figurines, the were-jaguar is the dominant motif and many are of children.

The Olmecs also made fine stone masks; some of these are quite small and served as pectorals. But of all the works of the Olmec sculptors, perhaps the most striking are neither the colossal heads nor the diminutive figures, but the life-size statues in the round; those in true Olmec style come from the heartland and so far twenty have been found. All represent naked men, often seated and with hands resting on knees or legs. Among the most splendid is 'The Wrestler', remarkable not only for its strength and realism, but for the precision with which the human body is carved (Figure 2, p. 27). Another notable piece is the 'Man of Las Limas', called after the place where it was found. It represents a typical Olmec personage with 'football' helmet bearing in his arms an apparently dead child. Paradoxically it is in the earliest of these statues in the round that the human anatomy is the most skilfully rendered and many come from San Lorenzo. However the finest stone reliefs, as we shall later see, belong to the post-San Lorenzo era.

Unlike the more numerous stone masterpieces, Olmec mural paint-ing has only come to light fairly recently, and in places far distant from the heartland. This by no means implies that in La Venta there were no murals, but merely that in such a climate they could not survive.

On the main highway from Mexico City to Acapulco, a short way beyond Chilpancingo, the state capital of Guerrero, a dirt road leads off to the Juxtlahuaca Cave, at the end of a long and narrow valley. The cave had been known since the 1930s, but had attracted little attention until in 1966 Carlo Gay penetrated its deepest recesses and discovered paintings that were pure Olmec in style. One of the oddest features of these is that they are as carefully hidden from the common view, as are some of the great Palaeolithic rock paintings of Europe. They are separated from the outside of the cave by a whole series of chambers, in one of which were found a number of human skulls. At the end of these lies the Gallery of Drawings; they are set in an obscure recess and could only have been painted with the aid of pine torches.

The principal mural displays a single Olmec figure, reminiscent of others portrayed in rock carvings and on stelae. This majestic chief has a black beard and a headdress of green quetzal feathers. Whereas many Olmec chiefs are portrayed in the nude, he wears a tunic pasted with bands of red, yellow and black; over his left shoulder hangs what seems to be a brown cape. The jaguar element is as usual present, in the form of gauntlets and anklets of jaguar skin. In his right hand he carries a kind of wand directed towards a small goatee-bearded figure with black face and red body. On another wall of the innermost chamber is painted a great snake, bright red in colour, that faces a feline crouching as if ready to attack the serpent; its head and body are also red, but over its back is a spotted skin.

Since this important discovery, another remarkable example of Olmec mural art has come to light at Oxtotitlán, two kilometres east of the village of Acatlán and only about ten kilometres north of Juxtla-huaca. Unlike the latter, the murals of Oxtotitlán were not hidden from public view; they stand on a cliff face in front of a cave and in two shallow grottoes. The painting on the cliff portrays a very stylized human figure, elaborately dressed and seated on a jaguar-like mon-ster. But by far the strangest painting, situated in one of the grottoes, portrays a man with typical Olmec features, dressed in a tight-fitting black costume; his right arm is raised towards the head of a jaguar. The work is almost unique in Olmec iconography in portraying a figure that is purely human, facing another that is a true jaguar. And in contrast to the generally sexless nature of their art, the mural is phallic, the jaguar's tail passing to the pubic area of the man, whose phallus extends to the rear of the animal. This human figure and his attendant jaguar, with a sexual connection between the two, are clearly important as religious symbols.

Figure 7. Oxtotitlán mural showing head
of Olmec figure in ritual attire

In addition to their achievements as the first great carvers of stone and painters of murals, the Olmecs invented the art of writing and the technique of recording calendrical dates on stone. This feat came as a kind of afterthought, when San Lorenzo and La Venta already lay in ruins; in these sites there are no calendric glyphs.

For a long time scholars had been familiar with the Mayan method of recording time, which supposedly they had invented. This system, known as the Long Count, consists of a tabulation of days elapsed since a notional base date, when the calendar was first created. Using bars for the number five, and dots for one, together with a stylized shell for zero, Maya inscriptions recorded dates in the form of five numerals to be read from left to right; these denoted the number of units of 144,000 days, 7,200 days, 360 days, 20 days, and one day that had elapsed since the notional base day, probably falling in the equivalent of 3113 B.C. The earliest Maya date from the great site of Tikal corresponds, according to the more widely accepted Thompson correlation, to A.D. 292.

A great stir was therefore created in 1939 by Stirling's discovery, mentioned above, of Stela C in Tres Zapotes, which showed on one side a Maya-type date hundreds of years earlier than any from the Maya land, and on the other an Olmec were-jaguar. The inscription was incomplete, since the stela had been broken, but enough of it remained for Stirling to be able to interpret the date as 31 B.C.,

Figure 8a. Glyph-like drawing in Oxtotitlán mural   Figure 8b. Olmec face in profile, Oxtotitlán

although Mayanists at the time rejected this reading. The stela, together with a strange Olmec carving known as the Tuxtla statuette, bearing a date of A.D. 162, were crucial to the argument, then brought forward for the first time, that the Olmecs had created Mexico's earliest civilization, and had even invented the art of writing and recorded dates.

Admittedly Stela C had obviously been used twice over, and its inscribed date, though long before the first from the Maya land, was very late in terms of Olmec chronology. Since these discoveries, the reading of the year on Stela C has been confirmed by other dated stelae found at El Baul in Guatemala and Chiapa de Corzo in south-eastern Mexico, which also predate the Maya by several centuries. In addition, in Monte Alban, whose Phase I corresponds to the later stages of Olmec civilization, a system of recording dates by bars and dots was already in use, together with a simple form of glyphic writing.

In the Olmec heartland a form not only of date recording but of writing came to be used, and David Joralemon has identified no less than 182 symbols in their art that appear to have had a glyphic meaning. Hence, while the Olmecs did not evolve the wide range of glyphs used by the Mayas, it was they and not the Mayas who initiated both the principle of glyphic writing and the actual system of bar and dot dates. Therefore, in addition to their key role in the development of sculpture, painting and monumental architecture, they were also the inventors of the calendar and pioneers in those calendric studies that were basic to Mexican civilization.

THE FELINE GOD

The main forms of Olmec art are easy to describe but much harder to interpret. While the modes of expression are varied the theme is constant: the cult of the human or were-jaguar, though snakes and birds are also present. Sometimes the beings portrayed are entirely human, even if their majestic bearing suggests that they possessed the jaguar's strength. In other cases the figures are more animal than human; the many children almost invariably have jaguar paws and other feline traits – or at times wear a jaguar mask – unless they are hunchbacks or cripples, apparently regarded with special awe by the Olmecs, as by certain other peoples.

Such feline figures are not really animals at all, but humans with animal traits, a theme that was to prove recurrent in Ancient Mexico, where throughout history warriors and priests continued to wear animal garb. Among the many felines, Mexican art almost invariably depicts the true jaguar, whereas the puma played the same role in Peru. While the jaguar is only the third largest of all the felines, it is the largest spotted cat. Its massive head with rounded face is well suited to be represented as half-human. In addition, it has a distinctive feature, a furrow that runs along the top of the head, formed by folds in its loose scalp. This furrow evidently became for the Olmecs a jaguar symbol, and, as a V-shaped cleft, is added to human faces as a token of the all-pervading jaguar cult, linked with fertility, since at times plants sprout from the cleft.

Man and jaguar are alike in that they both hunt a broad variety of other animals; they only differ in the latter's preference for swallowing his prey raw, while man eats his cooked, a theme that Claude Lévi-Strauss has explored in depth in *The Raw and the Cooked*.

American anthropologist Peter Furst has often stressed the role of the jaguar not only in pre-Columbian art, but also in the mythology of tribes that still exist in South America; these feline cults are related to forms of shamanism basic to the religions of the higher civilizations of both North and South America, though today they survive more in the latter.

For instance, among the Majo of Bolivia, a supernatural jaguar is venerated in a temple hut, and is attended by his own shamans. These are recruited from the privileged few who have actually survived attack by a jaguar in the forest and are therefore looked upon as special favourites of the cat god. Among the Majo, if a hunter kills a jaguar, he must remain for several days in the temple, while special offerings are made. The Olmecs, while they venerated the jaguars, also killed them, since their chiefs are often shown with adornments made out of their skins.

For the Majo and other Bolivian tribes, the jaguar is the original lord and ruler of their species. In South America, under the influence of higher cultures centred upon Peru but extending into Bolivia, the jaguar cult became institutionalized, served by temple priests. The Shipaya tribe of North Brazil still worships a feline creator and cultural hero. Here also, as in earlier times, this divine being is not a pure animal but a human creator who assumed jaguar form when he became angry. Among the Chibchan Kogi of Colombia he is also cast in the role of tribal ancestor; like the Olmecs, they are the 'people of the jaguar', and their traditional forbears were wild jaguars. Hence among native tribes of South America the notion of the man-jaguar not only existed in the past but remains very much alive today. Certain groups in the Amazon region of Brazil even use the same basic word for shaman and jaguar: when they grow old, these shamans are transmuted into the animal simply by donning its skin – an apparent carry-over from the ancient practice of wearing feline masks, or, like the figure in the Juxtlahuaca mural, a jaguar pelt.

This identification of man and jaguar not only applies to adults; even the Olmec child-feline concept lives on among the Tacana Indians in Bolivia. Their great Jaguar Shaman in 1961 told German anthropologists Karin Hissink and Albert Hain of the legend of a twelve-year-old boy who flew off into another world on the back of a giant-winged jaguar.

Many creations of Olmec religious art were seen only by the artist and the priests who buried them. The coloured mosaics were interred, and the huge pits crammed with ceremonial axes and figurines are unique in Ancient Mexico. It is by no means clear if the colossal heads were exposed to public view, since many of those found in San Lorenzo had been ceremonially buried, though this may have been done some time after they were carved.

The manner in which monuments were buried makes it clear that this was part of a solemn ritual, rather than a last-minute gesture in face of hostile invasion. The systematic way in which they were defaced required an effort second only to that needed to carve them; one method was to chip a series of little oblong slots out of the smooth surface. The colossal head in the garden of the National Museum in Mexico City is one of the most mutilated. It has seven such slots in the back of the head, and sixty dimpled holes picked out of its face.

Apart from the mystery of all the buried and defaced objects, the religious message contained in Olmec art is elusive. Their beliefs seem to be rooted in a more primitive religion based on shamanism and even totemism, whereby each tribe identifies itself with a particular animal, who is both its progenitor and protector. Often the beast in question has a mystic bond with the tribal chief, himself descended from a part-animal hero. The concept was not altogether absent in late pre-Columbian times; the Aztec rulers claimed as ancestor the semi-legendary Quetzalcoatl of Tula, the Plumed Serpent God; the jaguar was an important emblem of their all-powerful Smoking Mirror God.

Contemporary tribal shamans of the Americas, being magicians as much as priests, are credited with supernatural gifts, such as the art of healing. They enter into ecstatic states and have the power to transform themselves into animals, a notion present in Olmec art. But if these Olmec jaguar-like figures were still part-shaman, intellectually they paved the way for the priests of later cultures; their dating system shows that they had studied the motions of the sun and moon, and their architecture suggests an ability to measure distances. At the same time, if no longer pure shaman, they were still magicians; such man-jaguar scenes as those of the Juxtlahuaca Cave must have been thought to possess a magic potency, since they were not visible to the ordinary worshipper. Certain aspects of shamanism, such as peyote and other hallucinogens, survived in Mexico up to the Conquest.

Hence, Olmec religion is to be understood as much in the light of what went before in Mexico as of what came after. The jaguar, portrayed on occasion as copulating with a woman, is to be seen as both totem and creator, with whom their kingship is intimately linked, and the rulers in particular were the jaguar's children. In the absence of the lion that figures in coats of arms in Europe as a symbol of power, the jaguar was the undisputed king of the jungle. As we have seen, throughout the Americas the large feline remains a natural choice as tribal symbol, and is still sometimes thought of as a child.

Among the Olmecs also, the jaguar is not only the emblem of the ruler, but embodies the notion of childhood. In a purely physical sense this is not surprising, since the snub-nosed feline has features more like those of an infant than an adult. But the true meaning of the child-jaguar may be different: throughout the world, whether among Mexicans, Polynesians or Carthaginians, the child has been associated with human sacrifices; in later pre-Hispanic cultures it came to be the favourite victim of the Rain God, Tlaloc. By its very nature a child is an ideal sacrificial offering, because, being innocent, it is the purest intermediary between man and his gods, from whom it was so recently parted at birth. Other evidence exists of human sacrifice among the Olmecs, in the form, for instance, of severed heads without their bodies in the Olmec-type site of Tlatilco; Stirling found an instrument in Tres Zapotes which he took to be a sacrificial knife.

The frequent representation in Olmec statues of a man carrying a were-jaguar child has an obvious interpretation, since the attitude of the latter often makes it seem that he is dead rather than asleep. These infants were surely sacrificial victims being offered to the gods as the highest gift; when sacrificed as an intermediary between man and the jaguar god, in a sense they themselves became the jaguar, and as such were portrayed as half animal. Possibly, since they bear no marks of violence, they were drowned, like the infants who in later times were sacrificed to Tlaloc, and who also became the god.

Thus, in résumé, Olmec religion may be seen as a cult of the jaguar both as lord and progenitor, inseparable from kingship and government, and as child victim; the original myth perhaps sprang from the story of a primordial ruler of part-jaguar descent, who sacrificed his own child.

Certain evidence suggests that the feline stood for earth as much as for vital strength and that an essential part of its worship was an earth cult, in its turn related to fertility. In late pre-Hispanic times the jaguar represented the earth and was particularly associated with caves. The fertility aspect of the cult among the Olmecs is visible in certain scenes containing a phallic element.

On the other hand, while the association of jaguar with earth and fertility is close, the link between this jaguar deity and the Rain God, Tlaloc, is apt to be exaggerated. Tlaloc undoubtedly inherited certain feline traits that have been traced step by step from Olmec art to that of Teotihuacan by Miguel Covarrubias. But the Olmecs suffered more from an excess than from a lack of rain; moreover among the Mayas the jaguar was equally associated with the sun, and in their representations of its nightly course under the horizon the face of the sun takes the form of this animal. In a cult dedicated to earth rather than to

Figure 9. Man and were-jaguar child

rain, there would be a more natural tendency for so many objects to be immediately buried, though not necessarily accompanied by human remains; many of these were of jade, which to the Mexicans was not merely a precious stone, but also a symbol for the heart of the earth.

Far from being a kind of Rain God, as is at times suggested, I see the omnipresent Olmec feline not only as the progenitor of the tribe, linked with kingship and with child sacrifice, but also as an earth or fertility deity, who presided over the vegetation cycle, so vital to the well-being of the people. The Olmec legend embodied the story of the sacrifice of a child were-jaguar, a rite that was frequently recalled in works of art and probably re-enacted in offerings of real children, wearing masks and other jaguar accoutrements; the cult, as we shall see, spread to many parts of Mexico. Also present in Olmec religion was the Fire God (who also came to be associated with earth) and perhaps a rudimentary version of the Plumed Serpent. However, the fully-fledged Mexican pantheon with its plethora of deities, as we know it from later times, did not yet exist in its entirety and was only gradually developed. Olmec religion seems to represent a half-way stage between tribal shamanism and the complex religious system of later times.

THE UBIQUITOUS OLMECS

Olmec creativity in their homeland was remarkable. However, their achievement was not confined to a single territory like, say, the Huaxtec culture that was to flourish further north on the same coast; by virtue of their vigorous expansion, the Olmecs rank as one of the four all-embracing civilizations of Mexico.

While a colossal head had been found in the nineteenth century in southern Veracruz, it was not until 1928 that George Vaillant first discovered Olmec-type remains in Tlatilco on the outskirts of Mexico City. On the one hand, certain Olmec finds, such as rock carvings or murals in pure La Venta style, suggest a physical presence, or at least visits by Olmec craftsmen. In other distant places, however, numerous portable objects have been found belonging to a second category, since they could conceivably have been brought from the heartland; a third type of penetration occurs in places whose art forms show certain affinities, but are not pure Olmec, having been adapted to local tastes and conditions; such forms are usually called Olmecoid.

The mural paintings from the state of Guerrero, described above, belong to the first category. They are a hundred per cent Olmec, and could hardly have been painted without the help of an artist from the Gulf Coast homeland. And though stone monuments are lacking in Guerrero, a great abundance of smaller objects has been found there, particularly jade figurines; most of the Olmec pieces in private collections come from that region.

Equally representative of the purest Olmec style are the petro-glyphs of Chalcatzingo in the state of Morelos, about seventy kilometres south-east of Cuernavaca. Two of these were found in 1934 and others were discovered more recently. After a longish walk from the village of Jonacatepec, one is rewarded by the sight of one of the greatest of all Olmec works of art, known as Petroglyph I. Carved on an overhanging rock, this relief, three metres high, depicts a single richly-attired figure with huge headdress, seated on a throne inside what seems to be a cave, though it has also been taken to be the mouth of a great monster. The seated ruler carries a ceremonial bar not unlike those later shown in Maya reliefs. The style is very similar to that of Stela 3 of La Venta. The second relief shows a typically Olmec scene; on the right a reclining figure with goatee beard is portrayed; his bare body and bound wrists indicate that he is a captive. Facing him are three men dressed as warriors and brandishing clubs or batons. The phallic posture of the captive suggests some kind of fertility rite.

Figure 10. Relief from Chalcatzingo

Excavations at Chalcatzingo have yielded surprisingly few smaller Olmec objects; in contrast, in the nearby site of Las Bocas, also in Morelos, a number of Olmec figurines have been found that recall those of San Lorenzo in the heartland. A third site, Gualupita, situ-ated in the suburbs of Cuernavaca, has also yielded such typically Olmec objects as a crouching were-jaguar figure, wearing a jaguar skin.

In the central Valley of Mexico no carvings or paintings have come to light, such as those mentioned above, that would by themselves indicate the presence of Gulf Coast Olmecs. One important site is Tlapacoya, where Olmec figurines are found in the earliest levels of occupation. However, their influence in the Valley of Mexico is above all to be found in Tlatilco. In this open village site with no monuments or even mounds, a vast store of buried Pre-Classic objects have been unearthed, mostly clay figures and lifelike effigy vessels that are not at all Olmec in style. But in addition to these, a number of other clay figurines have been located that are so typically Olmec as to recall those of La Venta, though stone Olmec-type pieces are rare, compared with the quantity found in Guerrero. A distinguishing feature of these Olmec-type objects is that, according to radiocarbon dates, they belong to the thirteenth century B.C., and therefore coincide with the earliest dated phase of San Lorenzo.

Archaeologists are far from agreeing about the nature of this Olmec penetration of Tlatilco. Ignacio Bernal has called it a 'colony', owing to such markedly Olmec traits in a profusion which he interprets as a physical presence, rather than a mere trade relationship; Coe also uses the word 'colonial' in this context. On the other hand, Ronald Grennes Ravitz, in writing of their influences in the Mexican Plateau, says that it would be a distortion of the truth to describe Tlatilco as Olmec, or even Olmecoid, in any sense that might imply the existence of some kind of pan-Mexican state under the aegis of the Gulf Coast Olmecs.

Whatever the true status of Tlatilco, such limitations certainly apply to the great site of Monte Alban, near Oaxaca in south-east Mexico, whose earliest phase might be described as Olmecoid, but never as Olmec. The main monument of this early Monte Alban dates from about the sixth century B.C. and is called the Temple of the Dancers, so named after the series of reliefs of sexless figures, whose strange postures makes it look as if they are dancing or even swimming. While they are far from being typically Olmec, they have thick lips and flat noses, and convey a general impression that at least could be called Olmecoid. The extent to which Olmec influence is really present in these reliefs has been questioned and it has been pointed out that they are considerably later than La Venta. Bernal describes the style of the 'Dancers' and other Monte Alban monuments as a variant of the pure Olmec, from which it differs considerably. Other Olmecoid remains have been found in the nearby site of Dainzu, excavated by Bernal in the 1970s. Moreover, glyphs and bar-and-dot numerals have been found in Monte Alban; this is the earliest known writing in Mexico, since it is older than that found in the heartland, from which it also differs.

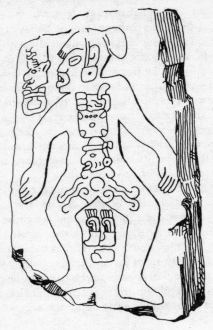

Figure 11. Dancer, Monte Alban

So far only examples have been given of penetration within the frontiers of present-day Mexico. Among these should also be included the Olmecoid traits in the well-explored site of Chiapa de Corzo in the state of Chiapas, near the Guatemalan border, as well as in Tonala, Chiapas, where stelae and petroglyphs show strong Olmec influence. Such influences spread even further into Guatemala and beyond. In Guatemala itself, an Olmec-style relief has been found near Quetzaltenango; a petroglyph at San Isidro Piedra, near the Pacific Coast, is in the purest La Venta tradition and portrays a man who brandishes a clublike weapon, recalling in many details the Chalcatzingo rock carvings. In the Classic Maya site of Uaxactun a temple base situated at the lowest level is decorated with masks that present certain Olmec motifs and a rather similar temple was found at the Maya site of Tikal, but it has since been covered over.

The petroglyphs carved on all four sides of a boulder at Las Victorias, two kilometres east of Chalchuapa, in the Republic of El Salvador, constitute the known limits of Olmec penetration beyond Guatemala, and are 700 kilometres distant as the crow flies from the heartland. The four figures depicted are crudely carved but none the less are typically Olmec, and even wear the characteristic 'football' helmet.

Such far-flung but varied traces of penetration pose many questions; any answer must be linked to the chronology, in the heartland and elsewhere, of the several phases of Olmec civilization. Fortunately in this respect radiocarbon dating, if it cannot provide a detailed history, at least offers pointers to the sequence of Olmec expansion and helps us to set them in historical perspective.

San Lorenzo, as we have seen, flourished from 1200 to 900 B.C., according to its radiocarbon dates. It is generally considered that, since San Lorenzo presents a fully developed culture, an Olmec formative stage must have developed elsewhere, perhaps in the Tuxtla Mountains, though Coe also writes of a probable early or pre-Olmec phase in San Lorenzo itself. Coe, however, presupposes that many basic traits, such as the use and transportation of huge stones, the elaborate iconography and even the drainage system were first invented in some place as yet undiscovered. During any such initial phase arose the cult of the jaguar, which already appears as a fully-fledged religion in San Lorenzo and La Venta. This proto-Olmec phase remains an enigma, since it is not really known at what time or in what place Olmec culture took on its very distinctive form.

The chronology of the heartland presents marked differences between the radiocarbon dates of San Lorenzo and La Venta, of which most but not all are several centuries later; as compared with 1200 to 900 B.C. for the main efflorescence of San Lorenzo, 900 to 600 B.C. are the more generally accepted dates for La Venta's most creative phase, though its total lifespan was longer. La Venta therefore brought forth a second flowering of Olmec culture. The violence of the upheaval at the time when San Lorenzo fell is demonstrated by the frenzy with which its monuments were smashed.

San Lorenzo is partly contemporary with Early Pre-Classic, or Early Formative in Mexico as a whole, while La Venta belongs more to the Middle Formative level. During the third and final Olmec phase, corresponding to Mexican Late Formative, La Venta was in turn virtually abandoned, while Olmec or Olmecoid culture survived in Tres Zapotes. To this closing and in some ways decadent phase, running from about 500 to 100 B.C., none the less belongs one of their greatest feats, the system of glyphic writing and dates, first found on Stela C of Tres Zapotes with its 31 B.C. date. Cerro de las Mesas, some twenty kilometres east of the Bay of Alvarado, is usually regarded more as a Classic than an Olmec site, though its earliest remains are distinctly Olmecoid and the dates on its first monuments were arranged exactly in the style of Stela C of Tres Zapotes. The beginnings of Cerro de las Mesas are Olmec in other respects, such as the burial of deposits of greenstone and jade axes, carved in an unmistakable, if degenerate, Olmec style.

This three-phase chronology for the heartland is basic to the mapping of Olmec expansion into other regions, where the dating of Olmec or Olmecoid traces varies greatly from place to place. In some sites such traces correspond to the great age of San Lorenzo, in others to the apogee of La Venta, while in Monte Alban they mainly belong to the third, or post-La Venta period. Influences therefore reached the rest of Middle America in successive waves of varied form and intensity. Particularly in the Valley of Mexico and in some sites of Morelos, these influences belong to the first phase, when San Lorenzo was in its prime. Olmec-type objects in both Tlatilco and Tlapacoya have been dated to between 1300 and 900 B.C., while for Olmec sites in Morelos we have dates ranging from 1356 to 1190 B.C. and only Chalcatzingo is later. The Las Bocas phase in Morelos is clearly early, since its hollow pottery figurines are extraordinarily like those of San Lorenzo. In Tlatilco the graves with Olmec-type objects, also more or less contemporary with San Lorenzo, are the oldest of all. These early examples of Olmec style, as we have seen, consist of smaller objects that could have been imported, rather than of large works of art that had to be executed *in situ*. Hence, during this early phase, Olmec merchants were already covering great distances, even if they took no artists with them.

Whereas these Olmec vestiges in the Valley of Mexico and in Morelos thus belong to the San Lorenzo phase, others outside the heartland correspond more to the second phase, marked by the apogee of La Venta. The Guerrero murals are more related to La Venta than to San Lorenzo, and those of Juxtlahuaca are thought to date from between 900 and 700 B.C.

Similar dates seem to apply to Chalcatzingo. Like the Guerrero murals, its rock carvings relate more to La Venta than to San Lorenzo, and archaeologist Daniel Grove dates them to about 900 to 800 B.C. Recently in Chalcatzingo three stelae have been discovered somewhat recalling those of Izapa, a site that, as we shall see, is more post-Olmec. Grove also assigns to the same period as the Chalcatzingo rock carvings the rather cruder petroglyphs of Las Victorias in El Salvador.

In Oaxaca, the 'Dancers' of Monte Alban I, often described as Olmecoid, correspond more closely to the third, or post-La Venta, Olmec phase. However, archaeologist Kent Flannery has identified village sites in the Oaxaca Valley as belonging to a pre-Monte Alban culture. The San Juan Formative phase in the Valley of Oaxaca is dated on the basis of both pottery and radiocarbon to between 1200 and 900 B.C. While its art forms are not basically Olmec or even Olmecoid, certain Olmec traits are present, such as representations of were-jaguars, some of which even have the U-shaped cleft in the head. Therefore an early as well as a late phase of Olmec influence is discernible in Oaxaca. This is also true of Chiapas, where certain Olmec remains belong to the early period, while others, such as those of Tliltepec, correspond to the latter part of the La Venta era, say from 700 to 500 B.C.

To the late phase belong not only the 'Dancers' but also the carvings in nearby Dainzu. The early Monte Alban glyphs, so important in the history of writing in Mexico, are also related to this final period; when Tres Zapotes still flourished; a rather unaccountable gap of 260 years exists between its Long Count glyphs and the first known Maya inscriptions in Tikal; this does not mean that no monuments were made during this intermediate period, but merely that none has been found.

It is hard to trace any step-by-step development from this late Olmec culture that leads directly to Maya art forms. Certain clues, however, are provided by the important site of Izapa on the Mexican Pacific Coast, very near to the Guatemalan border. Its art is clearly transitional between Olmec and Maya. The Izapa artists evidently passed on to the Mayas of Mexico and Guatemala the stela-altar complex, in which a round altar stands in front of a flat stela, elaborately carved. The florid baroque style of the stelae of Izapa has much in common with the Maya; at the same time Izapa is derived at least in part from late Olmec style, though basic differences exist, particularly the absence of the standard Olmec were-jaguar and baby face, indicating a radical departure from their religious beliefs. In the heartland itself the religion seems to have changed, since stelae from this final period in Tres Zapotes are more like those of Izapa than of La Venta.

STATE AND EMPIRE

The nature of Olmec cultural penetration of parts of Middle America outside the heartland has been seen to vary greatly, as regards its dates, its nature and its intensity. As a consequence, archaeologists differ as to how and why it came about. The argument mainly revolves around the key question as to whether the Olmecs came to other parts of Middle America as warriors or as traders. The same question arises, as we shall see, concerning the Teotihuacan expansion more than a thousand years later.

Michael Coe is a leading exponent of the 'imperial' point of view, referring to the Olmec heartland as a 'pristine state, bent on conquest, tribute and proselytizing'; in addition to dominating the Valley of Mexico, he believes that the Olmecs physically controlled the present-day states of Morelos, Puebla and possibly Guerrero. He is at the same time conscious of the importance of trade for the Olmecs, particularly in order to obtain jade, but he uses the word 'conquest' in the same context, and writes of 'warrior traders', rather on the lines of the Aztec merchants, who even fought their own campaigns.

Coe is far from being alone in his deductions. Peter David Joralemon supports this view of a far-flung empire, based on both trade and tribute. Ignacio Bernal takes an intermediate attitude, applying the term 'colonial' to Olmec influences in Tlatilco, but denying that a similar situation existed in Oaxaca. Grove takes an opposite stance and sees the adoption of Olmec forms and symbols throughout Highland Mexico as a borrowing of beliefs by peoples who themselves had little or no contact with the Gulf Coast. He regards trade as the most likely vehicle for this spread of ideas and objects, constituting a kind of status-borrowing from a more complex culture. He further considers that many of these highland sites evolved as commercial rather than as religious centres. In the case of the Guerrero murals, Grove is prepared to concede the possible presence in the two sites of an Olmec élite at one stage in their existence; they, like other sites, were situated on a principal trade route.

The exact nature of the proven Olmec penetration of the Highlands is largely a matter of personal opinion. My own belief is that they came more as traders than conquerors. Such commerce, however, would hardly have been limited to trade in the orthodox sense of the word, implying a mere exchange of goods for others of equivalent value. A more special relationship may spring up between a sophisticated people who trade exotic materials and their more primitive suppliers; such exchanges may involve a mechanism of ritual visits, the adoption of members of one group by the other, and even the exchange of wives. In the course of such exchanges, the élite of the simpler society may tend to imitate the behaviour of these visiting traders, and to adopt in part their religion, with its subtler symbolism and its gaudier trappings; by so doing, this élite would enhance its status among its own people. Hence the mechanisms of trade could explain not merely the presence of Olmec objects, but the imitation of certain forms of worship, especially among peoples who themselves already aspired to a higher level of culture, and whose élite was therefore more susceptible to the refinements of Olmec art and the mysteries of the were-jaguar cult.

Such relationships could take centuries to develop. Olmec influence in the earliest phase of their expansion, from 1200 to 900 B.C., takes the form of objects almost identical in style to those of the heartland, found extensively in both Central Mexico and Guerrero. Only during the second, or La Venta phase from, say, 900 to 600 B.C. do we find murals and rock carvings that point more directly to the adoption of Olmec beliefs and to the physical presence of certain artists, brought in to paint and carve works that had become a necessary adjunct to such beliefs. But even in these cases, the signs of Olmec culture are confined to a few traits or art forms. The pottery, for instance, of Chalcatzingo is non-Olmec and in no highland site do we find such basic features as altars, colossal heads and mosaics. In the final phase, lasting almost until the Christian era, relations between the heartland and such sites as Monte Alban and Chiapa de Corzo were less direct, since there was no precise imitation of Olmec art or religious symbols.

These observations are perforce based on what is known to date, and major finds of Olmec murals, petroglyphs, or even smaller objects in other zones, or the discovery of other La Venta forms, so far confined to the heartland, would transform the picture, already modified by the Guerrero murals.

In considering whether the Olmecs ever conquered an empire, population is surely a key factor. Some of the principal vestiges of their culture in Central Mexico belong to the San Lorenzo period, and it is to this early presence that the word 'colonial' has been applied. But Coe puts the population of San Lorenzo at 1,000, and estimates that 2,000 men could have built the site. Even supposing that San Lorenzo controlled most of the Olmec heartland at one time, it would have been most hard to recruit expeditionary forces from people living scattered in hundreds of small settlements. Equally, the population of the Island of La Venta was tiny, and it is hard to see them garrisoning Morelos and Guerrero in order to paint their murals and carve their petroglyphs.

No true comparison can be made between the Olmec heartland, in whose main centres the population could be counted in thousands, if not hundreds, and metropolitan Teotihuacan, which housed, as we shall see, up to 200,000 people, not to speak of Aztec Tenochtitlan, known to have conquered far and wide.

For the same reason, Olmec expansion is not to be compared with the performance of Tula. The Toltecs occupied Chichen Itza in the Yucatán Peninsula in about A.D. 1000. This occupation *did* involve some form of military conquest. But the Tula-Chichen relationship is quite different: *every* element of Toltec culture is found in Chichen. On the other hand, in the different regions of Mexico reached by the Olmecs, their traces are highly selective: in one place we find murals, in a second rock carving, in a third small figurines, and in a fourth glyphic writing and dot-and-bar dates. But in no place do we find these traits together.

Moreover, nowhere in the rest of Mexico are some of the most striking elements of Olmec culture to be found at all. Not only are the distinctive types of stone statues absent; in no site did people from La Venta build anything like their own fluted pyramid, whereas the architecture of later civilizations was copied widely. In most places people borrowed certain elements but continued to make pottery and even figurines in their own local style.

The importance of jade and other greenstones to the people of Mexico is hard to overstate. To the amazement of the Spaniards, native rulers valued them far more than gold; for the Olmecs greenstone was the main form of wealth, and objects made of these materials would also have been highly prized export items. In return, they received the raw stone; and in particular jade. It is known that the Classic Mayas obtained their jade from the Montague River Valley in Guatemala, and Guerrero was probably the source of supply for the bluish jade also used by the Olmecs; Chiapas was an important source for serpentine. Hence the search for fine stone could alone explain the two main lines of Olmec expansion, one to the north-west beyond the Valley of Mexico into Guerrero, and the other south-east into Chiapas and Guatemala. Obsidian was already a key material and also had a certain bearing on Olmec trade routes. From the start, San Lorenzo obtained obsidian from Guatemala and from the Valley of Mexico and later began to import it from the Pachuca region (north-east of Mexico City), which was to become the main supplier of future cultures.

Even the works of art executed *in situ*, the paintings and carvings, do not necessarily imply physical conquest. In Cacaxtla, near Tlaxcala, murals were found a few years ago that are not wholly Maya, but show a marked Maya influence. But no one ever suggests that the Mayas conquered Cacaxtla; the artists, if they were trained in the Maya land, are assumed to have been brought there by traders, who perhaps formed a special relationship with their customers in that place. This does not preclude the possibility that small groups of Olmecs lived in, say, Chalcatzingo, but without any thought of physical domination. Throughout the history of Middle America cases arise time after time of groups or colonies of one people settled within another, and this seems to have been quite a common practice, whether in Teotihuacan or Tenochtitlan. The Aztecs not only had foreign colonies in their own capital; their merchants also settled in places such as Xicalango, which lies a considerable distance east of La Venta and was not part of the Aztec Empire; had they wished to do so, they could have brought with them Aztec craftsmen from Central Mexico.

And while they may differ as to the nature of Olmec expansion, there is more agreement among scholars as to the existence of a unified political control within the heartland itself, though more excavation could clarify this point. It is hard to envisage a whole series of small independent centres, each with a population of barely a thousand, which included San Lorenzo, La Venta and a number of other unexcavated sites. They must surely have been grouped, if not into one unit, then into several. Only on such a basis could long-distance trade have been organized, and labour recruited to build the sites.

Many arguments have been advanced that La Venta was a true capital, controlling the whole heartland. But for the first and last part of the Olmec era, La Venta did not exist; however, it does stand head and shoulders above any known rival during its great period from 900 to 600 B.C. and it is not illogical to suggest that the heartland was then united into one state, with La Venta as a single capital, or as the leader of a league of several city-states, a pattern that later emerged with regularity in Ancient Mexico.

Whether it was the work of one or several political units, the overall Olmec achievement was prodigious. They did so many things undreamed of before their time that they are often called the parent civilization of Mexico. This may be an exaggeration, if it implies that all that followed stemmed exclusively from their genius. Certainly, however, they set a pattern which was to serve succeeding cultures; even if these were not wholly derived from the Olmecs, the debt which they owed to them was immense.

3

TEOTIHUACAN:
THE BIRTH OF A CITY

A NEW BEGINNING

The Olmecs had left their mark throughout the length and breadth of Middle America. On this foundation others were to build, as heirs to these pathfinders, who invented ceremonial architecture, monumental sculpture, mural painting and glyphic writing. The all-pervading Olmec culture was followed by others more diverse and regional; of these one only, as we shall see, was to escape from this regional mould, and set its stamp upon the rest.

The Olmec achievement nurtured two distinct trends, one native to the cool Central Plateau and the other to the tropical Caribbean lowlands. The Altiplano, since Olmec times, has brought forth art forms that are dramatic but austere; its architecture is geometric, precise and grandiose, while that of the Gulf Coast and of the Maya land is curvilinear and flamboyant. Such traits characterize the people of the two territories: the inhabitants of the plateau tend to be reserved and taciturn, while those of the coast are gay and extrovert, a contrast still visible in Mexico today.

The new cultures, which blossomed from about 200 B.C. to A.D. 800, belong to what is known as the 'Classic' period. This term is still generally used even in specialized works, though scholars have often proposed others, less tied to a Mediterranean context. 'Classic' is a fairly apt name for the cultures of the Altiplano, notable for their sobriety and purity of line; it is, however, also used to describe the more exuberant art of the Maya of that period.

This volume is mainly devoted to the Classic cultures of the Altiplano, whose essence was expressed in ceremonial centres made of earth and stone, covered with lime and plaster, many of which survive. Buildings were usually set in a planned complex round one or more plazas; rigidity of line was relieved by stone sculpture and painted

63

murals. In addition to their massive groups of temples, the Classic cultures have other common traits, in part an Olmec legacy: the worship of a similar but not identical pantheon of gods; the playing of the ritual ball-game; the use of some system of signs and glyphs; the development of a wide commercial network. The peoples of this genial age were ostensibly more dedicated to the arts of peace than of war; only towards the end the warriors came to the fore, as Classic gave way to Post-Classic, which was overtly militaristic.

Notwithstanding the marked differences between the regional cultures that followed the Olmecs, in varying degree they came to be overshadowed by Teotihuacan. The other major centres of the plateau, such as Monte Alban, not to speak of those of the Maya land, had their own peculiar genius. Teotihuacan, however, stood astride the Classic age of Middle America, and by virtue of this universality it must serve as our central theme in describing the period. Contemporary cultures will be treated in the context of their nexus with the great metropolis.

Visitors to modern Mexico, intent upon reaching the remoter and more exotic sites, easily forget this unique role of Teotihuacan in the Classic efflorescence. For sheer size it has no rival, and at its zenith the city covered an area of twenty square kilometres, more extensive than its contemporary, Imperial Rome. Even today it is an awesome place, with its two giant pyramids and its solemn rows of temple platforms. To the Aztecs, living a thousand years later, it seemed that these ruins were the work of giants, a belief strengthened by their discovery in the vicinity of bones of mammoth, long since extinct, that they took for those of humans.

Fray Bernardino de Sahagún explains that Teotihuacan means 'The Place where Men became Gods', and states that it had always been the burial place of kings. This belief was current at the time of the Spanish Conquest, when the main avenue was known as the Street of the Dead, though tombs are notably absent.

Olmec culture had managed to survive in part of its home territory almost until the Christian era. However, in much of the Altiplano the last trace of its presence vanished as early as 600 B.C., and an interlude followed known as the Late Pre-Classic, characterized by low platforms and simple clay figurines, and by the absence of the more sophisticated art forms brought into Central Mexico by the Olmecs.

The first attempt to break out of this rustic pattern, and to achieve something more grandiose, was made not in Teotihuacan, but in Cuicuilco. Disaster befell this site at the very moment when Teotihuacan began to be important, and Cuicuilco is therefore in a sense its forerunner, even if it is no longer proposed that refugees from the site founded Teotihuacan, whose origins are remoter. Cuicuilco is set in an eerie landscape formed by broken blocks of black lava, created when a small volcano called Xitla erupted at the very beginning of the Christian era and caused it to suffer the fate of Pompeii. The principal monument, visible from the main highway leading out of Mexico City to the south, is a round building some 17 metres high and 100 metres in diameter, with three inwardly sloping tiers of varying height; its top is reached by a ramp on the west side and by a stairway on the north. Other altars and pyramids exist in the neighbourhood, one of which was excavated in 1968 in the course of work on the nearby Olympic Village. A new suburb of Mexico City now covers much of the Cuicuilco complex, the details of which remain unknown.

The Valley of Teotihuacan is an extension of the much larger Valley of Mexico; its situation is strategic since it stands astride the easiest route to the Valley of Puebla. Though the landscape was then less bare than today the soil was never very fertile, except for the area watered by springs. As late as the 1920s so little was known of the site that it was still thought that Teotihuacan pottery was contemporary with the Aztecs, who flourished a thousand years later. Now, however, meticulous research offers a vision in depth of the city's development. Teotihuacan's emergence from village status, and its rise and fall in the course of a millennium, have been charted step by step in reports of the Teotihuacan Mapping Project, directed by archaeologist René Millon of Rochester University. In the course of this mammoth task, a computer data file was created that stored 281 separate items of information relating to each of the 5,000 sectors into which the city was divided for the purpose. These sectors were not plotted in the form of arbitrary squares and rectangles, but were made to correspond as closely as possible to architectural units or to clear spaces, such as plazas and streets.

This computer data file is probably the largest store of archaeological information ever assembled. It was copied on to 50,000 IBM cards, and involved the study of over one and a quarter million sherds and artifacts. Following this task, a clearer picture emerged of how the city rose to greatness and finally declined. An outstanding feature of the work was the gathering of large amounts of material belonging to the earlier stages of the city's existence; this made it possible to trace its expansion.

Accordingly, Millon and his colleagues, far from presenting the traditional once-and-for-all picture of past glories, have studied the silent stones of Teotihuacan in such a way as to re-create its history. Such a feat has seldom been matched in Old World research, where the task of breathing life into an ancient culture was often aided by decipherable texts. A generation ago, one could only have written of Teotihuacan in a descriptive rather than a historical sense. Now, however, at least in broad outline, we can retrace its own past from early beginnings to final collapse, while work in other places has revealed the extent of its influence on the rest of Mexico. Mexican archaeologists have meanwhile restored and revitalized the site, and in the course of their work uncovered mural paintings on a scale that offers at least a basis for the study of its religion.

However, it remains in doubt if much, if anything, will ever be known of the rulers who guided its destinies; their names and deeds are unrecorded, and, failing ampler texts, the archaeologist has no means of bringing them back to life. As a result, the history of Teotihuacan remains anonymous.

THE COURSE OF EVENTS

It has now been discovered that Teotihuacan enjoyed a prehistoric, or pre-monumental, phase. In this period, from about 600 to 200 B.C., the site of the future city was the home of small village groups, and the whole valley had a population of perhaps 6,000. These villagers tilled the soil, and were easily able to supplement their basic diet with fish and other products from the nearby Lake of Texcoco, as well as with game from the sparsely populated countryside.

The last part of this incubatory phase witnessed the creation of a very large village, spread over six square kilometres, mainly in the north-west part of the future city; it was hardly a town but a conglomeration of small buildings, divided by open spaces. Modest stone structures were erected, of which a few stood on the site of the future main axis, the Street of the Dead. In addition to these, archaeologists also found embryonic traces of the obsidian industry that became all-important in later times, and four obsidian workshops were located in this extended village. By 200 B.C., the Teotihuacan perimeter already housed some twenty per cent of its future population and this part of its history, formerly ignored, is now regarded as important.

Before this village phase came to be recognized, the city's history had already been divided into four separate stages or eras, prosaically called Teotihuacan I, II, III and IV. For simplicity's sake I prefer to use this terminology, traditionally employed by Mexican archaeologists, though American scholars have a different nomenclature, in which the Tzacualli phase approximately corresponds to Teotihuacan I, Miccaotli and Tlamililolpa to Teotihuacan II, Xolalpan to Teotihuacan III and Metepec to Teotihuacan IV. Specialists now tend to use these names, rather long and hard to memorize.

Teotihuacan I runs from 200 B.C. to A.D. 0, and marks the birth of a true city. By the end of Teotihuacan I it housed at least 40,000–50,000 inhabitants, of whom most lived in the north-western part of its final perimeter. During this period the population of the surrounding countryside actually began to fall, as part of a deliberate policy of concentrating the people within the urban limits. This emergence of a real city brought about a change in the life-style of the region, as revolutionary as that which took place when people first began to farm the land and to live in small villages.

During Teotihuacan I, the city took on its definitive shape, squarely based on the formal north-south axis of the Street of the Dead. This spinal cord does not follow an exact north-south orientation, but a line with an inclination of 15° 30′ east of north. The reasons for varying angles of deviation from true north in so many Mexican sites have been endlessly debated. Teotihuacan, like Cholula, Tula, and the main temple of Tenochtitlan, belongs to a 'family' that shares a similar, but not identical orientation. In the case of Teotihuacan, the theory that the buildings face the point where the sun sets on the longest day has been discarded as incorrect. It has been more plausibly suggested that the Street of the Dead was built to face the setting of the Pleiades at the time when it was constructed, though it is difficult to determine exactly where the constellation then vanished from view on the western horizon, whose contours may not have been identical to those of today.

There was nothing modest about this first urban period, which witnessed the creation of the most spectacular buildings of all, the Pyramids of the Sun and Moon; the Aztecs so described them to the Spaniards, but it is not likely that they were ever really dedicated to the cult of the Sun and Moon, seldom much in evidence in the art forms of Teotihuacan.

The Pyramid of the Sun was a once-for-all undertaking, in contrast to the more gradual process of enlargement of a smaller nucleus, common to many Mexican monuments. A tunnel 110 metres long was cut through its axis in 1935, and demonstrated that the huge mass was

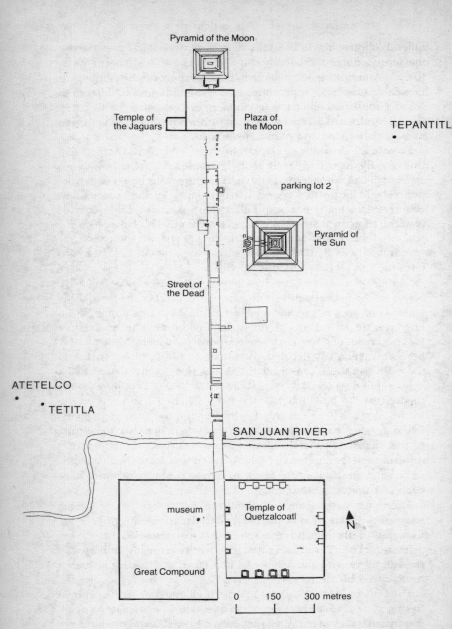

Figure 12. Plan of Teotihuacan

built out of great blocks of adobe as a single work; it contained only one earlier and smaller structure.

In all, twenty-three temple complexes belonging to Teotihuacan I have been identified, each formed by three temples built round a closed patio; sometimes a low platform encloses the fourth side. These complexes, which are typical of Central Mexico, are of modest proportions in comparison with the Pyramids of the Sun and Moon; many of them are situated along the Street of the Dead, then in the process of construction. Most of the final perimeter of the city was already inhabited, if only lightly, and in the north-west part a true town of three square kilometres existed. Building during Teotihuacan I was on a scale suggestive of a great centre not only for trade, but for religion.

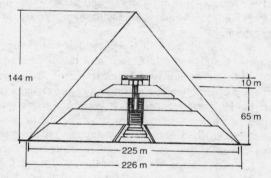

Figure 13. Pyramid of the Sun at Teotihuacan
set against triangular outline
of the Pyramid of Cheops in Egypt

The following period, Teotihuacan II, runs from A.D. 0 to 350 and witnessed its progress from city-state to metropolis, with wider ramifications. New building was concentrated in the southern part of the city, beyond and below the Pyramid of the Sun. The outstanding monument of the period is the Temple of Quetzalcoatl, noted for its sculpted façade. The great compound on the opposite side of the Street of the Dead, probably the chief market, dates from this time. The Pyramid of the Moon and the plaza in front were also then completed.

Not only had Teotihuacan become a great city, whose impact was felt throughout Ancient Mexico; it now began to attract groups of people from other regions. Its limits already embraced their maximum area of twenty square kilometres, and the strictly planned layout assumed its final shape. Teotihuacan seems to have fulfilled some kind of master plan, which took several centuries to complete and was perhaps subject to modification from time to time.

Teotihuacan II was notable for both its monumental sculpture and its architecture. In addition, a new kind of pottery came into vogue, known as 'Thin Orange', made of fine, polished orange clay, and so called because it is often as thin as an eggshell. Cups, bowls and effigy vases of men and animals, made of this material, have been found all over Middle America, often at great distances from Teotihuacan; hence it is important as a guide to the extent of the city's influence. Among the best examples of Teotihuacan pottery were the cylindrical tripod vases, often fitted with lids on top, surmounted by a bird. Many of these tripod vases are decorated in plano-relief, though the finest have been stuccoed and painted with sacred scenes, in the same manner as the murals.

These vases somewhat recall the typical bronze vessels of the contemporary Han Dynasty in China, and this likeness has led to suggestions that the design is of Chinese origin, though sheer coincidence is a more likely explanation. As I have explained in detail in another book, *Voyagers to the New World: Fact and Fantasy*, the Chinese had no ships that could reach Mexico at the time. Whole volumes have been dedicated to proving that Mexican civilization was imported from China, or elsewhere in South-East Asia. But the notion that Chinese mandarins directed the building of Teotihuacan amounts to sheer fantasy. The city has no parallel anywhere in Asia. Moreover, the Chinese plainly lacked the urge; though as early as A.D. 10 they landed in force in Korea, they did not even establish themselves in Japan until A.D. 552, and yet islands exist from which Korea and Japan can both be seen on a clear day.

Teotihuacan III (A.D. 350 to 650) is the age when the city reached the zenith of its power and glory, and its population rose to a figure of nearly 200,000. Monuments were built on a massive scale and the ruins that we see today, often built over others of an earlier date, mostly belong to this period. Even the Temple of Quetzalcoatl, dating from the previous era, was now covered by a larger and less decorative building. Teotihuacan III structures were added to the Pyramid of the Moon, in harmony with the imposing plaza of this era that stands in front of it.

Many of these buildings were restored during the programme of work undertaken by the Mexican National Institute of Anthropology between 1962 and 1964, directed by Ignacio Bernal. The scope of this great project has made it possible for the present-day visitor to gain at least some impression of the city's former grandeur. Numerous wall paintings were also discovered during these excavations; most belong to Teotihuacan III. The north-west part of the city continued to be the most densely populated, but it underwent less modification than the rest and is sometimes therefore called the 'Old City'.

The final phase, Teotihuacan IV, beginning in A.D. 650, was much shorter than the two preceding periods and lasted barely a century. At its end, the main buildings were burned and furiously wrecked.

After this cataclysm, the city collapsed – for reasons that will be studied later – and was soon reduced to mere thousands of squatters huddled among the ruins. The population was dispersed rather than slaughtered and the surrounding valley continued to be intensely cultivated; many village sites have been found, mostly quite small in size, that belong to the succeeding Toltec era. By Aztec times, the capital of the region was the town of Otumba. The Teotihuacan perimeter was not altogether abandoned and the four villages now located within the archaeological zone are known to have existed in the period immediately before the Conquest. According to one report, a stone statue stood at the top of the Pyramid of the Sun at this time; the same account states that the Emperor Moctezuma II and his priests used to come and make offerings at this shrine. Whether or not this is true, archaeologists discovered a small shrine, associated with Aztec pottery, in front of the Pyramid of the Sun.

THE MONUMENTS

Teotihuacan, far from being typical, differs notably from other Mexican sites. Most of these housed quite a small population. Usually described as ceremonial centres, many consist of a single group of monuments clustered round a main plaza. Teotihuacan, however, with its long central axis flanked with an infinity of palaces and patios, is built on a grander scale.

Today only the bare bones of the former metropolis lie exposed. It lacks the luxuriant flora of the Maya centres, or the breathtaking panoramas of hill-top sites, such as Monte Alban. However imposing the concept, the monochrome vistas of pyramids and platforms present a challenge to the visitor's imagination that is hard to meet without a basic knowledge of the city's past glories.

No account of Teotihuacan would be complete without some description of its monumental centre. I shall confine this to the most important buildings, and add something more about the standard dwellings and their layout when writing of the way of life of the average citizen.

If time permits, the best way to see Teotihuacan is to spend a night at the Villa Arqueológica Hotel and to visit the site at a reasonably early hour, before it becomes thronged with tourists, led by guides who, in their efforts to embellish the past, give full rein to their inventiveness.

As one approaches the site by the main highway, its greatest monument, the Pyramid of the Sun, can be discerned from afar, though its man-made bulk tends to merge with those natural hillocks from which, shorn of its stucco and paint, it differs little in form and colour.

This planned city was centred upon a main axis, the Street of the Dead. It is not really a street, since its central portion consists of a series of rectangular plazas, separated from each other by stairways, made to overcome the rise in level from south to north; it has equally little to do with the dead, as few burials have been found there. The Pyramid of the Moon dominates the northern end of the avenue; further to the south, it skirts the Pyramid of the Sun, from which it is separated by an ample plaza, and after crossing the San Juan River, the avenue reaches the complex known as the 'Citadel' (Ciudadela).

To the north of the Citadel, stretching as far as the Pyramid of the Moon, a line of important buildings flanks the Street of the Dead, off which smaller streets led, occupied by the many apartment compounds. Although it lacks tombs, it was essentially a *via sacra*, designed to overwhelm the viewer and impress upon him the power and glory of the city's gods.

The style of the main buildings, except for the largest of all, the two pyramids, is fairly uniform. In the series of platforms along the Street of the Dead, the dominant motif is the sloping base (*talud*), surmounted by a vertical parallel plane (*tablero*). These *tableros*, rising one above the other, were usually painted, and were therefore in effect monumental pictures, set in a stone frame. This style of architecture, so typical of Teotihuacan, served as a model for countless pyramids in other sites; in each place the ratio of sloping and straight portions was varied in such a way as to present a distinct profile to the viewer.

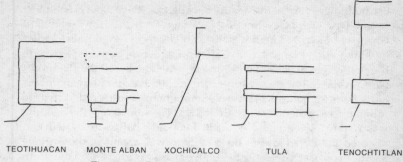

TEOTIHUACAN   MONTE ALBAN   XOCHICALCO   TULA   TENOCHTITLAN

Figure 14. Typical *talud-tablero* temple profiles

The core of nearly all the temples and platforms was made out of a porous and reddish stone, resistant to weather and light in weight. But as in all Middle American architecture, this rock was never visible through the invariable coating of plaster. Though vast quantities of quicklime were needed to make this lime plaster, not one of the ovens used for this purpose has been located in Teotihuacan.

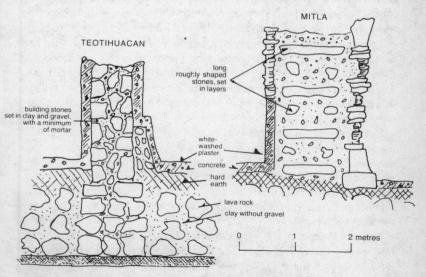

Figure 15. Comparative method of building walls in (a) Teotihuacan and (b) Mitla, Oaxaca, showing the core of stones, set in gravel, and covered by external layer of whitewash plaster

Teotihuacan's main landmark, the Pyramid of the Sun, is the highest building in Ancient Mexico outside the Maya land. Its almost square base (222 by 225 metres) is as large as that of the Pyramid of Cheops in Egypt, though it is not as high. As in Egypt, these earlier buildings are the largest. Don Carlos de Sigüenza, born in 1645, made the first archaeological dig in Mexico, when he bored the Pyramid's base. In the following century, in 1746, the Italian antiquarian Lorenzo Boturini made a map of the monument and recorded that he found traces of Sigüenza's borings; he still assumed that the building was hollow. Eventually, in 1908, Leopoldo Batres excavated and restored the Pyramid, but his treatment was drastic in the extreme and he even used dynamite to remove an outer structure on the south side, of which a few traces still remain. The long stones that project from this flank supported this outer structure; they did not serve, as is often suggested, to hold its coating of stucco.

The monument, as we now see it, consists of five great sloping bodies surmounted by platforms; built before the more standard formula was evolved, these inclined walls do not support vertical *tableros*. The interior is almost entirely formed of dried mud, covered on the outside by stone that is cut but not polished. Owing to its great height, it was made to vary from later buildings in another respect: the stairway that leads to the top is divided into sections, separated by flat platforms which also serve to give the modern visitor a chance to rest his weary legs, before completing the climb to the top. In common with other Mexican structures of its kind it is not a true pyramid, like those of Egypt, but a truncated cone that ended not in a point, but in a flat space where the temple of the god was placed; such temples were also made of stone but often had a thatched roof.

Contemporary with the Pyramid of the Sun is the other great mound known as the Pyramid of the Moon, which fortunately escaped Batres' demolition squad. It also consists of four great sloping platforms that formerly supported a temple at their summit. It is thirty-five metres high, but because it is built on higher ground than the loftier Pyramid of the Sun (sixty-four metres), their tops stand at the same level.

Directly in front of the Pyramid is the Plaza of the Moon, a formalized series of twelve platforms that deserves to rank among the world's finest squares. Like those in front of the Pyramid of the Sun, the plaza platforms were built much later than the main structure, at a time when the *talud-tablero* pattern was firmly set. The Pyramid of the Sun may impress by sheer bulk, but the appeal of the smaller monument is more delicate; towards dusk the play of shadows on its façade reflects both the vigour and refinement of this early style.

The Temple of Quetzalcoatl belongs to Teotihuacan II; it dates from about A.D. 200 and is also therefore to be counted among the earlier buildings of a city that was to thrive for five more centuries. Situated in the great sunken courtyard known as the Citadel (Ciudadela) below the Sun Pyramid, on the same side of the Street of the Dead, it lay buried beneath a latter-day structure, removed by Manuel Gamio in his important work on the site from 1917 to 1922. The western façade, which is all that remains of the original temple, is unique among the monuments of Ancient Mexico. Built in the early days of the *talud-tablero*, it consisted of six *tableros* of finely cut stone, divided from each other by a very short sloping *talud*; only the four lower tiers survive. In the centre of this façade is an enormous stairway, whose balustrades are decorated by serpent heads in high relief, another trait that was to be copied in many sites. The vertical *tableros* bear two alternating motifs: the first is a great stone serpent head, stylized and yet realistic, that emerges from a circular collar of rigid and regular plumes, resembling petals; the second is even more stylized and features the typical goggle eyes of the god Tlaloc. These motifs are carved as if floating on water, set with shells, and vestiges of their paint are still visible. At the top of the structure which later covered this façade a thick layer of shells was found, below which were placed human bones and skulls, together with many small jade counters and other objects.

A new large-scale archaeological project was started in 1980 by the National Institute under Mexican archaeologist Rubén Cabrera. While important work is also being carried out in two palace compounds on the west side of the Street of the Dead, another major objective is to investigate further and to restore the Ciudadela. The two extensive buildings on each side of the Temple of Quetzalcoatl are being fully explored; unusually large rooms have come to light, a find which reinforces the notion that these structures served as an administrative centre for the city.

In addition, a large compound or plaza is under study on the north side of the Ciudadela, to which it is joined by a stairway, recently discovered. Circular buildings, of a kind previously unknown in Teotihuacan, have come to light. The most fascinating discovery made during 1981 in this complex is a large cache of moulds for making ceremonial clay figures, wearing adornments and elaborate headdresses. The complex clearly included a very special workshop that produced no domestic pottery, but specialized exclusively in objects used in the ceremonial centre, of which it forms part. The outer walls of the compound show clearly that it underwent a long series of reconstructions, a feature that will be left visible after the present project is completed.

The nearest rival in sculpture to the Temple of Quetzalcoatl is the Palace of the Quetzal Butterfly (Quetzalpapalotl), restored in the 1960s. Situated behind a large platform on the west side of the Moon Plaza, it is entered through a patio formed by twelve quadrangular pillars; they are carved with stone reliefs, highly symbolized, and adorned with creatures that are part bird and part butterfly, from which the palace takes its present name. The butterflies are unmistakable but the birds look more like owls than quetzals. Once the fractured pieces of these pillars were reassembled, archaeologists were able to estimate their height and that of the cloister ceiling and could then complete the only reconstruction of a roofed building in Central Mexico.

The Palace is the best surviving specimen of the architecture of Teotihuacan III, to which so many of the main monuments belong; it covered an earlier structure, known as the Temple of the Jaguars, named after its feline mural painting. Like the façade of the Temple of Quetzalcoatl, this artistic jewel had been simply buried beneath a later building.

While the serpent heads of the Temple of Quetzalcoatl and the pillars of the Palace of the Quetzal Butterfly can be seen *in situ*, two other giant figures, though divorced from their original setting, help to give an idea of the grandeur of the city's sculpture. The most famous is the great carving that now stands at the entrance to the National Museum of Anthropology. Until a few years ago, it remained embedded in the rock out of which it had been hewn, some twenty kilometres south of Teotihuacan, presumably because its carvers lacked the means to move it to its intended site; when it was taken to Mexico City, a millennium and a half later, a special conveyance had to be brought from Texas for the purpose. The figure is known as Tlaloc, but is more likely to be his sister, the Goddess of Terrestrial Water, since it wears an unmanly skirt. In the National Museum stands another statue of the Goddess of the Waters, three metres high, that was found near the Pyramid of the Moon in 1860, and impresses by its grand design and by its delicate detail. These carvings are strictly architectural, and adapt the human figure to geometric shapes, in harmony with the essence of Classic Teotihuacan building, the invariable pattern of slope and panel.

Figure 16. Bird columns in Palace
of Quetzal Butterfly, Teotihuacan

Teotihuacan stoneworkers also carved countless masks, apparently intended as votive offerings, though no tombs of importance have
been found. The style of the earlier masks is related to those of Olmec
times; the later ones present a more triangular outline, with narrow
horizontal eyes, thin lips and a half-open mouth. The Aztecs were
also great makers of masks, and the tradition thus persisted from the
beginning to the end of pre-Hispanic civilization.

ART AND RELIGION

In its formalized sculpture, Teotihuacan never surpassed the Olmecs.
In the art of wall-painting, however, it was unrivalled. Almost all
excavated wall surfaces were once adorned with complex figures and
signs; so far, forty structures with paintings have been completely or
partially uncovered, and 350 murals have been found, taken mostly
from the lower walls; these represent only a fraction of the original
total, numbering perhaps tens of thousands, constantly repaired or
repainted.

Some knowledge of its mural art is basic to an understanding of the
city, and of what it stood for. In terms of pure craftsmanship, this
school of New World painting might be classed with that of Florence
in the Old, though its masterpieces are poorly preserved. Moreover,
the interest of this painting is not confined to its aesthetic qualities, for
it is also our only guide, however unsure, to the nature of the gods
who ruled the Classic cosmos. Unlike in Italy, where frescoes were
mostly confined to churches, cloisters and *palazzi*, those of the Mexican metropolis formed a background to the lives of rich and poor
alike, since they are found on the walls not only of temples and
palaces but also of apartment compounds where ordinary citizens
lived and worked. They adorned buildings both in the centre of the
city and in the outskirts.

These murals, far from being buried as offerings like the Olmec
jade, were made for the living. Teotihuacan was a painted city, and
these paintings are the very essence of its being, telling us not only of
its religion, but of customs and ceremonies, clothing and adornments. One learns, for instance, that a version of the ball-game was
played, though no courts have been found. According to one illustration, the ball was propelled with sticks rather than with the body, as
elsewhere.

The Mexican art historian, Miguel Covarrubias, aptly described the

painting of Teotihuacan as austere and distinguished, gay and graceful, and intensely religious. Many themes are related to nature: water
and mountains, trees, fruit, flowers, maize, cacao, butterflies, owls
and other birds, shells, snails, jaguars, coyote dogs, serpents and
armadillos. Abstract shapes and forms also abound, many of which
depict the headdress, mouth-mask, tongue and fangs of the mighty
Tlaloc: others derive from stylized versions of jaguars' paws or of
other animals.

The murals are painted in characteristic native style, without the
use of perspective. Space is illustrated by placing the more distant
objects higher up and the nearer ones lower down. As in Egyptian art,
the leading dignitaries are often drawn larger than other people. The
paintings are anonymous, and the very notion that an artist should
sign his work would have struck an Ancient Mexican as grotesque, for
they belonged to the gods, not to the craftsmen who created them.

The first important murals were discovered by Leopoldo Batres in
the late nineteenth century in a building that he named the Temple of
Agriculture. They have since almost vanished and we are left only
with Batres' own copies. As the name of the temple implies, they
display a wide range of produce that is being offered to the gods. At
the bottom, as in so many instances, turquoise-green waves are
drawn; above these, various figures are shown in the act of bringing
their offerings, which are heaped in front of them in two piles, from
which spirals of smoke pour forth.

The art of mural-painting was at its height between A.D. 450 and
650, when Teotihuacan's cultural influence was felt throughout Mexico. The most famous of all is the Tepantitla painting, discovered in
1942 in a palace or residence situated a short distance behind the
Pyramid of the Sun. Only part of the original mural survives, but a
reconstructed copy of the whole can be seen in the National Museum
in Mexico City. On the upper level are two paintings of Tlaloc, who
wears a towering crown of foliage, studded with water symbols, birds
and flowers. The god presides over another scene in the lower half, so
animated that it is almost like a comic strip; painted on a red background, a host of diminutive naked figures are seen at play, grouped
round a mountain on which tropical trees grow, and out of which two
rivers sprout. These little people are engaged in a variety of activities:
bathing, cutting flowers, resting under trees, taking fish from the
rivers, dancing and chasing butterflies as large as themselves. From
their mouths emerge stylized speech scrolls, as if they were shouting
or singing.

Because the element of water pervades this scene, Mexican archaeologist Alfonso Caso called it Tlalocan, the place which in latter-day Aztec legend was the paradise of Tlaloc as Rain God; it was then conceived as the place where the clouds were formed and the souls of the dead gathered. It was reserved for the elect of the Rain God: those who died by drowning, from epilepsy or from venereal diseases.

Figure 17. Ball-court player
in Tepantitla 'Tlaloc' mural

Anthropologist Peter Furst interprets this so-called paradise scene in quite a different way and suggests that the great tree above the frontal deity is not a vegetation symbol at all, but represents the Morning Glory vine, whose hallucinogenic seeds were treated as divine in Aztec times and are still used today to induce a state of ecstatic intoxication. For Furst and certain others, the central figure is not Tlaloc or any other male deity, but an earth and fertility goddess.

Most visitors see the frieze of the Temple of Jaguars, which lies on the standard tourist route. Not many, however, are taken to the 'Tlalocan' mural, and even fewer view the two other great series of paintings. In the first of these, Tetitla, lying some distance to the west of the principal monuments, occur four representations of the god Tlaloc, dressed once more in a huge feather headdress. His upper face takes the form of a bird, below which protrude white fangs, characteristic of the god. From his hands flow drops of water and other fertility symbols, such as seeds. Tetitla's interest is not confined to its murals; it is also a superb specimen of a palace compound, divided into a veritable maze of patios, temples and small rooms, some little more than cubicles. On almost every wall one sees vestiges of murals, many of which are decorated not with men and animals, but with strange and undecipherable symbols.

A few hundred metres from Tetitla lies a rather different palace, Atetelco, also outstanding both for its architecture and murals. It is built round a series of open spaces; the most striking is the White Patio, decorated on three sides with friezes of alternating coyote dogs and jaguars wearing sumptuous feather headdresses and with long speech scrolls coming out of their mouths. Enclosing these motifs and acting as a kind of frame is a net, adorned with feathers and with jade counters. The net, used to hunt aquatic birds, is an important element in Teotihuacan art.

Many Teotihuacan murals present a great frontal head, sometimes combined with other figures seen in profile; for instance, in the Tlalocan painting the frontal deity with his ritual paraphernalia and huge headdress is flanked by attending celebrants. Another favourite theme consists of processional profile figures, either humans dressed in part-animal costume or animals behaving as humans. Jaguars are numerous, as well as birds, and spotted dog-like creatures appear in Tetitla. Some of its paintings are almost abstract, lacking men, animals and recognizable objects which can tell us what they mean.

In art that employs perspective, the normal purpose is to portray a scene, to create a window into nature and to produce a likeness. In contrast, Teotihuacan painting presents images which had a specific meaning for the viewer not as lifelike objects, but as symbols, whose message often now escapes us. Among the rich store of glyphs and symbols, certain leading themes or complexes stand out. Of these, the most important is the so-called Rain God complex, in which certain forms, such as shells, drops of rain and rich vegetation predominate, in combination with plumed serpents, jaguars and coyotes. A second complex emphasizes the butterfly theme, while a third is centred upon a predatory owl, armed with arrows and a shield.

The Yale art historian, George Kubler, in his analysis of Teotihuacan's obscure iconography, stresses that the artist's main interest was not to draw likenesses of objects and of humans. More often he depicts hybrid beings, bird-serpents, double-headed jaguars, feathered jaguar-serpents, and even the human figure is often compounded, a bird's beak being combined with human hands. The images of jaguars – often wearing human dress – are not natural jaguars, but relate to the image or concept for which that animal stood. And in addition to these odd, if recognizable forms, fifty-seven signs have been identified that are almost certainly writing glyphs.

From this Kubler, in offering what he calls a provisional answer to the riddle, deduces that the artist, whose interest in recording appearances was so limited, uses symbols as a form of writing in order to convey a meaning. He even suggests that some symbols are in effect adjectives, used to describe qualities. Verbal statements may be included, as when a roadway marked with footprints denotes the act of walking on the part of jaguar-headed men.

Kubler suggests that the frontal figures in the murals are cult images, while those shown in profile are human celebrants or priests. He utters a timely warning against the common assumption that, despite the 800-year time-interval between Teotihuacan and Aztec art – whose iconography is better understood – they form part of an unbroken chain and that the same symbols therefore mean the same thing for the two peoples. But just as the Classic Orpheus and the Christian Good Shepherd assumed like form but unlike essence, so the feathered serpent, for instance, may come to mean different things in the course of a thousand years.

Figure 18. Tepantitla 'Red' Tlaloc

The same reasoning applies to the 'Rain God' Tlaloc. Though we do not know what language was spoken in Teotihuacan, Tlaloc is a Nahuatl name, commonly believed to derive from *tlaloa*, meaning 'to run'; hence the association with flowing or falling rain. But Nahuatl scholar Thelma Sullivan has convincingly argued that a truer rendering of the name is to be found in the word *tlalli*, meaning 'earth'.

Admittedly throughout Mexican history earth and rain gods tend to be associated, since both earth and rain are linked to fertility and to the ripening of corn. Moreover, earth gods lived in caves, which often covered springs. Water was unquestionably a leading element in Teotihuacan imagery and many marine objects figure in its painting and sculpture. The cult of Tlaloc pervades the mural art of Teotihuacan, just as Christian themes predominated in that of Europe; his worship attracted pilgrims from afar, and his goggle-eyed image was copied throughout Mexico. However, it is dangerous to assume that just because in Aztec times Tlaloc was mainly the Rain God, he perforce played the same role in Teotihuacan. Here Tlaloc was King of the Gods and as such becomes the bounteous creator and source of all fertility, transcending the simple role of Rain God, to which he was later relegated.

Jade counters that fall from Tlaloc's hands may, as is often suggested, symbolize water, but they could equally stand for riches and tribute, since jade was held to be more precious than gold. The drops of liquid, often reddish in colour, that fall from his fangs as well as from his hands are usually taken for water but could just as well be blood.

A further clue as to the true essence of Tlaloc, and to the mystique of Teotihuacan as holy city and place of pilgrimage, has come to light in recent years. In 1971 Ernesto Taboada, then in charge of the archaeological zone, chanced upon the remains of a stairway that led to a cave-tunnel through the bedrock underneath the Pyramid of the Sun and ending in a series of chambers in the form of a cloverleaf.

This subterranean cave must have been known when the Pyramid was built. In remote times, like many others, it may have been the outlet of a spring. The four chambers of the cloverleaf at the end of the cave-tunnel are divided by man-made walls. As interpreted by archaeologist Doris Heyden, the tunnel suggests some kind of cult, of which these chambers formed the inner sanctuary.

The cave centre lies exactly below the middle of the Pyramid. Its discovery gave substance to Millon's own reasoning; for some time his intuition told him that Teotihuacan owed its unique holiness to some pristine sanctuary beneath the main pyramid. Since the Earth God's traditional home was a cave, this early shrine adds force to the notion of a link between Tlaloc and earth, as well as water.

4

THE WORLD OF TEOTIHUACAN

THE TEOTIHUACAN EXPANSION

While it remains an open question how far, if at all, Teotihuacan was an imperial power in the military sense, its cultural imprint pervades the archaeological record. This impact can be traced almost to the United States border in the north and to Guatemala City and beyond in the south; it was present not only on the Pacific but also on the Gulf Coast, where it reached into the Maya land; it began to be felt in the first two centuries of the Christian era, well before the city reached its prime.

Just as the Mapping Project put Teotihuacan itself in a new perspective, so the work of other archaeologists now tells us much more about its widespread influence in other regions. To plot such influences would produce a patchwork quilt, since their nature and intensity varied greatly from place to place and there would also be blank spaces in such a map, where they were absent altogether. Teotihuacan's impact was particularly strong in regions bordering both the Caribbean and Pacific littorals. In the present-day state of Guerrero, in an area lying halfway between Mexico City and Acapulco, jade masks, figurines and other objects of undoubted Teotihuacan inspiration abound. In Guerrero, Teotihuacan was merely following in the footsteps of the Olmecs. But unlike the latter, its culture spread much further to the north-west along the Pacific coastline; at the site of Ixtepete, near Guadalajara, such traits are so marked as to give rise to suggestions that people from the metropolis were physically present. These cultural tentacles stretch as far as Chametla, near the modern Mazatlan, some 1,400 kilometres distant from Teotihuacan itself. Traces of Teotihuacan-type civilization, lasting right up to its fall, have also been found in the states of Durango and Zacatecas, in the region that lies midway between Chametla and the Valley of Mexico.

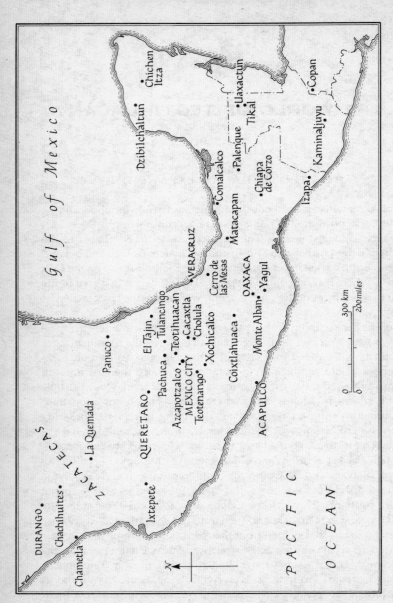

Gulf of Mexico

Chichen
Itza

Dzibilchaltun

Uaxactun
Palenque   Tikal   Copan
Comalcalco
Chiapa   Kaminaljuyu
Matacapan   de Corzo
Izapa

VERACRUZ

Cerro de
las Mesas   OAXACA
El Tajin   Cacaxtla   Yagul
Pachuca   Tulancingo   Cholula
Azcapotzalco   Teotihuacan   Xochicalco
Panuco   MEXICO CITY   Coixtlahuaca   Monte Alban
Teotenango

QUERETARO   ACAPULCO

La Quemada

DURANGO   ZACATECAS
Chachihuites
Ixtepete

Chametla

PACIFIC

OCEAN

N

300 km
200 miles

MAP 2. *THE TEOTIHUACAN ERA*

The Teotihuacan sphere of influence thus embraced a vast territory to the north-west that had been *terra incognita* to the Olmecs; by Aztec times, as we shall see, the bounds of civilization had receded and much of it was once more the home of nomad hunters. Teotihuacan's penetration along the Gulf Coast was equally strong, both in the Huaxteca to the north and in the Cerro de las Mesas area much further south. Beyond this, in the very centre of the Olmec heartland, the site of Matacapan, which still awaits a fuller study, has yielded remains whose architecture and pottery bear the stamp of Teotihuacan almost as strikingly as those of Kaminaljuyu in Guatemala, to be discussed later. On the other hand, in the land between the Huaxteca and these more southerly enclaves, Teotihuacan influences are far less conspicuous. This region was the home of the Tajin civilization, to be described in the next chapter. El Tajin created a style all of its own, though it used the *talud-tablero* formula.

Beyond Tabasco, Teotihuacan also penetrated the Maya region and some but not all of the Classic Maya centres opened their doors to its culture. The greatest of all, Tikal, in northern Guatemala, was among the sites where this penetration is the most visible, though Teotihuacan-inspired objects found there admittedly form a smallish fraction of the total. In Tikal one even finds vestiges of *talud-tablero* architecture, together with the goggle-eyed Tlaloc design on handbags and shields, and images of the god are carved on at least four stelae of the fifth century A.D. Thin Orange pottery, another sure pointer, has appeared in Maya sites in Guatemala, as well as objects made from the green obsidian characteristic of the metropolis. Thin Orange was also found at Copan, the important Maya site in the Republic of Honduras. Trade and commerce between the two regions tended to be reciprocal, and art historians have pointed to Maya influences in a few Teotihuacan murals; Maya polychrome pottery has also been found in what is known as the 'merchants' quarter' of the metropolis, and to a lesser extent in other parts of the city. It is not known how far Teotihuacan gods were worshipped and their rites copied in the Maya cities, though in Oaxaca Teotihuacan-type objects have been found, associated with gods not hitherto depicted there.

The metropolitan penetration of the Maya region began soon after A.D. 300 and reached a climax between A.D. 400 and 500. The Maya, as we have seen, dated their monuments by a system of glyphs, combined with dots and bars, that can now be read and correlated to our own calendar. This known Maya chronology has provided the best method of fixing that of the middle phases of Teotihuacan, whose products have been found in association with Maya monuments and pottery bearing glyphs. Since the mid-seventies, a breakthrough has been made in interpreting these glyphs and some of the powerful dynasties of the Classic Maya are now being identified. Any notion that the rulers of Tikal were in any way subordinate to Teotihuacan is surely exaggerated, notwithstanding the evidence of high-level contacts between the two places.

Figure 19. Teotihuacan-style figure
on Stela 32, Tikal, Guatemala

However marked the city's influence in the jungles of northern Guatemala, it pales before the intensity of its presence in the site of Kaminaljuyu, now submerged beneath a modern suburb of Guatemala City, few of whose dwellers are aware of its existence, let alone of its significance. The parallels between Kaminaljuyu and Teotihuacan are so arresting that archaeologist A. V. Kidder was led to suggest that the former was a colony of the latter.

The typical *talud-tablero* formula is omnipresent in the temples of Kaminaljuyu. The site enjoyed a long history; by 500 B.C., long before Teotihuacan came to the fore, it had already reached its maximum extent. Only much later, in about A.D. 400, did Teotihuacan make itself felt, but the exactitude with which its forms were then reproduced suggests that they were imported direct from their place of origin; in this period, known as the Esperanza phase, Kaminaljuyu enjoyed a cultural renaissance as a replica of Teotihuacan, complete with its typical sculpture, architecture and Tlaloc murals. Such extraordinary parallels have led to suggestions that Kaminaljuyu was for Teotihuacan a key military base, whose purpose was to control the rich lowlands of the Pacific Coast. Supporting evidence for such a theory is, however, unsubstantial. Uncanny similarities do exist between the two centres, but also the differences are so marked as to call in question the 'colonial' status of Kaminaljuyu. For instance, clay figurines, stone masks and Fire God braziers, traits so typical of Teotihuacan culture, are absent.

Kaminaljuyu was far from being an isolated outpost and Teotihuacan influences are also present in the Oaxaca region in south-east Mexico, some halfway between Kaminaljuyu and the metropolis. These are mainly found in the great centre of Monte Alban, though the proportion of Teotihuacan-type objects found there is small by comparison with Kaminaljuyu.

While Teotihuacan traits thus appear in the site, Monte Alban created from earliest times a distinctive style of its own. The civilization of the Zapotecs, and of the Mixtecs who later supplanted them, has a unique place in the pre-Columbian past. Because it was more a regional culture, lacking the universality of Teotihuacan or Tenochtitlan, it remains marginal to our theme, and only the briefest account, which does scant justice to its grandeur, can therefore be given.

Many vestiges of these past glories survive today, and Monte Alban is a 'must' for travellers to Mexico, to be combined with a visit to the city of Oaxaca, with its ornate churches and bustling market. The whole Valley of Oaxaca is studded with monuments of pre-Hispanic and colonial times; as a synthesis of the finer elements in Mexico's past, it has no rival. Monte Alban, which will forever be linked with the memory of Alfonso Caso, the Mexican archaeologist who excavated the site and revived its ancient glories, is best seen shortly before dusk. High up on the hill a huge platform was cut out of the living rock, 750 metres long by 250 metres wide. On this platform, situated 400 metres above the modern city and the valley, a spacious plaza was then constructed, flanked on all sides by temples, tombs and ball-courts. These pyramidal structures are joined by broad platforms, on which stood palaces and dwelling houses; all were once stuccoed and painted. The large ball-court is built in the form of a capital I; above the sloping surfaces are stone stands for the spectators. While the plaza buildings that are visible today mainly date from the fifth to seventh century A.D., a few – as already mentioned – derive from late Olmec and early post-Olmec times.

The full significance of the ceremonial centre to the people of the

Valley of Oaxaca remains a mystery, though the abundance of tombs suggests that, unlike Teotihuacan, the rulers and nobles of neighbouring communities lie buried there. No source of water has been found; for this reason, if for no other, it must be assumed that only a privileged few dwelt on the site, while the common people had their homes down below, outside the ceremonial area.

The subterranean tombs that have been found are one of the main features. Many consist of an elaborate chamber, complete with antechamber, roofed by a corbelled vault. The best preserved is Tomb 104, adorned with fine frescoes, hurriedly painted while the dead man awaited burial. At the top of the façade, which is a reproduction in miniature of a temple, a niche contains an urn in the form of a man, whose headdress is like that of the Teotihuacan Tlaloc. The door is a single slab and the interior contained rich offerings, including specimens of the clay urns that are so typical of Monte Alban. The style of the murals also recalls Teotihuacan, though some of the gods are different; the most important of these was a rain deity called Cosijo; the Plumed Serpent is present and a bat god was also of special importance.

The use of glyphs may have actually originated in Monte Alban, as we have seen, and by the time of its Classic efflorescence a fully-fledged writing system existed. These glyphs are numerous but, apart from some dates, few have yet been deciphered.

Teotihuacan influence in Monte Alban is more stylistic than fundamental, notwithstanding the uniform *talud-tablero* profile of the monumental architecture. The great burial urns, however, are unique to Monte Alban, while the types of people depicted in its murals and the day-signs associated with their names differ from those found in the metropolis. Since both El Tajin and Monte Alban developed their own styles, they serve to show that Teotihuacan's impact had certain limitations. Unlike Kaminaljuyu, in Monte Alban we are in the presence of an indirect influence more than a direct penetration; the site clung to its own identity and while both Olmec and Teotihuacan traces were in turn perceptible, they were never predominant.

Moreover, Mexico in the Classic era brought forth other cultures that have even less to do with Teotihuacan. Among the most singular is that found not far from the city of Veracruz, known as Remojadas. Typical of this are seated human figures carved in stone, both male and female; some are warriors and ball-game players, but the most familiar of all are the smiling female heads, whose expression almost recalls Leonardo da Vinci's *Mona Lisa*. In spite of their frozen, if enigmatic, smiles, the realities of Ancient Mexico make it more likely that they were sacrificial victims, their look of anguish masked by a simulated grin induced by a hallucinogenic draught.

Another art form that has no parallel in Teotihuacan derives from the present-day states of Colima and Nayarit on the Pacific littoral. The region has been inadequately studied, but a great variety of clay figures have been recovered, mainly by amateurs, from multichambered stone tombs, abundant in western Mexico in the Classic period, though unrelated to Teotihuacan. Tombs of a similar kind have also been found in Ecuador, and this gave rise to the notion that they were first introduced into Mexico by sea voyagers. This may be quite possible, though if such contacts took place, they were more probably made by people who followed the coast, and navigated coastal creeks, than by travellers across the open sea between Ecuador and Mexico, whose winds and currents are notoriously treacherous.

In Nayarit very large clay objects have been found, painted in black, white and yellow on a reddish background. They even include model ball-courts, with the game in progress. Most familiar of all are the Colima clay figures. Models of these are sold in every tourist shop in Mexico today, while for the benefit of those in search of something more 'authentic', numerous fakes have been produced with such skill that they are hard to distinguish from original pieces. Particularly famous are the Colima figures of little pot-bellied dogs of the hairless breed that figured as a delicacy in Mexican banquets. They are moulded in every attitude, playing and even dancing together. Other vessels represent birds and reptiles as well as human beings.

THE HOME BASE

Teotihuacan's influence on many distant regions was, as we have seen, extensive but variable and even at times debatable. However, a consensus prevails as to the concept of a home or metropolitan area, whose culture was so identical to that of the parent city as to make it probable that it was brought under physical control. This home territory embraced the Valley of Mexico, together with the south-east part of the state of Hidalgo, centred upon Pachuca, and stretching as far as Tulancingo to the north-east. Here one no longer finds a hybrid style, combined with local influences, since the typical Teotihuacan traits are present in their entirety. The city itself had absorbed much of the population in its vicinity, and these provincial centres were therefore fairly small, housing two or three thousand people each.

The abundance of Teotihuacan remains in the Puebla Valley to the south-east suggests that this also formed part of the home territory. Moreover, the valley contained a great centre, Cholula, situated some 100 kilometres from Teotihuacan, and capable of serving as a second capital, just as the Aztecs drew strength from a close alliance between Tenochtitlan and nearby Texcoco.

Cholula was no mere satellite, but an important city in its own right, and one which was to outlive Teotihuacan and survive until Conquest times. Its site (also provided with a Villa Arqueológica Hotel) is another 'must' for the modern traveller, who can combine this visit with a trip to Puebla, so rich in colonial monuments. As the visitor descends into the plain, after a spectacular drive through the pine forests and snow-capped volcanoes of the Sierra Nevada, he sees before him, glittering in the sun, the tiled domes of a myriad of churches. The most conspicuous of these stands at the top of quite a large hill. Only when one gets closer can it be seen that this is no natural elevation, but a great man-made mound, the largest structure in the New World, one of the biggest ever made by man, and bulkier than any of the pyramids of Egypt.

The Cholula of Aztec times stood on another site, and the earlier pyramid was already a great green hill and remained so until excavations were started in 1931 and it came to be realized that it was a man-made monument, whose base measured 400 by 400 metres. At that time over three kilometres of tunnels were bored through its mass, in order to study the successive cultural levels that lay buried beneath it.

By 400 B.C., Cholula was already occupied and its earliest platforms were built of mud and stone; in the course of its history the great pyramid was rebuilt and enlarged six times. Its *talud-tablero* profile is similar to that of Teotihuacan, though coastal influences, particularly from El Tajin, are also present. It was a great trading centre in Classic times, and was to remain so throughout its long history; among the objects found in the site are some from Monte Alban and Xochicalco.

In the late 1960s and early 1970s, the Mexican National Institute of Anthropology decided to investigate more fully the great mound, so far known only by tunnels bored into its sides. The project was headed by the veteran archaeologist Ignacio Marquina. The pyramid is so huge that to excavate and reconstruct the whole monument would have been a gargantuan task. Instead, the work was confined to the south side; even this more limited undertaking, involving a fraction of the entire structure, required the removal of hundreds of thousands of tonnes of earth. As a result, a whole complex of temples, palaces and plazas were uncovered, some painted with fine murals. Among the major discoveries was an imposing square, named the Plaza of the Altars owing to the presence of great thrones on each of three sides; a fourth could not be found. This plaza formed the approach to the pyramid, the rest of which remains uncovered. The presence of three thrones gave added force to the notion that Cholula – and possibly Teotihuacan – were governed by several co-rulers, rather than by a sole king.

A sensational find was made by archaeologists who bored into the pyramid and located an older structure, of which one whole wall was painted with some of the most striking frescoes ever found in Mexico. These were called 'The Drunkards', since they portrayed a series of paired figures, larger than life and richly adorned, facing each other and holding up, as if in a toast, beakers of pulque, the sacred beverage of Ancient Mexico, drunk mainly as a religious rite; according to one tradition, pulque was invented in Cholula. These frescoes were painted in about A.D. 200, half a millennium before the fall of Classic Cholula.

It was once thought that the city had held out as a bastion of civilization for some time after the fall of Teotihuacan. But the excavations proved that the ceramic phases in the two sites are closely linked, and Classic Cholula seems therefore to have also fallen in about A.D. 750. However, unlike Teotihuacan, it staged a comeback; a slow recovery set in that took centuries to complete; the pyramid fell into disuse but a new Cholula arose under the site of the modern town, and became a thriving centre in the closing centuries of the pre-Hispanic era.

STATE AND EMPIRE

It is nowadays agreed that Teotihuacan was in every sense a true state. The very scale of construction, even in quite early times, could only have been the product of a mature society, far removed from the tribal level. Apart from the religious monuments, domestic architecture reveals marked social and material differences, more characteristic of a state than of a tribal polity. There are huge dwellings that can justly be called palaces, others are medium-sized, and finally some are little more than huts.

It was, moreover, much more than a mere city-state, owing to its control of nearby territory and its penetration of remoter regions. To assess the significance of this Teotihuacan penetration, the differences between the metropolitan zone and the more distant lands are crucial. In outlying areas the intensity of its influence, while ever-present, varies from one place to another and the extent of its military conquests has accordingly been hotly debated.

It has been argued with some force, first that Kaminaljuyu, and conceivably the south Veracruz-Tabasco region, were imperial provinces, because of an assembly of Teotihuacan traits so striking as to suggest an armed presence. It has even been proposed that in other places, such as Oaxaca, and the Huaxteca on the Gulf Coast, commercial contacts are on such a scale as to suggest some sort of physical control. Such opinions are based on what is known of the methods of Aztec merchants, who tended to confine their operations to regions already under Aztec rule, or at least marked for future conquest. Hence it is argued that Teotihuacan merchants must also have operated under a military umbrella.

Both similarity of style and intensity of trade are therefore advanced as proof that Teotihuacan, if it did not conquer every corner of such remoter regions, at least controlled strategic points. But to equate trading links with armed assault, and to maintain that Teotihuacan merchants acted as a military vanguard, is to invoke once more the tenuous dogma that all the earlier peoples of Mexico must have acted exactly as did the Aztecs. Scholars nurtured on Old World traditions are tempted to conjure up visions of far-flung empires whenever they see an impressive array of pyramids and plazas, as in Teotihuacan. Others are eager to detect signs of imperial rule wherever the art and architecture of one place is copied in another. But the archaeological record normally offers proof of contact rather than of conquest, and the leap from trade links and artistic parallels to assertions about political control is long and hazardous.

Sanders and Price, in their significant work *Mesoamerica: The Evolution of a Civilization*, insist that such similarities of style, particularly in temple architecture, are to be taken as evidence of physical control over a given area, on grounds which they describe as 'obvious'; according to their line of reasoning, a local group might purchase portable foreign objects as exotic household baubles and as offerings for their dead; however, such a group would be reluctant to supply the manpower to build monuments in honour of foreign gods. Hence large-scale ceremonial architecture of an alien style is taken as proof that outside force gained control over the local surplus labour.

This logic has certain flaws. England in the eighteenth century adopted Palladian architecture for the houses of its ruling class. The style originated in the Venetian Republic, but this does not prove that England was a province of Venice. Thereafter, 'Chinoiserie' became fashionable in England, both for building and decoration. According to the thinking of Sanders and Price, if England's 'surplus labour' was used to build the Brighton Pavilion for the Prince-Regent, this suggests that the country, freed from the tyranny of Venice, had promptly become a Chinese colony.

In another context, Sanders maintains that Teotihuacan not only conquered far and wide, but even set out to impose on much of Mexico its techniques of government, based on a hereditary ruling class, a centrally administered judiciary, an efficient corvée labour system, combined with the levy of tribute and backed by a professional military caste. He discerns types of domination, varying from true colonization in Kaminaljuyu to a more diffuse, less intensive control in Tikal; in that site Teotihuacan's impact was more commercial than political and in a very recent discussion attended by the author, Sanders tended to lay less stress on its military presence elsewhere, and to emphasize the part played by its merchants.

Notwithstanding such opinions to the contrary, the manpower available to Teotihuacan was surely not adequate to subjugate vast regions of Mexico on a long-term basis; admittedly the city population was large, but it stood alone, lacking the satellite centres that ringed the Aztec capital and supplied their cannon fodder. The latter could thereby draw for military service on a population nearly ten times larger than that of Teotihuacan.

Moreover, while it will later be explained that in Teotihuacan militarism was gaining ground at the time of its fall, if not before, there is little in its art and architecture at its apogee to suggest any obsession with war and conquest. Notwithstanding the presence in murals of eagles and jaguars, which later became symbols of war, the imagery of Teotihuacan does nothing to glamorize the warrior. There is little evidence, as occurred later in Tula and Tenochtitlan, of a close identity between ruler, priest and soldier. Teotihuacan is more often described as a theocracy; paradoxically, this theocratic view has itself been used as evidence of an imperial role. It has been argued that the special status of the city as the mecca of an Islam-type proselytizing religion, with Tlaloc in the role of Mohammed, led to physical expansion in quest of spiritual conquest, of a kind sought by the Spaniards. But such proselytization is an Old World concept, and it is hardly realistic to credit the rulers of Teotihuacan with a fanatical intent to save the souls of peoples who already worshipped similar gods.

To supply the needs of the city, a vast empire was surely not required, and local resources, supplemented by those of the rich lagoon that lay nearby, and of the fertile soil of the Valley of Mexico, would have been quite enough to feed its people. From the wealth of available data, it is estimated that with the tools and methods of cultivation then used, the Valley of Teotihuacan alone, including both the irrigated area along the River San Juan and the larger zone where crops grew only in the rainy season, would have provided enough of the staple food, maize, for 150,000 to 175,000 people.

Admittedly, religious rites in the great metropolis required some contact with the tropical lowlands; central to all worship and to war was the wearing of regalia, resplendent with the plumes of birds native to the tropics, as illustrated in the murals. Such regalia included ornaments of jade and turquoise as well as jaguar skins from the tropics. In addition, shells and other marine objects proliferate in Teotihuacan religious art, and huge quantities were imported. However, to imply that luxuries could never be obtained through commerce, either directly or through intermediaries, and that feathers could not be had without using force, is an uncertain premise. The demand for coastal produce was not confined to Teotihuacan, and existed throughout the Altiplano. The very abundance of Teotihuacan products exported to such regions suggests that, unlike the Aztecs, who left meagre traces, they were in a position to obtain their finery by peaceful trade.

Thin Orange pottery and cylindrical effigy vessels were important export items. But in addition to these, the metropolis seems to have gained a virtual monopoly in the obsidian trade over a vast area. The obsidian flake, with a cutting edge so fine as to compare with a steel razor, was much the most efficient cutting tool ever made by Stone Age man; the making and marketing of the product was as basic to the economy of Ancient Mexico as, say, the steel industry in recent times.

In particular the green obsidian from Pachuca appears in quantity wherever Teotihuacan influences abound; it is unmistakable and can be recognized even without any laboratory test. Solid mounds of this green stone, mined throughout the ages, are still visible in the area today. Teotihuacan housed concentrations of obsidian workshops, and it is calculated that these could have produced supplies of finished implements to serve the needs of literally millions of people.

In addition, raw obsidian was traded and high-quality cores from Pachuca have been found in Monte Alban.

In Tikal not only was the green Pachuca variety found but also grey obsidian from Otumba, near Teotihuacan, and – even more signi-ficant – obsidian from a source near Kaminaljuyu. This suggests that Teotihuacan expansion was closely linked to trade and that its thrust-ing merchants, under state auspices, among their various activities had monopolized the mining and marketing of Middle America's most important raw material. This would help to explain the Teoti-huacan presence not only in distant Kaminaljuyu, near an extra source of supply, but even in southern Veracruz, that would have served as an entrepôt for trade with the Maya land, where obsidian was sold in exchange for cacao and other luxuries.

While accepting as a fact Teotihuacan control of its 'metropolitan' area, I therefore question the vision of far-flung military conquest and view the long-distance expansion of the metropolis more as the work of merchants than of soldiers. Such expansion might in some ways be likened to that of the United States in recent times, when commercial enterprise on a huge scale also helped to implant elements of Amer-ican culture in many countries without deploying armed force. In contrast, where the British traded in past centuries, the imperial flag often followed this trade.

The Olmecs may serve as a parallel case. While Michael Coe, as we have seen, argues in favour of their physical conquest of, say, the Valley of Mexico, other scholars reject this view. As in the case of Teotihuacan, the Olmec impact was most varied, ranging from sites that merely imported Olmec ornaments to others that faithfully copied their bas-reliefs, though not their colossal heads, nor the cloverleaf-shaped mound of La Venta. Hence, in far-off places, pre-cisely the same problem arises in the two instances: why, if these 'subject' peoples imitated some traits of the heartland, did they reject others?

The Olmecs were patently too thin on the ground to conquer and hold large areas. The same surely applies to Teotihuacan, whose sphere of cultural influence coincided with that of the Olmecs to an almost uncanny degree. Conceivably, the metropolis might have sent a once-and-for-all expedition to seize, say, Kaminaljuyu, but not to hold it as a kind of colony. Similarities of style could then have followed a 'Hellenistic' pattern, just as the impact of Greece remained strong in the Near East long after Alexander's tide of conquest had ebbed. In like manner, though the Byzantine Empire made a fleeting conquest of Italy in the sixth century A.D., this short-lived triumph led to the faithful reproduction of Byzantine symbolism and art forms, particularly in Norman Sicily, centuries after the last Byzantine soldier had left the peninsula.

Not only does Sanders take an 'imperialist' view of Teotihuacan's global role. He is also a leading figure among those who see Mexican civilization mainly as a by-product of its ecology; in particular he affirms that Teotihuacan built up its techniques of government as a response to the requirements of 'hydraulic agriculture'. In other words, it grew from tribe to state because a strong central authority was needed to control its irrigation system. This line of reasoning may help to explain the birth of Old World civilizations, such as Egypt, Mesopotamia, and even China; when applied to the New World, however, it is less convincing. Any visitor to Teotihuacan can see for himself that a good deal of imagination is needed to equate the meagre flow of the San Juan River and its springs with the Nile, the Euphrates and the Yellow River.

René Millon, on the basis of his own ample data, takes the opposite view. In challenging the ecological approach, he points out that Teotihuacan's irrigation system, based on mere springs, was on too modest a scale to have been the deciding factor in its explosive expansion.

None the less, even if the need to control water supplies was not the crucial factor in the city's rise, this could not have occurred without firm government by a ruling élite. Little, however, is known as to its nature. After studying the entire perimeter of Teotihuacan, Millon became convinced that government was centred upon the Citadel in the south, whose function was in part religious. Though part of this complex (including the Temple of Quetzalcoatl) dates from early times, it never lost its original importance, since further buildings were erected there in the last century before the fall of the city. The Citadel contains twin palaces, each with the same overall plan, another feature that might suggest the presence of two rulers, housed in a sacred setting. It is also possible that the Pyramid of the Sun had two temples on its summit, since the earlier pyramid beneath it almost certainly had two shrines on top.

Political and religious functions were thus closely interlocked, and the priesthood surely played a leading part in government. These clerics learned to know the movements of the sun, moon, stars and planets; in particular, they were familiar with the cycle of Venus, so important to the Classic Maya, and in later times basic to the cult of the Plumed Serpent. By virtue of their knowledge of calendrics, the priests were able to direct the economy, telling people when to sow and when to reap. By observing the heavens, they learned to measure time, distance and angles; such studies enabled them to draw up the exact plans for the layout of the city, and hence to control its greatest capital investment, the long-term construction programme.

Furthermore, the painting of the countless murals, with their symbolism, required the guidance of the priests, who themselves figure so frequently, more often dressed as jaguars, birds, coyotes, adorned with quetzal plumes. Art and architecture unite in suggesting that Teotihuacan was a hieratic state and the very number and size of its temples suggests the presence, as in Christian Rome, of a vast clergy. These priests and prelates were concerned not only with ritual, but with the pursuit of power. In the gods' names they summoned the labour to build the city's temples and palaces, imposed its fiat upon nearby provinces, and traded with remoter lands.

THE CITY AND ITS INDUSTRIES

Teotihuacan was in every sense a city. In contrast, even the largest Maya centre, Tikal, was not fully urbanized; it housed a bare fifth of the numbers of Teotihuacan, though spread over an area just as large. However, Tikal's rural zone was quite thickly populated.

It is not easy to draw the line between a city and a ceremonial centre; certain sites that lie somewhere halfway between the one and the other have been described by Ignacio Bernal as 'dispersed cities'. The mere presence of class distinctions, of a ruling hierarchy and of specialized artisans does not in itself merit the term 'city'. Population is the key factor, and for this a density of over 2,000 per square kilometre may serve as a useful yardstick.

Covering an area of twenty square kilometres, with a population running into six figures, Teotihuacan is unquestionably urban and thereby differs from other centres of its time in the New World. Moreover, it was outstanding in the scope of its crafts and industries, which employed at least a third of its people. In terms both of numbers and of wealth, it therefore stood head and shoulders above its rivals; the majestic monuments, the genial artisans and the enterprising merchants combined to give it a status that was unique. In its heyday, tens of thousands of outsiders attended the festivals and the markets, and its riches were increased by its fame as both shrine and emporium for people from far away.

This vision of a great city with its countless streets and houses, as opposed to mere clusters of temples and priests' dwellings, has emerged from Millon's Mapping Project. None the less, while the archaeologists can chart the layout of such streets, they cannot reconstruct them, and it is hard for the modern visitor to picture for himself how these teeming and narrow thoroughfares must have looked. The nearest approach to such a visual reconstruction might be Pompeii, contemporary with early Teotihuacan, whose contours were held fast for posterity in a mould of volcanic ash. Based on a grid pattern, its layout was more like that of a modern Mexican town than of, say, a medieval city in Europe.

Millon further discovered that the city's north-west quadrant was not only the most densely settled of its four quarters and therefore the most urbanized, but also housed the largest number of craft specialists, many of whose workshops he identified. The walled precincts found in the course of his survey are a striking feature of this part of the perimeter. A group of these compounds, situated west of the Pyramid of the Moon, would have virtually shut off this area from the rest, forming an enclosure that could only be entered at one or two points.

The people of Teotihuacan lived not in single family units or homes, but in apartment compounds that constitute one of its more unique features. In all, no less than 2,200 of these have been identified and this figure has been used as a basis for calculating the total population. By A.D. 100 the population already amounted to some 40,000. At this time, however, while temples were built of stone, domestic dwellings were still made of adobe and other perishable materials; limited numbers of people went on living in such structures even after the compounds were erected.

In the third century A.D., a revolutionary change in the pattern of housing took place, when the apartment compounds came into use; according to the archaeological evidence, this development coincided with a major expansion in the obsidian industry. The compound seems to have been designed for urban life in a city that was already bursting its bounds as the demand for its products grew and more and more people settled there. Whatever the reason for an increasing concentration within the perimeter of farmers as well as artisans – uncharacteristic of Middle America as a whole – the advantage to the ruling élite of such a step is obvious. When most of those who worked the land were housed within the city limits, it became easier for the state to intervene in the agricultural as well as the industrial sector of the economy.

Apart from a few of the largest and most spacious, these compounds, at one time invariably described as 'palaces', were not mainly lived in by people of high status, and were the standard dwellings for the masses. This point came to be understood after the whole perimeter was mapped and such great numbers of them were found. Henceforth the standard family unit was no longer a house, but an apartment, and the layout of rooms, patios and entrances implies that a number of families occupied a single compound. Accommodation tended to be crowded; in a typical structure, measuring about 60 metres square, between 60 and 100 people would have lived; probably they were united by some bond of kinship, or by adherence to a common craft. A study of skeletal remains in one unit indicated that the men were more closely related to each other than the women. Some kind of corporate ownership seems probable and there is no reason to believe that the compounds belonged to the state. The rapid changeover from individual houses to apartment blocks has its social implications. In Ancient Mexico people were used to living surrounded by open spaces, and closer confinement must have created new tensions, if not conflicts, such as could only have been kept in check by a strong government.

Though most compounds were far from being palaces, some were much larger than the average, measuring up to 150 metres square. But whether large or small, they are not single family abodes, being clearly divided into separate sections by high windowless walls, while narrow streets divided the structure from other compounds. Quite often such units are L-shaped, with a row of rooms facing the street, connected with another row at right angles to the first. Once these compounds became the standard form of housing, they were equally to be found on the edge of the city, where space was no problem. Most of those that have been excavated have at least one major patio with one or more temples facing it. The principal temple, if there is more than one, is usually on the east side of the patio. The best-studied compounds seem to have been rebuilt at least three or four times.

A visitor to Tetitla, some distance from the centre, can form an idea of what such compounds were like, though it is not exactly typical, since it is built on a grander scale than most. Rooms, patios, porticos and entrances conform to a set plan, though this may not be immediately apparent today, as one threads one's way from one part of the partially restored structure to another, in search of the many surviving vestiges of murals.

Though the larger 'palaces' were obviously reserved for people of high status, they were not always built near the centre. This in itself is unusual, since in other sites the houses of the nobles were often clustered around the main ceremonial buildings. In addition to such luxury dwellings, other compounds have been explored where people of lower status lived; typical of these is Tlamililolpa, where burial offerings show that its occupants, crammed into teeming tenements, were fairly humble. The crowded pattern of life endured throughout the history of this compound, though it was rebuilt several times.

The contrasts between rich and poor were not unlike those that future archaeologists might discern if they retraced the ground plan of New York and made separate studies of, say, Park Avenue and Harlem. Then as now, both rich and poor lived in buildings based on the concept of housing many family units within a larger edifice. Just as occurs today, within the framework of this concept, the well-to-do in Teotihuacan enjoyed much more spacious quarters, though even in these the rooms are by our standards minute.

In the course of mapping the layout of the compounds, the archaeologists made another major discovery: they found that one sector had been inhabited mainly, if not solely, by people from the Oaxaca region. This special quarter reveals the cosmopolitan nature of the city; it is probably not the only ethnic enclave, though it is the only one whose details have so far been studied. The dwellers of this colony did not sever all contact with their home town, since some are buried after the Oaxaca fashion, in stone-lined tombs, complete with antechamber; in one case, set into the wall was a stela, made from a re-used block of stone and bearing glyph and number in pure Oaxaca style. This stela is not portable, since it weighs over 270 kilograms, and must therefore have been made in Teotihuacan. Two funerary urns, so typical of Oaxaca, were also found, and people who lived in this *barrio* continued to make domestic utensils in their native style.

Excavations in the Oaxaca quarter suggest that it first came into existence in about A.D. 400, at a time when links between Teotihuacan and Oaxaca were at their closest; the two urns belong to that period. The Oaxaca-style tomb and stela are much later, and date from A.D. 700. The tomb shows that the people who had been living in this quarter for several centuries still clung to the funerary cults of their homeland. Yet in other respects they adopted the ways of their neighbours, choosing to dwell in Teotihuacan-type compounds, containing temples that followed the local pattern.

Certain parts of the city can be identified with specific crafts. For
instance, a quarter for potters and one for those who moulded clay
figurines have been found. Nearly 150 ceramic workshops have been
located, together with fifteen for the making of figurines. But by far
the most numerous were compounds, complete with workshops, for
cutting obsidian tools; in all, over 400 such workshops were unearthed. Two large concentrations of these obsidian workshops were
found, one behind the Citadel, and the other near the Pyramid of the
Moon; its artisans occupied one of the great walled compounds of the
sector.

Occupations such as wood-carving, leather-working, together with
the weaving of cloth and matting, were major crafts, but the places
where such perishable items were made cannot be traced. Building
was another major occupation, but it is hard to locate the homes of
those who worked on the great constructions. Part of this labour force
would have consisted of people who tilled the land at other times of
the year. In all, of the 2,200 apartment compounds located, at least 400
were evidently lived in by craftsmen of some kind, and by their
households.

THE PEOPLE AND THEIR DAILY LIFE

Much has been written about the gods of Teotihuacan and their
ministers. Less, however, has been said about the humbler people,
who worked on the land or in the workshops, and their way of life is
hard to reconstruct. Today archaeology may shun its former role as a
mere chronicle of priests and princes, and strives to shed equal light
on the life of the common people. But in Ancient Mexico it is far from
easy to pierce the veil of anonymity that shrouds their existence. They
usually lived in perishable dwellings, and, unlike the modern
worker, owned few consumer gadgets that posterity could unearth.
At least in Teotihuacan, many ordinary citizens dwelt in stone buildings. None the less, no one thought to paint or carve the likeness of a
potter or a peasant and one gleans next to nothing of their way of life
from the countless frescoes, which more often portray an overdressed
Tlaloc, flanked by exotically clad priests.

Rich and poor alike lived and worked in a grandiose setting.
Resplendent in their coat of gleaming stucco, the central monuments
were a dazzling sight. The sheer size of the city affected its people,
who had to walk even larger distances than those living in smaller

places. Since the Street of the Dead was a sacred avenue, it was hardly to be used as a mere pathway for ordinary citizens to go to the market opposite the Citadel, or for those trekking back from work in the fields. Probably they had to take a more devious route, except when attending ceremonies.

In Teotihuacan, even to get from one end to the other of the urban zone involved a longish walk. And apart from the need to fetch food, water was not always near at hand; the River San Juan, at least nowadays, is often a mere trickle; the shore of the Lake of Texcoco was quite a long way from those who lived at the opposite end of the metropolis. A few wells have been found but these were more for ceremonial use, such as that discovered in the plaza north of the Ciudadela this year, and which provides a very limited supply of water.

Though the city itself was extensive, quarters within the compounds tended to be cramped and people would have spent much of their time out of doors in patios, streets and open spaces. As in other parts of Ancient Mexico, life followed the course of the sun, and except where ritual chores, such as temple sweeping, dictated otherwise, people would have gone to bed at sunset and risen with the dawn. Lighting in the Teotihuacan compounds must have been rudimentary; any attempt to light up, say, Tetitla, would have soon blackened its murals.

Another factor affecting life in the Teotihuacan Valley is the rather marked extremes of temperature. These are noticeably greater than in the central Valley of Mexico; in ancient times much of the latter was covered by lagoon water, which had a moderating effect, and nowadays the Valley Centre is partly shielded by the modern city. While the sun can beat down fiercely by day, the nights in Teotihuacan for most of the year are chilly, if not cold, and winter frost is not infrequent. Scholars often write of rain as the vital gift of the gods, and are apt to forget that then, as today, the main enemy of the farmer in the Teotihuacan Valley was not so much drought as early frost or hail.

People in the region still have a saying that if corn has not sprouted by St John's day (24 June), it will be destroyed by St Michael's (29 September). But in non-irrigated land it is difficult to plant the seed in time for it to sprout and ripen early; in 1979 I happened to spend 29 September near Teotihuacan and witnessed one of these untimely night frosts. On this occasion three frosts in succession devastated the crops, which are lost in this way about once in every seven years.

During the chilly Teotihuacan nights, the stars would shine with an intensity still visible in rural Mexico, far from the city smog. An almost eerie silence prevailed, broken only by the barking of dogs, since turkeys screech during the day, and by the blowing of horns and shells in the temples. In the compounds, the concentration of huddled human bodies would have been the only form of heating and the best aid to keeping warm at night. There were no woollen garments, and the common people dressed mainly in clothes made of maguey fibre; in Aztec times they were forbidden to use quilted cotton, which was reserved for the upper classes, but could wear rabbit fur.

Apart from slaves, the common people fell into two main categories, artisans and farmers. Of these, the former were probably the better off, deriving a higher status from their special skills. They also enjoyed the major advantage of living close to their place of work. For owing to the concentration of much of the rural population in the city, many of those who tilled the fields lived a considerable distance from their work. We can imagine the long trail of people setting off at dawn to their long day's toil, and returning at dusk. Similar sights can still be seen in rural Mexico, but with a difference: today one is struck by the number of animals – goats, sheep and even cattle – that accompany the returning workers. In former days these did not exist and goods had to be carried by the people themselves. At times of harvest they would have come home laden with produce for the market, borne on their own backs.

While plenty of signs of ancient cultivation are still visible in the form of terraced hillsides, we do not know to whom the land belonged: whether to the state, to a hereditary caste, or to the cultivators themselves. To infer from what is known of Aztec landholding is mere speculation; apart from other factors, the ecologies of Teotihuacan and Tenochtitlan were far from similar.

The many nets illustrated in mural paintings show that hunting and fishing were major pastimes; they would have offered the best means of adding to the protein content of the standard fare of beans and maize, spiced with chilli. Domestic dogs and turkeys were eaten mainly by the upper classes.

The Lake of Texcoco was rich not only in fish, but in aquatic birds and other fauna regarded as edible. These lagoon fauna were hard to exterminate, but a population of the size of Teotihuacan would eventually have depleted the supplies of land animals, such as rabbits and deer; however, they would have been more plentiful than today, when they are all but extinct, though many towns in Mexico still bear such names as Tochtepec (Place of Rabbits) and Mazatepec (Place of Deer).

The women, when not helping in the fields or tending the children, had many other tasks, of which weaving cloth was among the most important. Shopping in the market was another time-consuming activity. In view of the size of the urban zone local markets must have existed, if only on a small scale, though they have not been found.

In general, the people's life was monotonous, if not austere; but as in so many ancient communities, this monotony was relieved at frequent intervals by the great religious festivals, involving much dressing up, dancing and singing. These ceremonies, apart from their entertainment value, were an essential part of the lives of the common people. Many were linked with the vegetation cycle and with fertility gods in one form or another; to neglect them would be to imperil the crops. In Ancient Mexico due attention to such rites was just as indispensable to the process of obtaining a good harvest as the physical act of sowing and reaping.

DECLINE AND FALL

Teotihuacan, after prospering for almost a millennium, in the eighth century A.D. suffered a major disaster, ending in total collapse. Ample evidence proves that the city was sacked, burned and partly destroyed. Unmistakable signs of fire have been found in many of the temples that line the Street of the Dead and particularly in the Palace of the Quetzal Butterfly, near the Moon Pyramid. Not only were its wooden roofs burned; the sculpted columns around the main patio were torn apart and then thrown into a large pit. The monumental stairway of the Moon Pyramid was deliberately wrecked, while the platforms surrounding the plaza were pulled down and their remains scattered. Many of the offerings buried in front of the main temples were also plundered. The huge statue of the Goddess of Water, Tlaloc's spouse (sometimes described as his sister), that probably stood on the Moon Pyramid, was found at a distance of 150 metres from this monument. The new excavations now in progress even reveal traces of fire in the massive wall at the back of the Ciudadela.

In the 1962–4 excavations charred beams were taken from the roofs of the buildings that lined the Street of the Dead. These yielded radiocarbon dates most of which ranged from A.D. 150 to 300. Such dates made little apparent sense, since they belonged to the most recent structures on each location, supposedly erected nearer to A.D. 600 than 300. As already explained, the Teotihuacan chronology is based on that of the Classic Maya, deriving from the association of Teotihuacan objects of a given period with dated Maya monuments, though archaeologists are now trying to escape from this dependence on Maya dating by means of closer dating of Teotihuacan itself. None the less, if three centuries were added to the estimated age of Teotihuacan III buildings, the generally accepted Maya chronology – based on glyphs – would also have to be drastically revised.

An explanation for the apparent anomaly however exists: in Middle America it was the custom to build at successive intervals, often of fifty-two years, new temples on top of the old, which were dismantled and used as filling for the superstructure. In interpreting their dates it must be borne in mind that the radiocarbon method, when applied to wood, gives the year – within a specified margin of error – of the death of the tree from which the wood was taken. Normally, when a tree is cut down and hence dies, its timber is quickly used in some building, which can thus be dated, since its construction can be assumed to correspond with the year of the death of the tree. But such calculations take no account of the Mexican custom of using beams from a previous structure, when a new and larger one was built on top of it. This was often the case in Teotihuacan, where nearby forests had been denuded and new timber was thus hard to find; it therefore becomes likely that the beams in question had been in use for several centuries before they were finally employed in these latter-day buildings.

The city seems to have reached the height of its power in the fifth and sixth centuries; in certain regions, such as Oaxaca, Teotihuacan influences already vanish in the seventh and eighth centuries, corresponding to Teotihuacan IV. During this short final phase, it still prospered, though the population began to fall. New construction is now known to have taken place in the Street of the Dead, even though the period was less creative than its predecessors, and the principal palaces and murals belong to Teotihuacan III. Therefore the great cataclysm is now believed to have taken place in the mid-eighth century, at the end of Teotihuacan IV. After this date much of the city was abandoned and its population dispersed into smaller settlements.

Evidence is coming to light that, in addition to the central monuments, the outer suburbs were also ravaged at this time. In 1979, American archaeologist Evelyn Rattray excavated a small palace at Hacienda Metepec on the outskirts of the perimeter. She found clear evidence that its occupants, who lived there during Teotihuacan IV, fell victim to armed assault; the palace had been burned and its ruins taken over by squatters who employed a rather coarse pottery, decorated with wavy lines, that came into wide use after the fall of the city; it abounded, as we shall see, in the early Tula. This information is significant, and much further work of the kind is needed in both inner and outer Teotihuacan in order to learn more about what happened at the end, and about the identity of the aggressors.

No major climatic change took place and economic causes for the collapse, while they presumably existed, are hard for the archaeologist to detect. None the less, it is known that in Mexico the environment began to deteriorate in fairly early times, and certain pre-Hispanic practices were apt to have a disastrous effect on the local ecology. It is surely no coincidence that four leading sites, Teotihuacan, Xochicalco, Mitla and Tula, are set in surroundings that are now barren, if not desolate. The excessive use of timber in Teotihuacan denuded the hillsides and led to soil erosion. Middle American builders employed wood on an immense scale; in addition to roofs supported by wooden beams, it was used for the nucleus of columns and pillars, and for door lintels. Much of this wood was not visible; in columns it was covered with rubble and stucco, and on roof beams by a layer of clay. In addition, huge quantities were burned in the making of quicklime. Lime plaster was invariably used to cover walls and floors and it has been calculated that hundreds of thousands of tonnes of this thick plaster would have been consumed for the purpose throughout the city.

The lack of pack animals, and of navigable rivers on which timber could be floated, limited long-distance hauling; instead, trees in the vicinity were mercilessly felled and the countryside for miles around was bared. Today other trees have taken the place of those destroyed long ago, but they are mostly of the Pirul variety, introduced, as the name implies, after the Conquest from Peru. With their clusters of red berries they are very decorative, but the wood is useless and for practical purposes they are little more than outsize weeds.

In addition to the damage done by deforestation, the need to fill so many mouths led to over-use of the soil, which deteriorated as a result. As can still be seen in modern Mexico, maize, if planted year after year, simply exhausts the soil; in the absence of large animals it could not be restored by the use of manure as fertilizer. This lowered productivity also had certain social effects, since people had to walk ever longer distances to their place of toil, as remoter lands came to be tilled. In addition, as game and wild animals were killed off in the immediate vicinity, hunting became less rewarding.

None the less, this ecological decline cannot by itself explain Teoti-huacan's collapse. A large proportion of the people could have been fed from the produce of its irrigated land, less vulnerable to seasonal fluctuations and to erosion. Moreover, if the city still dominated the metropolitan region, including the central Valley of Mexico with its rich lagoons, it could have imported ample food to make up for local shortages. Only military weakness would have endangered such supplies, and among the probable causes of decline the military factor therefore looms large.

Formerly archaeologists and historians tended to paint a rather idyllic picture of the Classic era in Mexico as a Golden Age, undis-turbed by the din of battle. They may rightly have insisted that in the art forms of Teotihuacan the cult of war and of the warrior, all-pervasive in later times, is absent. But if war was not yet the sport of kings and princes, this does not mean that warriors did not exist and that wars were never fought. The picture of Teotihuacan as a haven of peace has had to be modified over the years. The archaeological evidence suggests that it had brought its metropolitan region under its control, and it is hard to see how any such control could have been maintained without some use of force. Teotihuacan is no longer thought of as an open city; the very site is highly strategic, since it stands astride the easiest route between the two main valleys of Mexico and Puebla. Moreover, the great walls of the closed precincts in the north-west part of the city could have served defensive pur-poses and the group of walled compounds found by Millon could have been used to close off this area from the rest. Such compounds not only change our idea of how the city looked, but raise new questions as to its true nature; clearly it was not a defenceless giant, as previously described. Any assailant would have had to pass through the narrow streets while subject to assault from people on the roof-tops, as happened to Cortés when he attacked the Aztec capital.

Some time after the fall of Teotihuacan a crude wall was con-structed, part of which can still be seen today, which covered the front of some of the smaller pyramids that face the Street of the Dead, cutting off their access to the avenue. In addition, late in the city's history, defensive walls were built on the upper part of the Citadel. Most of this evidence of militarism comes from the closing era, and from the seventh century onwards, if battle scenes are lacking, armed figures appear in murals and on pottery vessels; some hold a shield and others a spear or crossed spears. Certain figures are illustrated with cotton armour headdresses or helmets that enclose the head and lower part of the jaw. Several hundred clay figurines of warriors dating from this period have also been found. Murals and pottery further suggest that the military orders, whose emblems were the eagle and the jaguar, and who were important in late pre-Hispanic times, already existed.

As early as the third century the existence of human sacrifice, inseparable from war, is implied by decapitated heads depicted in paintings; sacrificial knives have been unearthed, together with certain evidence of ritual cannibalism, and of human heads used as trophies; such heads are also frequent in Classic Maya art. Figurines have been found of the Flayed God, Xipe, whose cult demanded sacrifice. In other murals, jaguars and eagles are shown with trilobate objects below rather than inside their mouths, suggestive of hearts, from which fall red drops that seem to be blood. These recall the friezes of predatory animals gnawing human hearts found in Tula, whose culture was overtly militaristic.

Figure 20. Teotihuacan warrior in Atetelco fresco

In one Atetelco mural, seven priests or gods hold darts in one hand and a knife in the other. This knife is very similar to the instrument shown in an important painting in the Zacuala Palace, on which is impaled an object that art historian Arthur Miller describes as a heart or a cactus fruit; the two alternatives amount to rather the same thing; in later times at least, the reddish cactus fruit (*tenochtli*) was symbolic of the heart.

Certain ostensibly pacific murals can also be interpreted in other ways. Some of the so-called water seen to flow from the hands of the god Tlaloc is often nearer in colour to blood; in other cases, the drops fall not from the god's hands but from his fangs; unless he was given to dribbling, these could hardly be water. In the bottom left-hand corner of the famous 'Tlalocan' mural appears the figure of a man, whose hands and feet are firmly held by four others; his body is stretched out in the manner of a typical Aztec victim, and only the sacrificial stone is missing.

These signs of a greater stress on war (and sacrifice) are most relevant and this apparent change of emphasis is crucial. In Teotihuacan (and among the Classic Maya) it was more in the nature of a response to pressures, both internal and foreign. But in the succeeding era such tendencies gathered force, and war became an obsession. It has been shown that the cutting of the forests and the overcropping of the land weakened the economy; this in its turn led to social tensions, of which more will be said in the next chapter. Under such circumstances, any increased military effort proved vain, and Teotihuacan's hold on its metropolitan area was undermined.

In the century before its fall, no centres outside its own valley show evidence of Teotihuacan occupation; it is also probable that it had ceased to dominate the Cholula region. If the city still presented a prosperous façade, and if some artists still pursued their craft, such prosperity was more apparent than real in a community forced to fall back on its local resources at the very moment when these were curtailed. By this time the enemy was at the very gates.

In Ancient Mexico the settled peoples faced a constant challenge from less advanced tribes living to the north-west, beyond the bounds of civilization. This precarious and fluctuating frontier between settled and nomad territory tended to follow the dividing line between land where rainfall was enough for seasonal crops, and the arid regions beyond, inhabited only by gatherers and hunters. In post-Teotihuacan times this frontier between cultivated and arid land moved southwards, owing to a cyclical change in climate.

The ravaging of the ceremonial centre offers evidence that some outside invasion took place, though the destruction was so methodical that Millon suspects that the priests destroyed their own temples. Once disaster loomed large, it developed a momentum of its own; if outside enemies could not flatten the temples, their own ministers dismantled them stone by stone. This selective demolition, mainly focused on the Street of the Dead, was a monumental task. Not only does it recall the demonic force with which the Olmecs sought, at times vainly, to deface their images; in Teotihuacan itself a tradition of ritual destruction existed, and is visible in attempts to burn both the sides and front of the Temple of Quetzalcoatl, many centuries before the final fall.

Following the great disaster, the city was reduced to a regional centre numbering at first some 30,000 people, who lived on among the ruins, which they shared with the more primitive interlopers. Many others took refuge in the surrounding country in smaller villages and settlements.

The sixteenth-century chronicler Fray Bernardino de Sahagún, in Book X of his *History*, tells a story that can be linked to the fall of Teotihuacan, the first event in Mexican history to which a written source refers. He says nothing of *why* the city fell, but describes the scene as the 'wise men', the rulers, fled from the doomed metropolis:

. . . The wise men remained not long; soon they went. Once again they embarked and carried off the writings, the books, the paintings; they carried away all the crafts, the castings of metals. And when they departed, they summoned all those they left behind. They said to them: 'Our lord, the protector of all, the wind, the night, saith you shall remain. We go leaving you here. Our lord goeth bequeathing you this land; it is your merit, your lot. Our lord, the master of all, goeth still farther, and we go with him. Whither the lord, the night [and] the wind, our lord, the master of all, goeth, we go accompanying him. He goeth, he goeth back, but he will come, he will come to do his duty, he will come to acknowledge you. When the world is become oppressed, when it is the end of the world, at the time of its ending, he will come to bring it to an end. But [until then] you shall dwell here; you shall stand guard here . . .

What Sahagún writes of the carrying off of the books may be interpreted as a form of ritual destruction. These were the sacred texts of Teotihuacan that would have been meaningless if removed to any other context. Thus from the very outset, a parallel may be sought between the written word and the archaeological record, which reveals the purposeful dismantling of temples.

The friar goes on to tell how the different peoples left Teotihuacan, including a group of people from the Huaxteca, who returned to their original home on the Gulf Coast:

. . . And with shame the Huaxteca abandoned the land; they took all his people with him. All who understood the language moved together; they moved in a body. They traveled there from whence they came, to Panotla, now called Pantla. And as they went with great misgivings of the water, the sea, they settled there. These are called Teueiome, which means 'our neighbors.' And the name comes from their ruler named Cuextecatl. They are called Cuexteca . . .

Some people, whom Sahagún calls 'Toltecs', or 'Nahuas', left in the direction of the arid north-west, from which, according to his account, they were fated one day to return:

. . . And then these different people went [on]; the Tolteca, the Mexica, the Nahua. All the people, as they sought land, encountered the plains, the deserts. The one they worshipped accompanied them; he went speaking to them. No more could they recall how long they had wandered; for a long time they traveled over the desert. They went to settle at a place in the desert, in a valley among the crags, a very dangerous place. And the people wept; they were saddened, they suffered affliction; there was no more to eat, no more to drink . . .

Modern study and ancient metaphor stress the impact of a collapse, whose shockwaves were felt throughout Ancient Mexico. Power crumbled and the economy faced ruin as the main arteries of commerce were severed. The demand for luxury goods, confected for Teotihuacan's nobles, plummeted and the wealth derived from this trade vanished overnight. Such convulsions were followed by a spiritual crisis that had its material effects; when the city lost its religious aura, it was visited by no more of those pilgrims, who, like the modern tourist, added much to the trade balance. The fall of Teotihuacan, like that of Rome, three centuries before, left in its wake a disordered world, whose surviving cities were like planets in orbit round an extinct sun.

5

TULA

THE FIFTH SUN

Following the great exodus from Teotihuacan, forsaken by its 'wise men', Fray Sahagún records what his informants told him of the birth of a new world, known as the 'Fifth Sun', that took place in the ruins of the shattered city.

It is told that when all yet was in darkness, when yet no sun had shone and no dawn had broken – it is said – the gods gathered themselves together and took counsel among themselves there at Teotihuacan. They spoke; they said among themselves:

'Come hither O gods! Who will carry the burden? Who will take upon himself to be the sun, to bring the dawn?'

Thereupon one of the lesser gods, Tecuziztecatl, spoke up and said: 'O gods, I shall be one'. The gods then asked: 'Who else?'. But none dared and all drew back afraid. Since no one volunteered, they chose the little syphilitic god, Nanauatzin, as the second victim.

The two deities then did penance, one on the Pyramid of the Sun, and the other on the Pyramid of the Moon:

And this Tecuziztecatl: that with which he did penance was all costly. His fir branches were quetzal feathers, and his grass balls were of gold; his maguey spines were of green stone; the reddened, bloodied spines were of coral. And his incense was very good incense. Nanauatzin, his fir branches were made only of green water rushes, green reeds bound in threes . . . and for his incense he used only the scabs from his sores.

Following this fact, the victims were ritually attired, and bedecked with paper and feather adornments. The remaining gods settled themselves around the great hearth, in which the victims were to be immolated. The little syphilitic god cast himself boldly into the blaze, but his companion drew back four times before taking the plunge; he

was therefore the last of the two to emerge. The legend relates that
they were followed into the fire by a jaguar and an eagle; as a result,
the eagle's feathers were forever blackened, while the jaguar only
scorched himself before escaping, and became dotted with black
spots. In the Fifth World, in whose birth they partook, the eagle and
jaguar were to symbolize valour and knighthood.

After Tecuziztecatl emerged from the fire, one of the gods came
running, and cast a rabbit in his face. 'With it he darkened his face; he
killed its brilliance. Thus doth it appear today.' He accordingly
became the moon, whose surface shadows reminded the Mexicans of
the outline of a rabbit.

The gods who had been transformed into the sun and moon still
remained motionless and no dawn came.

Thus it became the charge of Ehécatl, the wind, who arose and exerted
himself, fiercely and violently as he blew. At once he could move him [the sun]
who thereupon went his way. And when he had already followed his course,
only the moon remained there. At the time when the sun came to enter the
place where he set, then once more the moon moved.

The allegory of the birth of the Fifth Sun, supposedly in Teotihuacan, expresses the spiritual resolve of Ancient Mexico not to
perish, but, phoenix-like, to rise from the ruins of the Classic World,
guided by new leaders, settled in new places, and comforted by new
gods. Middle American culture was now to assume different forms
that in many respects diverged from those of the past.

The period that followed the birth of the new sun is commonly
known as the Post-Classic. It was to reach its climax in the century
that preceded the Spanish invasion in 1519, and which witnessed the
sweeping conquests of the Aztec Empire. But between the fall of
Teotihuacan and the rise of the Aztecs over six centuries were to
elapse – a point not always made clear to visitors to Mexico, when
they survey the vestiges of both cultures.

During the earlier part of this long interval the centre of gravity
shifted, and Central Mexico came under the sway of the Toltecs,
whose capital was Tula, situated some sixty-four kilometres to the
north-west of Mexico City; its expansive phase was fairly short,
lasting from about A.D. 950 to 1150.

The spirit of the new age, whether in Tula, or in its sister-city in the
Maya land, Chichen Itza, is expressed in art devoted to warlike
themes, in contrast to the more serene forms of the Classic era. In Tula
stone reliefs and painted friezes depict warriors armed to the teeth, or

processions of predatory jaguars, coyote dogs and eagles, symbolic of war; from their fangs and beaks hang human hearts, dripping with gore. As compared with Teotihuacan, Post-Classic art seems rather grim and joyless, as if all the gaiety had gone out of life; a typical product of the new spirit is the 'chacmool', an angular figure of stone found in many places, including Tula and Chichen, and carved in a strange and contorted pose, with head deflected at right angles from the body. (See Figure 27, p. 150.) The chacmool invariably bears in his hands a stone vessel, which serves no obvious purpose, and was sometimes thought to contain some innocent tribute to the gods, such as flower petals. However, a latter-day chacmool, dating from Aztec times, holds a rather different vessel, more characteristic of the re-positories for human hearts offered to the sun. Also in this period appear the first-known skull-racks; they became a typical feature of Aztec architecture, often mentioned by the Spanish conquerors.

The Tula that we see today mainly dates from after A.D. 1000, or over two centuries after the decline of its predecessor. During the interval that separated the fall of Teotihuacan from the rise of Tula Middle American civilization was kept alive in three other centres: Xochicalco, El Tajin and Monte Alban. A certain change of emphasis is already visible in their architecture and art; for instance, Xochicalco stands on a steep hill and was strongly fortified, while in El Tajin the cult of death is paramount.

The dawn of a blatantly militarist age in Mexico is part of a world-wide pattern. Julian Steward, in writing of cultural change, defines the stages through which both Old World and New World cultures passed; after a Formative or Pre-Classic period came 'regional flores-cence', corresponding to the Mexican Classic, followed in time by 'initial conquests', identifiable with the early Post-Classic, or Toltec era. During this period, as defined by Steward, the warrior state came into being; in Mexico government became more secular, leading to an increase in the power of the palace at the expense of the temple.

Such changes are however ill-defined in Mexico in comparison with the Ancient Near East, where copious texts enrich the archaeological record. Discussion as to why certain 'empires' of the New World vanished, after a fairly short lifespan, has focused upon the Maya collapse. But the fall of Teotihuacan and its shrinkage from metropolis to village was just as spectacular and is part of the same story, even if it occurred rather earlier; certain basic factors probably accounted for both.

An aura of romance surrounds the fall of the Maya cities that for so long defied the rigours of the Peten Jungle, where few people have chosen to live ever since. Previous attempts to explain this 'mystery' as the result of plagues or earthquakes are nowadays largely discounted.

In the fall of Teotihuacan and of the Classic Maya cities, a like pattern emerges, even if the circumstances were not identical. A similar sequence of events may have brought about the end of La Venta and the other Olmec centres of Tabasco a thousand years before. And, indeed, the same problems might have eventually overtaken the Aztecs if the Spaniards had not put a premature end to their achievements.

The great cultures of Mexico, whether Teotihuacan or the Maya (to whom the word 'empire' has also been applied), were, economically speaking, giants with feet of clay, owing to the almost total lack of technical progress, and to the absence of any adequate means of transport; the nearby land was usually tilled in such a way as to ensure that crop yields would in time fall. And when, because of such improvident methods of cultivation, the fields lost their fertility, the only beast of burden to bring food from further afield was man himself, thus placing a further strain on human resources.

In addition, since there were no draught animals, not only was the wheel not used (though wheeled toys have been found), but the plough was never invented. Instead, the planting stick continued to serve but this implement had severe drawbacks. After the land had been cleared and cultivated, a thick crop of weeds would grow in the valleys; these then had to be left untilled, and agriculture was confined to the steep and terraced hillsides, since the planting stick could not penetrate the mass of weeds.

As we have seen in the case of Teotihuacan, such technical shortcomings were an obvious source of social tensions, and left a city more exposed to outside pressures, whether in Teotihuacan, Tula, or in the Peten Jungle. An imbalance arose between the demands of the city and the output of its hinterland. On the one hand, the need was felt to control the land over a wider area, owing to soil erosion near the centre; but at that very moment the will to maintain this vital hold was sapped. As will become apparent in dealing with the Aztecs, Ancient Mexicans never evolved any machinery of close control, like, say, the Romans, over other regions. Without such a system, it was very easy for the whole apparatus of state to fall apart in times of stress; while still in its prime, the Aztec Empire had to deal with constant provincial rebellions.

Perhaps because their population was a fraction of that of Teoti-huacan, and their food needs therefore less great, the Maya city-states lasted rather longer. The same reasoning applies even more to the Olmecs, whose numbers were still smaller, and whose decline was more gradual, even if a few individual centres collapsed quickly. Among the Mayas, whatever the internal tensions, outside pressures may have built up more slowly, since so many sites were protected by a wall of jungle. Moreover, their fall was not immediate; the romantic notion that the Maya civilization vanished overnight is now dis-counted; and in some major sites a decadent phase before the final end has been found, during which no more dated monuments were built and simpler forms of pottery came to be used.

Many causes have been suggested for the collapse of kingdoms in Ancient Mexico; among these, peasant revolt is often cited. But if ecological decline produced social stresses, they are unlikely to have led to armed uprising; class struggle is a European notion, less applic-able to societies such as Ancient Mexico, where any challenge to rank and privilege would have been an act of defiance against the gods. If such a challenge ever took place in Middle America, the god-fearing masses, sometimes described by writers as 'oppressed', would have been much more likely to take the side of a reactionary clergy. On the other hand, cleavages within the ruling class are a surer cause of weakness. Such rifts are all the more easy to envisage as nearby land produced less and food became harder to get, or had to be brought from further afield; this left a smaller cake to be divided up by the well-to-do, who were in the habit of taking the largest slice for themselves.

In *Sons of the Shaking Earth* Eric Wolf aptly describes the change from Classic to Post-Classic under the title 'The Coming of the Warriors'. He stresses the sociological factor, and the fatal flaw in the theocratic, or Classic, society, in the form of this basic imbalance between 'holy town' and hinterland, between city and province. As he puts it, both town and country grew in their involvement with each other, but the growth of the centre was more opulent and more obvious. While he, like others, over-emphasizes the likelihood of a popular reaction in the form of a physical clash between rich and poor, he rightly points to the contrast between the centre, bloated with wealth, and the poorer periphery; this made the state more vulnerable to attack from without, as well as from within.

Wolf himself underlines the other constant factor in the process of change: the threat of marauding interlopers on the fringe; they can sometimes be identified, as in Hacienda Metepec, as the bearers of a cruder pottery, representing a kind of throwback to pre-Teotihuacan styles.

Economic decline, leading to certain social stresses and a weakened response to external threats, is therefore a valid reason for the general collapse. In seeking its causes, however, due attention is seldom paid to the spiritual factor; in Mexico Teotihuacan came to be virtually abandoned, followed later by El Tajin, Xochicalco, Monte Alban, and the great centres of the Maya jungle. In the Old World, places such as Ur would suffer an eclipse and then rise to the fore again; Rome in particular was to become the 'Eternal City'. But in Middle America, Cholula alone had a genius for survival.

In Mexico a city was as much the residence of its gods as of ordinary mortals. As a rule, these gods tended to be judged by immediate results; if evil came to pass, then the local deities had forsaken their fold. When this was thought to happen, the city itself was shorn of its previous magic and ceased to be Wolf's 'holy town'. As Tenochtitlan, the Aztec capital, was about to succumb to the Spanish invader, the anguished cry went up: The gods have departed.' A loss of this aura of sanctity would help to explain the abandonment of many places, and the destruction of their idols.

Much evidence survives, whether in La Venta, in Teotihuacan, in the Peten Jungle, or later in Tula, of monuments methodically smashed and of buildings burned to a cinder. As we have seen, Millon suspects that in Teotihuacan the priests themselves destroyed their temples, and this may also be true of the Olmecs and others.

SUCCESSOR STATES

Of the cities that thrived in the Classic age, the great Teotihuacan, perhaps because of its very size, had been the first to fall. The Classic Maya centres survived for another century; in the largest, Tikal, the last stela is dated A.D. 869 and by A.D. 889 nearly all the main Maya cities had produced their last date glyph; the elaborate long-count system of recording time was abandoned.

Nearer to Teotihuacan in the Altiplano, Xochicalco to the south of Mexico City, Monte Alban further to the south-east near Oaxaca, and El Tajin near the coast of the Gulf of Mexico, continued to exist. To these should be added the more recently excavated Teotenango, situated near Toluca, to the west of Mexico City. Xochicalco seems to have survived the metropolis by about two centuries, while Monte Alban and El Tajin continued a little longer , perhaps until A.D. 1000. Teotenango still existed at the time of the Conquest. Almost all of what we know of these sites derives from archaeology rather than from written sources, except in the case of Teotenango, of which the seventeenth-century chronicler Francisco Chimalpain writes at length as a rival to Tula in the splendour of its monuments – an account that may be largely apocryphal.

Xochicalco, Monte Alban and El Tajin have been described by Wigberto Jiménez Moreno, leading historian of Ancient Mexico, as 'successor states' of the metropolis. This definition may be apt, but only tells part of the story, since much of their lifespan coincided with that of Teotihuacan. None the less, since their fall came later, they lived to provide a link between Classic and Post-Classic Mexico. Given the fairly low density of population at that time, there was enough land for all, and notions that these centres were part of a Teotihuacan 'empire', against which they fought a kind of war of independence, rest on no concrete evidence of any kind. To imagine Xochicalco or El Tajin dispatching armies to defeat Teotihuacan, rather, say, as Prussia crushed France in 1870, is once more to interpret Ancient Mexico in the light of modern European history.

These four centres, notwithstanding distinctions between them, have certain traits in common. The location of each is spectacular, and for the modern visitor they perhaps have a more ready appeal than the rather skeletal ruins of Teotihuacan itself, so close to Mexico City, and so swamped by visitors.

While, as previously explained, the earliest buildings of Monte Alban in the state of Oaxaca predate Teotihuacan, and go back to Olmec times, the site as seen today is mainly the product of the latter part of Monte Alban III, which coincides with the later phases in Teotihuacan and with the immediate post-Teotihuacan era. It had been built by the Zapotecs, who still inhabit part of the region, and whose capital was Monte Alban until they were driven out by the Mixtecs, several centuries after the fall of Teotihuacan, though the city had lost control of most of the surrounding region long before this.

Strongly influenced by Monte Alban, with which it shares many common glyphs, is Xochicalco, situated 113 kilometres south of Mexico City, just off the old road from Cuernavaca to Taxco. Xochicalco in its turn was to exercise a marked influence on Tula and other sites of the Toltec period; like Monte Alban, it commands a spectacular view over the valley beneath, and is also best visited about an hour before sunset. Its ruins sprawl over a whole series of hilltops, shaped into stone terraces and platforms, and cover over twenty-five hectares; only a fraction of this complex has been excavated. Just as in Monte Alban, no sources of water exist on the site, whose buildings were the preserve of the ruling élite. Hence it was not a city in the true sense, and estimates of the population range from 10,000 to 20,000, though this figure does not include the peasant cultivators living in the plain below. In this respect Xochicalco differs from Teotihuacan, where the farmers were grouped within the city limits; it recalls those Maya ceremonial centres, with which its layout and population are more comparable.

The Jesuit José Antonio de Alzarte (1737–89) described the site in his booklet *Antiquities of Xochicalco*; on his two visits he made a map, together with a few detailed drawings. This was the very first publication devoted exclusively to Mexican archaeology. Xochicalco was next visited by the French explorer Guillaume Dupaix, who wrote of it in 1806. By far the most striking monument is the Pyramid of the Plumed Serpent, located on the main plaza, situated at the very summit of the terraced platforms; the monument was so named after the reliefs that surround its base; it was first excavated and restored by Leopoldo Batres in 1910. Only the darkened basalt stone of the Pyramid of the Plumed Serpent is now visible; like most Mexican monuments, it originally bore a coat of lime plaster, and was painted in different colours; traces of this paint can still be seen. Between the coils of the serpents that undulate along the sloping base platform, dignitaries are seated cross-legged, with loincloths and headdresses of quetzal feathers, and adorned with jade necklaces, anklets, bracelets and earrings. Their posture and the style of carving recall other reliefs in the Maya site of Copan in the Republic of Honduras, whose ball-court is almost identical in design to that of Xochicalco, a design that was later adopted in Tula. The pyramids of Xochicalco also have a very distinctive kind of cornice, which came to be used in Tula.

Hence, having absorbed influences from Teotihuacan, the Maya land and from Monte Alban, which it then passed on to Tula, Xochicalco has deservedly been called the crossroads of Ancient Mexico. Such influences however are cultural, and when authors write of Xochicalco as 'without any doubt' the centre of militarist expansion from the southern periphery into the central highlands, they are merely speculating.

In 1960, Mexican archaeologist César Saenz, who for many years worked in Xochicalco, made a major find when he unearthed three stelae; these are now displayed in the National Museum of Anthropology in Mexico City, though replicas can be seen at the site. Their reliefs vividly illustrate the passage from the old era to the new since they depict both the Classic gods of Teotihuacan, predominantly the chief deity, Tlaloc, side by side with the leading gods of the Post-Classic era. Dating from about A.D. 700, these stelae are the first known portrayals of Quetzalcoatl, no longer a symbol as in the Teotihuacan carvings of plumed serpents, but a man, dressed in the elaborate regalia of the God of the Morning Star, in which he henceforth appears in Tula and elsewhere.

Figure 21. Stela I, Xochicalco

El Tajin, that other great survivor of the Teotihuacan débâcle, contrasts in many respects with Xochicalco; instead of being perched on an arid peak, it lies at a low altitude in a luxuriant tropical setting, amidst rich crops of maize, cacao and vanilla. However, like Xochicalco, it was founded when Teotihuacan already flourished, but survived rather longer, possibly until about A.D. 1100. Like Xochicalco, it was also first described by Alzarte in 1785.

The site is large and only a fraction has been excavated, mainly by José García Payon, who continued to work there until his death. Tajin's most famous monument is the Pyramid of Niches; it is not very big (less than twenty metres high), and rises in six tiers to an upper sanctuary. As its name implies, the temple is unique because it is honeycombed with niches; they number 365, one for each day of the year. It is not known if they had any special use; it has been suggested that they symbolized caves, revered as the dwellings of the Earth God.

Viewed from this monument, green mounds cover other ruins that stretch as far as the eye can see. In El Tajin, as in Xochicalco and so many other Mexican sites, the modern visitor sees a few excavated monuments surrounded by countless hillocks that conceal an infinity of ruins. To excavate and restore the whole site, and then to guard it adequately, would be a prodigious task. Moreover, the Tajin culture was by no means confined to Tajin itself. About a hundred kilometres to the south, near Quetzallan, lies the large site of Yohuallichan which has been little excavated but which also has a Tajin-type pyramid with many niches.

At some distance from Tajin's Pyramid of Niches stands another excavated complex known as Little Tajin, consisting of a colonnaded building with many small chambers. These, like so many pre-Columbian structures whose use is unknown to us, are conventionally called priests' palaces, for lack of a better description.

El Tajin is so rich in remains of ball-courts and in carvings of objects worn by players that its inhabitants seem to have been obsessed by the game. There were no universal rules for this ritual pastime, since courts in different places vary widely in size and shape, and in the angle of slope of their walls. The religious significance of the game cannot be overstressed and it figures in many codices, in which the players are dressed as gods. It was promptly banned by the Spaniards as the very essence of native devil-worship, and no record survives of exactly how it was played. The general aim was to propel a rubber ball, mainly with the aid of the body, either through a ring, or in certain cases into a niche in the wall.

The game was very ancient indeed, and Olmec reliefs show people who wear the typical ball-game accoutrements. Like many rites and beliefs, it changed over the centuries; not only did the rules differ, but its religious role was altered. In accounts of the immediate pre-Conquest period there is no apparent association between the ball-game and human sacrifice, though it may have existed. In Tajin, dating from, say, A.D. 800, as well as in Chichen Itza, several centuries later, the game was strictly sacrificial, and involved decapitation.

In latter-day codices the ball-court is conventionally drawn as two T's placed end to end, the form it takes in most excavated sites. A great number of ball-courts have been found, and amply demonstrate that it was an élitist rite rather than a popular spectacle, since the space on top, from which spectators would have been able to view the game, is very limited.

The principal court of El Tajin is sixty metres long, formed by two facing vertical walls, covered with splendid bas-reliefs. In one of these a player is sacrificed by the others, who brandish the ritual knife over his head. In a stela from a nearby site of the same period, seven serpents sprout from the neck of a decapitated ball player (as also occurs in a Chichen Itza relief). Portraits of the Death God abound in El Tajin, and his skull and skeleton are ubiquitous in sculpture and relief. With its morbid scenes of death and its plethora of skulls, El Tajin thus marks the passage between the serener Classic art forms and an age dedicated to the cult of war.

El Tajin, whose main pyramid is so unlike any other, also brought forth an unmistakable style of sculpture, distinguishable at a glance in any collection of the arts of Ancient Mexico. Characteristic of this style are those rather enigmatic stone carvings known as 'yokes', 'palms' and 'axes'. Mainly in the form of these objects, El Tajin culture has left abundant traces along the coast of the Caribbean for nearly 1,600 kilometres to the south-east of its birthplace, and others were found on the Pacific littoral near the Mexican-Guatemalan border.

The U-shaped yokes are intricately carved with convoluted scrolls and human faces. Yokes, palms and axes are connected with the ball-game, since in bas-reliefs and figurines they are worn by the players. However, the stone yokes are so heavy that players would have been helplessly weighed down by them. Clearly they were sacred symbols in stone, fashioned in imitation of protective belts of leather, actually worn for the game.

Less important than El Tajin, but more directly linked to the closing era of Teotihuacan, is Cacaxtla in the present-day state of Tlaxcala, where in 1975 well-preserved frescoes were found in a palace or dwelling; they combine traits of both Teotihuacan and Maya style. Cacaxtla obviously forms part of a larger complex, including other sites on nearby hills that are still unexplored; Cacaxtla itself is quite small, though its exquisite murals could hardly have been painted by a single artist, since they belong to two distinct periods. The discovery of this second site, in addition to Xochicalco, of about the same date and also with Maya influences, was both unexpected and important. No one knows how many virgin sites between Yucatán and Central Mexico might not also reveal Maya traits, and give added proof of Maya visitors to the Mexican Altiplano at the very end of the Teotihuacan era. Cacaxtla is essentially transitional; the finest frescoes, in which two majestic figures stand serenely poised on serpent and jaguar rafts, seem to belong to a different age to the bloody battle scene painted nearby that includes a body literally sawn in half and a warrior who grasps a fistful of human entrails.

From these brief descriptions it can be seen that the interval between the Teotihuacan and the Toltec eras was no cultural hiatus or Dark Ages, of a kind that followed the collapse of many Old World cultures. On the contrary, major bastions of civilization survived the fall of the metropolis. These centres, except for El Tajin, are defended hill-sites. In many respects they stand halfway between Teotihuacan and its ultimate successor, Tula; they are more war-orientated than the former, but less overtly bellicose than the latter; their role, if any, in toppling the universal but not eternal city is unknown.

THE GREAT TOLLAN

None of these 'successor states' was fated to become the true heir of Teotihuacan as the leading power in Central Mexico; none was situated in the key central valley, and all except Teotenango reached their zenith before Teotihuacan fell, and thereafter were on the decline.

Instead, the centre of gravity eventually shifted in a north-westerly direction to Tula, situated in a region known as the Teotlalpan, contiguous to the Valley of Mexico, from which it is divided by no major barrier. Then, as today, sedentary cultivation in this region was precarious: the vegetation is basically of a semi-arid type in which useless mesquite bushes, together with nopal and maguey cactus predominate; since the Conquest, the equally unusable pirul tree also flourishes there. In the rainy season a light grass cover sprouts, more suitable for small herds of goats and sheep than for regular crops.

The literal meaning of the name Teotlalpan in Nahuatl is 'Land of the Gods'. But to any modern visitor this might seem to be an incongruous title. To quote American anthropologist Sherburne Cook, the soil is thin, poor and at times almost non-existent. Except for the irrigated fields along the river, agricultural land consists of small plots scratched out of the cactus thickets on the hill slopes, and water comes from muddy reservoirs used to impound the precious rainfall. Such is the Teotlalpan, 'The Land of the Gods'. Cook concedes that conditions have grown harsher since Toltec times, owing to over-population and erosion, though the climate has not changed much. This process of erosion would have gathered momentum as the hillsides were shorn of trees; it continued in the colonial era and helps to account for the forlorn aspect of the land today.

The question therefore remains to be answered: why was the leading role in Middle America now assumed by a region that offered few apparent advantages, and was not as strategically located as Teotihuacan? In the first place, Tula's prosperity depended not on this desolate hinterland but on the richer land lying below the city, bordering on the River Tula, whose flow of water is copious and dependable. The disparity between this verdant river valley and the poor hilltops on which the ancient city stands is nowadays such that the very air that one breathes seems different; below it smells cool and fresh, while above it blows hot and dusty.

Moreover, the Teotlalpan is not without natural resources; in spite of its apparent barrenness, it yields abundant supplies of the basic pre-Columbian agricultural products: maize, beans, amaranth, pulque (the ritual drink), maguey cactus (for clothing fibres) and in certain parts, cotton. In addition, meat from wild animals was in those days more plentiful. Another major asset were the great obsidian deposits near Pachuca on its eastern fringe that had already been exploited in Classic times. The abundance of lime was also important, in view of the demand for making the thick stucco coating that enveloped the ceremonial centres.

To these assets, which made of the Teotlalpan at least a viable unit, might be added a location that favoured long-distance commerce, since it enjoyed easy access to the Gulf Coast to the east, and to the rich lands of the Bajío and beyond to the west. None the less, in comparison with the wondrous site of the future Aztec capital, Tenochtitlan, set in a rich lagoon that offered both food and protection, the advantages of the Tula region were meagre, though perhaps sufficient to refute any notion of the Toltec achievement as a kind of response to a challenge, in Toynbean terms, and a triumph over harsh and adverse conditions.

And while ecological factors may influence the course of events, they are seldom their mainspring. Modern devotees of ecological determinism, who tend to explain Ancient Mexican history merely as a by-product of such forces, omit from their reasoning the rise of the fledgling Tula, which does little to support their arguments. The site was neither ideal nor impracticable, and had no salient feature that could have made its rise to power predictable.

Tula is a Spanish corruption of the Nahuatl 'Tollan', meaning 'Place of Rushes'. The name was symbolical, and also signified 'metropolis', because rushes grow in such abundance and serve to convey the impression of multitude. As such, the name Tollan was sometimes applied by the Aztecs to their own capital, to Cholula, and even in retrospect to Teotihuacan.

Owing to their association with that precious commodity, water, rushes had a special significance in Mexico. And quite apart from any symbolic meaning, they were an important material; the best container, whether for individual shopping in the market or for bulk deliveries of tribute from conquered peoples, was the basket made of rushes. The standard mat, the *petate*, still widely used today, was also made of rushes. This versatile material therefore served everyone from the king to his humblest subject, since it was even used to make the 'chair of the gods', the ruler's throne. The image of the Aztec tribal god was carried in a case made of rushes during their migration, and the roofs of temples were often made of this material, rather than of straw. Thus Tula, as a 'place of rushes', would be a city possessing a highly-prized asset, which also symbolized water and fertility.

And just as the name Tollan, from being first applied to a single city, took on the more universal sense of metropolis, so also Toltec (Nahuatl 'Toltecatl'), meaning 'inhabitant of Tollan', came to be used to describe civilized or educated peoples. Fray Sahagún, for instance, applies the term 'Toltec' to those who lived in cities, whom he contrasts to cave-dwelling nomads, classed as Chichimecs.

In addition, in the literature of Aztec times 'Toltec' is often used to imply the possession of specific skills. For 'Toltecatl', Siméon's Nahuatl dictionary gives the translation 'artisan, skilled worker, artist' and only as an afterthought adds 'inhabitant of Tollan'. The Aztecs thus came to apply the term both to skilled artisans, and in quite a different sense to the former citizens of Tula, by then the legendary inventors of human civilization, of whom they were the self-proclaimed heirs.

The divorce of 'Toltec' from its basic meaning, and the aura with which the Aztecs surrounded the name, as embracing the great and the good, continued to perplex scholars who tried to reconstruct the Mexican past at a time when the site of Tula was known, but had not been restored. Aztec accounts were taken at their face value, in which the Toltec capital was described as a fabulous city, full of palaces and temples made out of pure gold and turquoise, adorned with precious feathers, and built by genial sybarites. Hence it became obvious that only Teotihuacan could answer to such descriptions, and it was therefore taken to be the true Tula and the capital of the historical Toltecs. This attribution was first made by Bishop Plancarte of Cuernavaca at the beginning of the present century, and was adopted by the most noted archaeologist of his time, Manuel Gamio, enthralled by the grandeur of Teotihuacan, as revealed by his work on the site from 1917 to 1922. Until the 1940s it then became common to write of the 'Toltecs of Teotihuacan'.

This identification, however, soon began to be questioned. Doubts had already been raised earlier in the century by the German Eduard Seler, and later by the Swedish archaeologist Sigwald Linné. But it was not until the Round Table Conference of the Mexican Society of Anthropology, held in 1941, that the wheel took a full turn. The conference, attended by many of the most distinguished Mexicanists of all time, resolved that Tula, Hidalgo, not Teotihuacan, was the Tollan of the principal historical sources. This conclusion was inspired by the reasoning of Wigberto Jiménez Moreno, who identified a series of place-names and geographical landmarks, associated in written texts with the historical Tollan, as still existing in the vicinity of Tula, Hidalgo. To quote a simple but specific example: Sahagún calls the Tollan, where the famous Topiltzin Quetzalcoatl ruled, Tollan Xicocotitlan (Xicocotitlan means 'Place near to Xicococ' and Xicococ in Nahuatl signifies 'Place of the Bee'). Jiménez Moreno pointed to the unmistakable hill, whose name has now been corrupted into Xicuco, that is today visible from Tula. In addition to such place names, linked only to the Tula region, Sahagún insists that Tollan was situated on a major river, a term hardly applicable to the rivulet that runs through Teotihuacan.

At about the same time people became aware of the importance of the archaeological site of Tula, till then overlooked, though it had been described by the French archaeologist Désiré Charnay in the 1850s. In 1941, the year of the Round Table Conference, Mexican archaeologist Jorge Acosta began a five-year series of excavations of Tula's central Acropolis, on which he published ample reports.

Acosta reconstructed the Temple of Quetzalcoatl, and restored to its summit the cyclopean atlantes that have become Tula's most salient feature. It became abundantly clear to Acosta that the ceramics of Tula had little to do with Classic Teotihuacan; in the lowest or oldest strata, he found pottery (known as 'Coyotlatelco') used by people who first settled in Teotihuacan after its fall.

BEGINNINGS

Many references to the Toltecs occur in the literature of late pre-Hispanic times, but their content is richer in legend than in history. In order, therefore, to establish who the Toltecs were and what they did, these ambiguous written sources have to be compared, and where possible reconciled, with the archaeological data now available.

It is now known that in Teotihuacan times the immediate vicinity of Tula was sparsely occupied. A modest Classic settlement was found at Julian Villagran, about two kilometres north of Tula's urban zone, and another at Tepeji del Rio, twenty kilometres to the south; Chingu, a rather more important site, lies ten kilometres east of Tula, and was probably at that time a kind of regional capital.

Both legend and archaeology indicate that the first people to settle in Tula itself came from the north-western confines of civilized Middle America. Archaeologist Robert Cobean in his Harvard doctoral dissertation made a study in depth of Toltec pottery, and did much to clarify the beginnings of Tula. He shows that the earliest sherds from the site (Prado, dating from A.D. 700–800) have forms and decoration similar to an older pottery from the Bajío, the region lying to the north-west of Tula. The people who came from here brought with them pots of a type that had been used in the Bajío before the foundation of Tula.

These migrants from the north-west who founded Tula are called Tolteca-Chichimecs in the historical sources. They reputedly came from a place called Seven Caves, the fabled home of all Chichimec tribes. But while 'Toltec' stood for sophistication, 'Chichimec' meant the very opposite, and applied to those nomads who roamed much of north-west Mexico when the Spaniards arrived; the latter describe them as without pottery or clothing, and often on the brink of starvation. The name 'Chichimec' literally means people who came from Chichimani, the 'Place of Sucking'. Chichimecs are thus to be seen as newly-born, or young peoples. Tolteca-Chichimec is therefore at first sight a meaningless term, implying both civilization and savagery. It really applies to people who stood at the lower end of the cultural scale, but who were beginning to improve their lot. Like so many of those migrants into Central Mexico from the arid north-west, the founders of Tula had already learned the rudiments of agriculture, and had adopted Mexican gods.

Robert Cobean explains that the second layer of Tula ceramics (Corral, A.D. 800–900), unlike the first, is closely related to those of the central Valley of Mexico. This tentatively supports written accounts of a second group that settled in Tula at a very early stage, and who came from the opposite direction, the south-east; unlike the first group of migrants, they were highly civilized. These people were called Nonoalcas, a term implying people who spoke Nahuatl poorly. Nonoalco, whence they came, literally means 'where the language changes'; it is situated in Tabasco on the Gulf Coast. In the course of their migration, the sources say that these Nonoalcas collected other Nahuatl-speakers, including people from Teotihuacan, which had lost much of its population at about this time. Fray Sahagún, in recounting the legend of the great dispersal from Teotihuacan, tells of a tribe called Toltecs, or Nahuas, who also left, and went to a far-off place in the desert (i.e. the north-west), where there was little to eat and little to drink. Eventually they returned in the direction whence they had come.

The historian Alva Ixtlilxóchitl also writes of these Nonoalca migrants and actually names a number of places where they halted on their way to Tula. His list has given rise to confusion, because it includes a town called Jalisco, which was automatically associated with the modern state of that name, lying some 500 kilometres north-west of Mexico City. But several Jaliscos (the name means 'Place of Sand') existed near the Gulf Coast, where most of the other places which the historian names can also be identified. According to Ixtlilxóchitl's account, before eventually reaching Tula, the Nonoalcas spent a long time in the Huaxteca, lying to the north of the present-day Veracruz. Quetzalcoatl, the leading Toltec deity, has certain Huaxtec traits and specific items of his attire, such as his conical hat, invariably shown in codex illustrations, come from there.

Archaeology concurs with written sources in suggesting that Tula had been founded as a mere village by people who arrived from the north-west, where their simple pottery had originated. The Nonoalcas, after leaving the Huaxteca, first stayed in Tulancingo, nearly halfway between Tula and the Gulf Coast, and then came to Tula, where they taught the first settlers more elaborate skills, including the building of stone temples. At the same time they introduced the worship of the Plumed Serpent God, Quetzalcoatl, who became the patron deity of Tula, and who derived as much from the Caribbean Coast as from Teotihuacan.

The early settlement in Tula, where the two streams of migrants from opposite directions joined forces, was centred on 'Little Tula' (Tula Chico), lying about 1¼ kilometres from the principal ceremonial centre of later times, often called the Acropolis. Not enough excavation of this early Tula has been done to give a realistic estimate of its size, but present evidence suggests that it covered four square kilometres, and had a population of some 20,000 people, though this may be an overestimate.

THE CITY

Tula is easily reached from Mexico City, and the drive takes a little over an hour. The journey may include a visit to the colonial monastery and museum of Tepotzotlán, with its ornate church and its graceful cloisters and gardens; in the restaurant adjacent to the monastery quite a good Mexican-style lunch can be obtained.

The pre-Hispanic Tollan stands on a limestone ridge overlooking the modern Tula de Allende, situated in the river valley below. The ancient city covered most of this L-shaped ridge on the higher ground, but it is not known whether any of its people lived in the valley, on the site of the present-day town.

The name Tula will always be associated with Jorge Acosta. Though he confined his work to the central plaza, he was able to establish a sequence, in terms of early and late Toltec phases. This he applied to architecture as well as to pottery, since he found substructures under the main buildings that he reconstructed. The profile of these early temples often took the form of a sloping *talud* surmounted by a plain *tablero* that is not typical of the later Tula, nor of Teotihuacan, but more of Xochicalco and of El Tajin. As a result of his work, Acosta concluded that the city reached its apogee shortly before it was partly destroyed in about A.D. 1150.

Tula's expansive phase, running from A.D. 950 to 1150, corresponds to what is usually called the Mazapa horizon, named after the typical pottery of the period, an unattractive red-on-brown ware first identified near Teotihuacan, and used by people who settled there in

Post-Classic times. Similar sherds are found over much of Middle America, and since they date from the period of Tula's greatness, are apt to be called 'Toltec'. In point of fact, very little pottery has been found in Tula itself that can truly be called Mazapa, and more characteristic of the city itself is a ware called Jara Polished Orange that is even coarser.

The Tula of this florescent period is a large city, about which present information is far from complete, since recent excavations have been limited in scale and are not to be compared with Millon's Teotihuacan Mapping Project. The site, much of which had not been

Figure 22. Plan of Tula

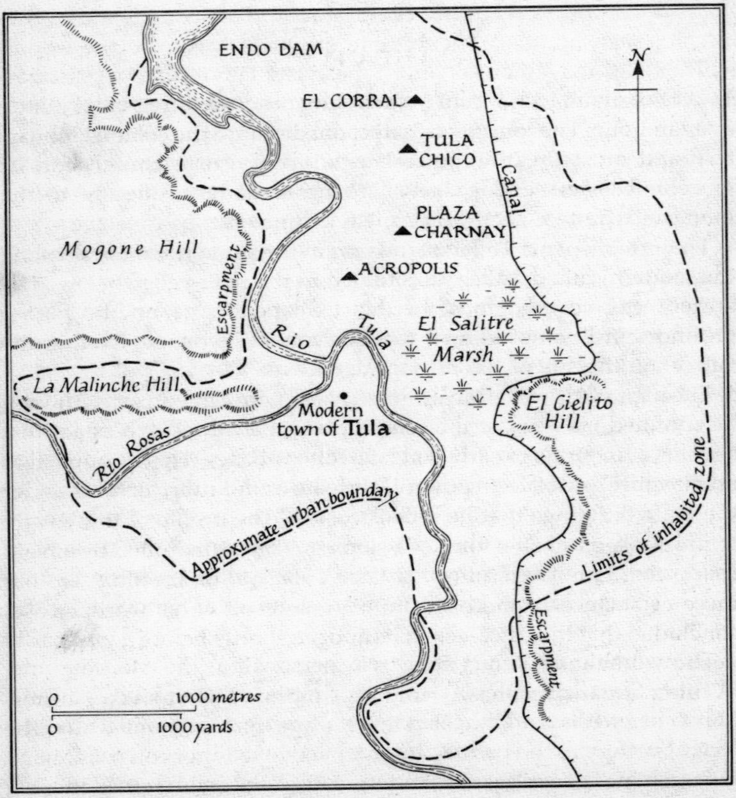

touched until recently, covers approximately thirteen square kilometres. While Charnay and Acosta had concentrated upon the Acropolis, much data on the rest of the site were obtained by the Missouri University Tula Project in the late 1960s and early 1970s; some work was later done by the Mexican National Institute of Anthropology, under the direction of Eduardo Matos. In all, three principal ceremonial centres have now been identified: the earliest, known as Little Tula, a second called the Plaza Charnay, and the principal group of monuments, the Acropolis. For the visitor the main interest still lies in the latter, which contains much the most impressive buildings, and has been more fully reconstructed.

The Acropolis consists of a spacious central plaza, flanked on the east by the largest structure, known as Building C, only partly excavated; on the west by a ball-court, explored by Eduardo Matos (no less than six ball-courts in all have been found in Tula); on the north side lies the main pyramid, the Temple of Quetzalcoatl, on the top of which stand the famous atlantes; these had lain for many centuries under the pyramid, smashed into fragments, and were probably not visible in Aztec times. A large colonnade, a unique feature of the Toltec period, marks the entrance to the temple. Acosta partly rebuilt its columns, then reduced almost to ground level; they formerly supported a roof, and from this great vestibule the élite of Tula could take part in the ceremonies performed in the plaza without exposing themselves to the midday sun.

The solemn cyclopean atlantes that crown the pyramid originally supported the wood-beamed roof of a temple, long since vanished; they represent not the Plumed Serpent God as such, but the same deity as the personification of Venus, the Morning Star. In this guise the god is dressed as a warrior, armed with the *atlatl*, or javelin thrower. His weapon has been described by space-fiction writer Erich von Däniken as a laser-beam thrower, brought to Tula by visitors from another world. But the *atlatl*, clearly visible in the atlantes' right hands, is the characteristic weapon of the period, as shown in many later codices. In their left hands the stone figures carry a sheaf of arrows, or javelins, the standard ammunition for the *atlatl*.

The worship of Venus as a twin personality, the Morning and Evening Stars, came to play a key role in the religion of the Ancient Mexicans, who carefully charted the planet's movements. Like the Aztec Sun God, who rose in the east every morning, Quetzalcoatl as Morning Star was a warrior, and in codices he is often shown with

pink and white body stripes, commonly used to portray prisoners
destined for sacrifice.

Certain chroniclers insist that Quetzalcoatl was really a benign
deity, who 'disapproved' of human sacrifice, and tried to stop it. This
fable derives from Conquest times, when their Indian subjects were
anxious to convince the Spaniards that not all their gods were devils,
and went out of their way to whitewash Quetzalcoatl, in order that
they could boast of at least one semi-respectable deity. But in certain
codices the god performs sacrificial acts, such as the gouging out of
the eye of a diminutive prisoner; in later times priests dressed as
Quetzalcoatl led the way in mass immolations.

Quetzalcoatl, as depicted in Tula, was a warrior and the patron god
of a warrior society; in the Post-Classic era, and probably before, he
was as inseparable from sacrifice as any other. The wars which the
Toltec soldiers fought served to obtain not only tribute, but also
captives for the altars of their gods, and the skull-rack in Tula suggests
multiple sacrifice as part of the process of war and conquest.

The atlantes are typical of the grim men-at-arms who proliferate in
the art of Tula: Toltec warriors wore a heavy pad of quilted cotton on
the left arm as a protection against arrows and a round shield strap-
ped on the back; their sandals are often decorated with feathered

Figure 23. Serpent
devouring skeleton from Tula relief

serpents, and their headgear, as worn by the atlantes, is a kind of
pillbox-shaped hat, topped by quetzal plumes and carrying in front a
bird flying downwards, a favourite Mexican adornment or symbol,
both in early times and late. On their breasts these Toltec warriors
wear a butterfly emblem, so stylized as to be barely recognizable as
such.

On the sides of the great pyramid are carved friezes in which processions of jaguars alternate with eagles, both gnawing human hearts dripping with blood. Behind the temple lies the Wall of Serpents (Coatepantli); its reliefs, carefully pieced together and put back in their original position, show a series of serpents swallowing whole human bodies, whose skulls emerge from their fangs.

The site of Tula is extensive and the average visitor, if he is able to find his way to the remains of Little Tula or of the Plaza Charnay, will be poorly rewarded for his longish walk. For whatever the scientific value of the work done on these key points in Tula's history, they have not been rebuilt. On the other hand, the Corral, about 1½ kilometres to the north of the main plaza and also excavated by Acosta, is well worth a visit. The central portion is round and was dedicated to the Plumed Serpent as God of Wind; such temples to the God of Wind were invariably circular, in order that the wind could blow freely round them. Adjoining the stairway of the Corral is a small altar with a sculpted frieze depicting the usual procession of

Figure 24. Eagle with human heart
in its beak

Toltec warriors; below them appears the equally inevitable row of skulls.

After viewing these buildings, together with the small selection of Toltec objects in the adjacent museum, the feeling remains that, however grand the scale of Tula, and however glorious its history, its culture was not only stern but sad. On all sides, one finds row upon row of the same warriors, predatory animals and skulls, without a trace of the finer and more playful touches of Classic murals. One is also struck by a certain coarseness of execution, which at times verges on the shoddy.

Fray Sahagún, in Book X of his *History*, gives an account of the principal monuments of Tula that bears little relation to what we see today:

Wherefore was it called a Toltec house? It was built with consummate care, majestically designed; it was the place of worship of their priest, whose name was Quetzalcoatl; it was the house of gold. For this reason was it called the house of gold; that which served as the stucco was gold plate applied, joined to it. One was facing west, toward the setting sun; this was the house of green stone, the house of fine turquoise. For this reason it was called the house of green stone, the house of fine turquoise. One was facing south, toward the irrigated lands; this was the house of shells or of silver. That which served as the stucco, the interior of the walls, seemed as if made of these shells inlaid. One was facing north, toward the plains, toward the spear house; this was the red house, red because shells were inlaid in the interior walls, or those stones which were precious stones, were red.

Figure 25. Jaguar from Tula relief

Sahagún recorded what his Nahuatl-speaking informants told him in their colourful but repetitive idiom, which gains effect by piling image upon image. He goes on to describe an even more exotic structure, in which feathers covered the interior walls. It consisted of four abodes: one facing east was lined with yellow feathers, one facing west with blue cotinga feathers; a house of white plumes faced south and another of red spoonbill plumes looked to the north. In addition to their accounts of fabulous buildings, Sahagún and others go out of their way to laud the genial and creative Toltecs, the very inventors of the human sciences; in such a catalogue of Toltec virtues, the artistic talent of Ancient Greece is combined with the subtle refinement of Byzantium.

But anyone who chooses to compare the saga with the reality of Tula's ruins, impressive though they may be, is in for a sorry surprise. It has to be remembered, however, that jade, turquoise, gold and even feathers were not just exotic materials, supposedly used in place of stone and stucco in the buildings of Tula and other cities. In a world where symbols counted for everything, they notionally conveyed the

Figure 26. Toltec standard bearer

idea of great riches, and in Aztec times were used to imply the receipt of tribute. These fabulous tales no more apply to the real city than do the exotic birds and tropical cacao bushes also associated with Tula in the same texts, but never really found at such an altitude. They are not part of the earthly Tula but of a mythical or other-worldly Tollan, representing for the Aztecs the source of all that is beautiful and good; in like manner the Book of Revelations describes the new and heavenly Jerusalem, 'a city of pure gold, like unto clear glass'. The emphasis on contrasting colours was also more religious than factual; as in

China, colours were linked with the four cardinal points, in their turn associated with important gods.

For the Aztecs of Conquest times, if their own capital, Tenochtitlan, was great, Tula had to be greater still. Skills and crafts, such as metallurgy, and even the art of writing – invented a thousand years before the Toltecs – automatically became the gift of these fabled forbears from whom all creativity derived. This rather doctored version of history merely served as a backcloth to Aztec grandeur.

Even if these idyllic accounts of Tula are not taken too literally, the present-day ruins show that it was indeed the city of the Plumed Serpent, the god Quetzalcoatl. It clung to this aura of sanctity and the first gifts given to the Emperor Moctezuma by Cortés, identified as the returned Quetzalcoatl, were reverently placed in the temple of that god in Tula, which was still his sacred city.

The name of this deity is derived from the Nahuatl *coatl*, meaning 'serpent' and *quetzalli*, 'green feather'; in addition to 'plumed serpent' it also conveyed the meaning of 'precious serpent', because quetzal feathers were so highly prized. The bird-serpent tradition is basic to Mexican symbolism, representing earth and sky, the terrestrial snake in unison with the celestial bird. Quetzalcoatl, as previously stressed, was much less prominent in Teotihuacan, where, if he appears at all, he takes the form not of a man but of a serpent, as in the famous temple that bears his name. At that time, he was at best an auxiliary of the principal god, Tlaloc.

Though the first known images of a human Quetzalcoatl were found on the Xochicalco stelae, which predate Tula, it is here that the god comes into his own and is frequently portrayed. Like most Mexican deities, Quetzalcoatl is a versatile god. Apart from his two roles as creator and the Morning Star, he was also God of Wind, and is usually shown in codices not only with his typical conical hat but also with a duckbill mask, the emblem of the God of Wind. Both as the green serpent that recalls the winding stream, and as the wind that comes before the tropical rain, he is closely associated with water, so precious in Highland Mexico. Most deities from Tlaloc onwards are in some way linked with fertility and with water. The great Smoking Mirror (Tezcatlipoca) of late pre-Hispanic times is ostensibly a sky god; yet he is also the jaguar, identified since early times with earth and hence with water. Even the great War God, the Humming Bird of the Left (Huitzilopochtli), partly derives from an older deity, simply called Opochtli, who was the fisherman's patron and one of the Tlaloques, or little Tlalocs, who dwelt in the lagoon on which the Aztec capital stood.

The last ruler was known as Topiltzin Quetzalcoatl, and legend suggests that the people who founded Tula were led by a man who also bore the god's name. Topiltzin, meaning 'Our Prince', was both a title and a personal name, and other appellations are also given for the last Toltec ruler. Tula may have had several rulers, presiding over the different ceremonial centres, though Little Tula had fallen into disuse before the city's fall. Plural rule was traditional in Mexico and, although the Aztecs and their allies of Texcoco each had a single king, subject city-states in the vicinity had three or even four monarchs.

Written sources say little about how Tula was governed, and the archaeological record tells even less. Tula, like Teotihuacan, is some-times called a 'hydraulic state'. The description may be misleading, if taken to imply that the city became powerful because it had a strong government, solely created by the need to harness its water supply – a theory better applied to the River Nile than to the River Tula. None the less, some form of irrigation was obviously necessary. Even today, when so much water is drawn off upstream for large-scale projects, the river still has an ample flow at the point where it reaches Tula, and irrigates extensive lands in the vicinity. The soil of its valley is fertile in contrast to the barren hills above, and it is inconceivable that the urbanized Toltecs should have been content to rely solely for their crops on a precarious rainfall – dependent on the caprice of the gods – while leaving the river valley untilled and its waters untapped. A city that depended for a living on the scanty seasonal rain of the Teotlalpan could never have grown so large.

Moreover, at one point on the river bank a kind of automatic or natural irrigation takes place; the land flanking the Tula River just below Little Tula is regularly flooded when the level of the stream rises in the summer rainy season. This would have prompted the Toltecs to control the flow of water by artificial means. When the Spaniards arrived they found large irrigation schemes in the region, and their accounts tell of many centres that harnessed the waters for growing maize and vegetables.

Irrigation schemes of a simple kind, even if they do not themselves force tribal peoples to adopt the trappings of a state, do require a fairly complex system of government. In addition, Toltec militarism implies a transfer of power from the temple to the palace, just as in Mesopo-tamia, where in Sumerian times the ruler of each city-state was the 'tenant and farmer' of the local god, whereas in the Babylonian era that followed, in the second millennium B.C., the palace took over much of the power of the temple.

The same forces operated in Mexico, though all accounts infer that in Tula the king continued to be priest as well as ruler. In this he stands halfway between the priest-ruler of Teotihuacan and the Aztec Emperor, who was a secular monarch, even if he performed priestly functions. Legend portrays the last Toltec king, Topiltzin, as living in an ivory tower, secluded from all but his own menials. Such stories are more likely to relate to earlier times; a cloistered tyrant might maintain his sway over a small city-state, but an empire cannot be conquered and held by a bizarre recluse.

In Tula, as in Post-Classic Mexico as a whole, the monarchy stood at the apex of a privileged military caste, whose members figure in the sculptured friezes that also portray eagles and ocelots, the emblems of the leading Aztec knights. As in Tenochtitlan, its warrior nobility surely claimed a generous share of the total wealth, including the richest lands. Art forms reveal a total dedication to war, and the Toltec state was impelled by the urge to impose tribute, particularly in the form of luxuries such as jade, feathers and ocelot skins. These exactions sustained the ruler and his palace and also enriched the military élite, who helped to further his conquests and on whom in return he lavished the choicest spoils of war. With trivial exceptions, even the most durable of such trophies, the jade, the gold and the turquoise, have not been unearthed in Tula; this is not surprising, since Sahagún mentions looting and devastation at its fall.

6

THE TOLTEC ERA

The Toltec Empire poses questions that are hard to answer: what impact did it have on the rest of Ancient Mexico during its apogee from A.D. 950 to 1150, and what territories, if any, did it conquer?

Historians differ profoundly on this. Wigberto Jiménez Moreno has always favoured a larger Toltec Empire, comparable to the known conquests of the Aztecs; on the other hand, earlier scholars, such as Daniel Brinton, went to the opposite extreme and denied that it ever existed.

In seeking to define, even tentatively, the limits of Toltec rule, two basic problems arise. First, in Ancient Mexico a cyclical notion of time prevailed; whatever happened in one era was a reflection of what had gone before and a foretaste of what would come after. The Aztecs saw their own empire as a repetition of Toltec triumphs. Hence, when they made conquests on the Gulf Coast of Mexico, they then assumed that the Toltecs must have done the same, though evidence to that effect is tenuous. The presence at the time of the Spanish Conquest of Nahuatl-speakers on the Caribbean littoral proves nothing, since it is not known when they went there.

Second, in view of the fragmentary written data on pre-Aztec times, the temptation arises to use pottery styles as a means of defining the bounds of empire. But this, as previously stressed, is a hazardous undertaking. If the extent of the Aztec Empire had to be estimated, not by detailed tribute-lists and other contemporary records, but by the presence of Aztec pottery, the conclusions would be largely negative. Extensive areas known to have been conquered, such as the Oaxaca region, reveal only the scantest traces of an Aztec presence. Moreover, ceramics associated with the Toltec era, which are found all over Mexico, do not serve as a pointer to domination by

Tula itself; they were not necessarily made in that city, and certain wares typical of the period were not found in Tula.

The highest current estimate for the population of Tula is about 60,000, with a further 60,000 living in the surrounding countryside. This total of 120,000 is rather less than the number housed within the city of Teotihuacan and amounts to a mere fraction of the manpower available to the Aztecs, which included not only the inhabitants of their own capital, but also those of the constellation of lakeside cities that so bedazzled the Spaniards when they first arrived; at that time the population of the Valley of Mexico numbered about one and a quarter million. It is hardly conceivable that one medium-sized city (other estimates of Tula's population amount to 30,000) could have seized and held – as is often suggested – an empire stretching east-wards to the Gulf, south-east to Oaxaca, and far into North-West Mexico, where even the Aztecs never set foot. Notwithstanding the much larger forces at their disposal, Aztec historians often remind us of the precarious nature of their rule; lacking a network of fixed garrisons, they fought endless campaigns against people they had already once conquered, but who then rebelled against the burden of tribute. They thus faced the need to wage several wars at the same time, a feat for which the Toltecs lacked the manpower.

Finally, supposing that the Toltecs *had* made conquests on the Aztec scale, there is no conceivable use to which a city the size of Tula could have put the avalanche of tribute derived from such a huge domain. Aztec tribute-lists do not explain how, even with a much larger population, such annual items as, say, a total of 123,400 cotton mantles could be absorbed, since the common people were forbidden to wear them. Had Tula conquered a territory stretching from the Atlantic to the Pacific, its people would have been deluged in tribute, and the streets of the city might literally have been paved in gold, as the more imaginative accounts suggest.

A maximum population of 120,000 in the Tula region could not have provided the men of military age needed for such conquests, after allowing for the inevitable quota of non-combatants: slaves, craftsmen, the aged, the young and the physically unfit. Admittedly much can be achieved with small numbers; King Henry V, for in-stance, set out to win the Battle of Agincourt with an army of only 6,000, comparable perhaps with the kind of force which Tula could have raised. But while battles can be won with tiny forces, it is much harder, as King Henry and his successors also discovered, to make lasting gains without more supporting troops.

An intimate relationship with far-off Chichen Itza is demonstrable, but neither the study of its pottery nor its architecture offers many clues as to Tula's other conquests, while written documents often reflect Aztec, not Toltec, achievements. In view of the rather short lifespan of Tula as a leading power, its triumphs were fleeting and left in their wake only limited traces.

Certain data as to the nature of the Toltec Empire come from the seventeenth-century chronicler, Francisco Chimalpain, who writes of three realms, Tollan, Culhuacán and Otompan, which exercised a joint sway, lasting for 191 years; at the end of this time their alliance fell asunder, and only Culhuacán survived as a leading power. Culhuacán is now a derelict suburb on the outer fringes of Mexico City. Otompan, or Otumba as it is now called, is situated to the north-east of Teotihuacan; however, the Nahuatl name simply means 'Place of Otomis', and could have applied to some other place inhabited by such people. This, however, is not likely, since the known Otumba became quite an important town in late pre-Hispanic times. Its location is significant; as a leading ally of Tula, it would have provided a link with the vanished glories of Teotihuacan, to which it lies so near.

At all events, the notion of a triple alliance conforms to the known structure of the Aztec Empire, ruled, as we shall see, by three cities, of which Tenochtitlan was merely the senior partner. It was hard, if not impossible, for one Mexican city-state to control an empire single-handed, without the help of partners, and this limitation would have applied to Tula quite as much as to its successor.

Culhuacán survived as the remaining bastion of Toltec power after the fall of Tula. When the Toltec Empire stood at its zenith, this city, situated on the fertile shore of the Lake of Texcoco, was not only a second capital, but also served as an ideal springboard for the conquest of the warm lands beyond the mountains to the south, the present-day state of Morelos. Since time immemorial the peoples of the high plateau were drawn towards this low-lying region, rich in cotton and those other luxuries required as status symbols by the military élite. The historical sources mention Toltec associations with Cuernavaca, now the capital of Morelos, and the Polished Orange pottery that is typical of Tula has been found in that region. Since this was a domestic rather than an export ware, it is more likely to be found in places where Toltec armies were present than in others merely visited by traders. Moreover, Xochicalco is also situated in Morelos; though it only survived into the earlier part of the Toltec era,

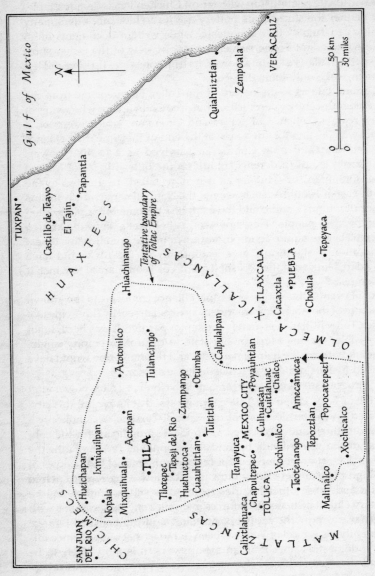

Gulf of Mexico

N

50 km
30 miles

VERACRUZ
Zempoala
Quiahuiztlan

TUXPAN
Castillo de Teayo
El Tajín
Papantla

H U A X T E C S

Tentative boundary of Toltec Empire

Huachinango

Tepeyaca
TLAXCALA
Cacaxtla
PUEBLA
Cholula

X I C A L L A N C A S

O L M E C A

Tulancingo
Atotonilco
Calpulalpan

Zumpango
Otumba
Tepeji del Rio
Tultitlan

Poyauhtlan
MEXICO CITY
Culhuacán
Cuitlahuac
Chalco
Amecameca
Popocatepetl

Huichapan
Ixmiquilpan
Actopan
TULA
Tilotepec
Huehuetoca
Cuauhtitlan

Nopala
Mixquihuala

Tenayuca
Chapultepec
Xochimilco
Tepoztlan
Xochicalco

C H I C H I M E C S

SAN JUAN DEL RIO
Calixtlahuaca
TOLUCA
Teotenango
Malinalco

M A T L A T Z I N C A S

MAP 3. THE TOLTEC DOMAIN

1. Olmec jadeite mask

2. Olmec bust of an old woman

3. Olmec standing figure

4. Olmec pendant of distorted figure

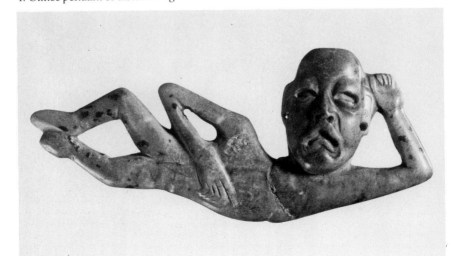

5. Pyramid of the Moon, Teotihuacan

6. Serpent heads from the Temple of Quetzalcoatl, Teotihuacan

7. Teotihuacan tripod vase

8. Court of the Palace of the Quetzal Butterfly, Teotihuacan

9. Teotihuacan statue, probably of Chalchiuhtlicue, Goddess of Water, standing outside the National Museum in Mexico City

10. Detail of a mural in the Tepantitla Palace, Teotihuacan

11. Teotihuacan stone mask

12. Stone axe from El Tajin

13. Detail of a relief from the Temple of Quetzalcoatl, Xochicalco

14. Pyramid of the Niches, El Tajin

15. Atlas figure from Tula

16. Carved jaguar from Tula

17. Toltec jaguar relief

18. Jaguar statue in Tula Museum

19. Tula atlantes

20. Atlantes from Chichen Itza

21. The caracol at Chichen Itza

22. Chacmool, Chichen Itza

23. The foundation of Tenochtitlan, from the *Codex Mendoza*. In the centre, the eagle alights on a cactus, surrounded by ten Mexican leaders

24. The plan of Tenochtitlan traditionally attributed to Hernán Cortés

25. A model of the ceremonial centre of Tenochtitlan. In the background is the Great Temple

26. A monkey wearing the facial duckbill mask of Quetzalcoatl

27. The goddess Coatlicue, mother of Huitzilopochtli

28. Aztec rabbit

29. The goddess Tlazolteotl

30. The Wall of Serpents at the pyramid of Tenayuca

31. Close-up of a serpent at Tenayuca

32. Close-up of a part of Tizoc's Stone

33. An Aztec tribute-list
in the *Codex Mendoza*

34. A seated Macehual, or peasant

35. A jaguar from the Temple of the Eagle
and jaguar knights in Malinalco

36. Aztec onyx jar

Tenochtitlan.

37. The first meeting between Moctezuma II and Hernán Cortés, as recorded in the Lienzo de Tlaxcala

38. Spaniards fighting Indians, from Dúran's *History*

it is a site from which Tula borrowed much. In a sense the latter is a more direct heir to Xochicalco than to Teotihuacan.

The southern limits of the Toltec Empire may be taken to have embraced part at least of the Valley of Morelos. In the east, it surely stretched as far as Tulancingo, mentioned by numerous sources as the place where the two ethnic groups, the Tolteca-Chichimecs and the Nonoalcas, traditionally joined forces; Tulancingo lay adjacent to the territory of the Huaxtecs, who occupied the coast. As can be seen from Map 3, this eastern sector of the Toltec domain would normally have included towns such as Actopan and Atotonilco, situated in a region which successive rulers of the Valley of Mexico found it easy to penetrate, owing to the absence of any natural obstacle.

Suggestions have often been made that the Toltecs made long-range conquests north and west of their capital. Evidence of actual conquest, as opposed to contact, is tenuous. Commercial ties are demonstrable; for instance, in the National Museum in Mexico City a copper disc can be seen that represents four stylized serpents and comes from Casas Grandes, the great site in Chihuahua, near the U.S. border. But the museum also possesses an almost identical disc from Chichen Itza, Tula's sister-city in the Maya land, and both these discs resemble an adornment worn by the atlantes of Tula. Even further afield in the American south-west, such Toltec emblems as a horned and feathered serpent have been found, and in the earlier Pueblo culture of Arizona, copper balls of Central Mexican origin date from Toltec times.

Cultural colonization of the north-west corresponds more to the Teotihuacan than to the Toltec era, when Central Mexican influences were already on the wane in the present-day states of Zacatecas and Durango, lying about halfway from Tula to the U.S. border. It is therefore hard to agree with American archaeologist Charles Kelley, whose work on the subject is notable, when he writes of penetration into this region, not merely of traders, but of 'militaristic Toltec nobles', during the closing decades of Tula's heyday. Cultural traits, and works of art such as copper discs, could be passed on by merchants from one place to the next and form a slender basis for firm historical conclusions.

Once again, potsherds are converted into people, and the presence of mere portable objects made in one place is taken as proof of its conquest of another. And yet no one pretends that South-East Asians conquered Scandinavia, just because Buddhist figures have been found there, brought by Norse visitors to Arab lands. It seems most uncertain whether Toltec military control stretched in this direction much beyond the Teotlalpan itself. From irrigated lands bordering the Tula River they could have more than satisfied their needs of the staple foods, maize, beans and chillis. The inducement was therefore far greater to expand in the opposite direction into the lowlands, not in search of maize and beans, but of turquoise, feathers and jade, without which no religious ceremony was complete; in the final analysis even the supply of food, in particular the sacred maize, depended as much on these rites in homage to the gods as on more material considerations, such as good husbandry.

The problem of the extent of the Toltec Empire has been further confused by the opening passage of a major historical source, the *Toltec-Chichimec History (Historia Tolteca-Chichimeca)*. This document lists twenty places that the Nahuatl text calls the 'hands and feet' of Tula. The term is however ambiguous, and successive translators have differed as to whether these people were really subjects or allies.

The matter is complicated by the inclusion in the list of a number of townships that were ostensibly very far distant from Tula itself. The German scholar Walter Krickeberg in the 1930s was among the first to seek their correct location; the names are divided into four groups of five, and he identified the cities of the second of these four groups with places on or near the coast of the Gulf of Mexico in the present-day state of Veracruz; these places still exist today and were fairly important in late pre-Columbian times. However, Paul Kirchhoff, another leading German scholar, identified other places bearing the same names but situated quite near to Tula itself. I consider that Kirchhoff is more likely to be right, in the absence of more concrete evidence that the Toltecs controlled the Gulf Coast.

Enclaves of Nahuatl-speakers still exist on the Caribbean littoral, where the use of this language became widespread. But these could have arrived at any time. Not only does Sahagún state that the 'wise men', at the fall of Teotihuacan, went east; other sources tell how in Aztec times, during the great famine of 1450–54, people sold their children to the inhabitants of the well-watered coastal regions in return for food.

Archaeology offers no proof of Toltec armed intervention in this region. José García Payon, the excavator of El Tajin, describes the pyramid of Castillo de Teayo, some fifty kilometres north of El Tajin, as contemporary with those of Tula, to which it bears a marked resemblance. This is certainly true, but like the proverbial swallow that does not make a summer, a single pyramid is a poor foundation on which to build visions of an empire stretching from coast to coast. For those who can spare the time, Castillo de Teayo is most worth a visit. Its Toltec-style pyramid is unique in forming the centre piece of the plaza of a small modern village. It is moreover one of few pyramids, outside the Maya area, that preserves part of the original temple that stood on its summit, which has disappeared from so many more familiar monuments. It is also unlikely that the Toltecs conquered the Valley of Toluca. Its capital, Toluca, is nowadays a bare hour's drive westward from Mexico City. Twenty-four kilometres to the south of Toluca lies the great site of Teotenango, founded about a century before Tula. The chronicler Chimalpain writes of wars fought between Tula and Teotenango, and mentions people who migrated from there to Tula. Román Piña Chan, who excavated and restored the site during the 1970s, stresses its connections both with late Teotihuacan and with Xochicalco, but insists that nothing specifically Toltec is to be found there, in contrast to recognizable remains of the Aztecs, who conquered the Valley of Toluca.

Chimalpain writes of a structure in Teotenango that he calls the Pyramid of the Toltecs; he says that it was built beside water, in which grew great rushes. He also mentions another temple, dedicated to the chief god of Teotenango, adorned with shrines studded with precious stones, recalling Sahagún's account of the marvels of Tula. The chronicler states that these monuments were so grandiose that the King of Tula became jealous and tried to destroy this rival to the splendours of his own capital.

Whatever the element of exaggeration in the chronicler's account of Teotenango, it remains an imposing site, easily reached from Mexico City. It was founded in about A.D. 700, during the closing stages of the Teotihuacan hegemony; at the lowest levels sherds are found related to the last phase in Teotihuacan. Founded much later than El Tajin or Xochicalco, the early Teotenango bridges the gap between Late Classic and Early Post-Classic. Unlike most other cities of Toltec times, it was still flourishing at the Spanish Conquest. The site is highly strategic; on one side it is protected by a great wall, while on the remaining three the abrupt slope of the mountain shields it from attack. Seen from afar, the protective girdle of stone might have been carved out of the rock by a creator god, and it was thus aptly named Teotenango, 'The Place of the Divine Wall'. The area of the ancient city is larger than that of the modern town below, which has 12,000 inhabitants, but whose houses are more concentrated. In pre-

Conquest times the élite probably lived on the fortified hill, while the remainder dwelt in the plain.

Whereas the lack of typically Toltec remains on the site does not in itself prove that the Toltecs never conquered Teotenango, its natural defences are so formidable that it was well placed to withstand their assault. Moreover, the Valley of Toluca, lying at an even higher and chillier altitude than the Valley of Mexico, offered no tempting spoils in the form of products not freely available to the Toltecs nearer home.

Much has been written about rivalries between Tula and the city-states of the Puebla Valley to the east, beyond the snow-capped volcanoes. This region was to play an important role in Aztec times, as an enemy rather than a conquered province, and its leading city at the time, Tlaxcala, became the faithful ally of Cortés. But in the Toltec era, Tlaxcala was not yet of any consequence, and the power of Cholula was temporarily eclipsed. Assuming, like the Ancient Mexicans, that history repeats itself, scholars are apt to suggest that if Cholula was important before and after the Toltecs, then it was perforce also Tula's great rival, and it is even credited with a leading part in the latter's decline and fall. But no archaeological or written evidence supports such a hypothesis. At the time of Tula's foundation the Great Pyramid of Cholula was almost abandoned. Simple structures on its flanks belong to the Toltec period, but their scale is so limited as to amount to little more than the work of squatters. In the course of the Toltec era, Cholula staged a very modest revival, but only after the fall of Tula did it achieve a more spectacular renaissance, which gave its name to the famous polychrome pottery of Aztec times and whose legacy includes important codices.

The Puebla Valley was settled at this time by people confusingly named the Xicallanca Olmecs, though they have absolutely nothing to do with the original Olmecs of the Gulf Coast; they are sometimes also called the 'Historic Olmecs'. They were not the founders of any major centre of civilization remotely comparable with Tula or even with Teotenango. Archaeologist Angel García Cook worked in the Puebla-Tlaxcala region and found many big villages contemporary with Tula, but no towns, suggesting a fairly low density of population. This picture has been little modified by the discoveries in Cacaxtla, mentioned above; the site is small; it did not necessarily belong to these Historic Olmecs, and was in any case not a potential rival to Tula. The Olmec-Xicallanca territory, including the Puebla Valley and stretching eastwards towards the coast, is to be seen more as a no-man's-land between the Toltec domains and the peoples of the littoral than as an empire in its own right.

None the less, if the peoples of the Puebla Valley were no military rival to Tula, their capacity as traders was important. At Guasave, on the Pacific Coast in Sonora, some 1,600 kilometres to the north-west of the Puebla region, in levels dated to between A.D. 900 and 1250, and hence coinciding with the Toltec era, a whole complex of artifacts has been found which are extraordinarily similar to those of Central Mexico; they are not, however, related to those of Tula, but to others more typical of the Puebla Valley. A few items had obvious connections with Culhuacán in the Central Valley and in Guasave ancient food remains include dragonfly eggs, a Valley of Mexico delicacy, collected from poles set in the middle of the salty Lake of Texcoco. This unexpected proof of trade between the Puebla Valley and the north-west is typical of a tendency for links to appear between two distant regions of Ancient Mexico, in the form of styles or objects of which no trace can be found in the lands that lie between them; of this the most dramatic example is provided by Tula and its bonds with Yucatán.

THE MAYAN MARCH

The relationship between Tula and Chichen Itza, lying some 1,500 kilometres to the east, is one of the great enigmas of pre-Hispanic history. In the case of Teotihuacan and Kaminaljuyu, already discussed, common traits in art and architecture are so marked as to imply direct contact, and perhaps some form of colonization. Between Tula and Chichen the similarities are even more arresting.

These uncanny parallels have often been described. To name only a few common art forms: friezes of warriors, chacmools, processions of jaguars, caryatids or atlantes to hold up roofs, and butterfly pectorals are found in both places. In addition, they share specific architectural elements: stairways with sculpted serpent balustrades; columns formed by serpent bodies with heads at ground level; skull-racks; halls filled with columns. Of such common features, the most evident to any visitor are the huge areas adjacent to both the Temple of Warriors in Chichen and the Temple of Quetzalcoatl in Tula, each filled with serried rows of columns; such colonnaded halls are unique in Mexico. And apart from details, the two sites are imbued with the same overall theme. Both display an austerity alien to the more exuberant Maya tradition and in stark contrast to its florid profiles. Not only are the emblems of death, the skulls and the predatory animals, present in profusion; the warriors depicted in friezes and reliefs are sartorially and physically identical; those of Chichen lack the typical Maya profile and are overtly Toltec.

Figure 27. Toltec chacmool of type also found in Chichen Itza

Mere similarities in pottery forms as, say, between Teotihuacan and Han Dynasty China, may legitimately be ascribed to chance. But between Tula and Chichen parallels are so close and so numerous as to defy this kind of explanation. To take a specific example of a pair of buildings, one in each city: the ball-court that occupies the west side of the main plaza in Tula, excavated by Eduardo Matos, though less imposing, displays all the main elements of the great court of Chichen. Both are on the west side of their respective plazas and share the same north-south orientation; they offer an identical profile of sloping court and upright wall, quite distinct from most other Mexican ball-courts; each has an impressive stairway on the west and a skull-rack on the east side; even their scale is comparable, and the Tula court is the second largest known after that of Chichen, measuring 120 metres from north to south.

The Chichen that thus became Tula's sister-city was a latter-day creation of Maya civilization, flourishing some time after the fall of the Classic Maya cities. Their more immediate successor, though also in part their contemporary, was a culture known as Puuc, named after some low-lying hills in south-western Yucatán; its earlier buildings coincided with the last phase of the Classic Maya, and Puuc then survived till the emergence of the 'Toltec Maya' style in Chichen in about A.D. 1000. Puuc architecture is very distinct from Classic or Toltec Maya. The lower façade of its long buildings is free of decoration, while the upper part is covered with exuberant stone mosaics, in which figure strange sky serpent masks with hooked noses, interspersed with criss-cross geometric designs. The most impressive Puuc site is Uxmal, some seventy-five kilometres south-west of Merida, the capital of Yucatán; not far from Uxmal lie two other important centres of this culture, Kabah and Sayil.

Chichen Itza was already fairly important in Puuc times; the round Caracol (meaning 'snail'), usually known as the Observatory, belongs to this period, and the Castillo, whose visible exterior is pure Toltec Maya, was superimposed on an earlier Puuc pyramid.

The Maya land had become a centre of attraction for people from the Central Plateau well before the rise of Tula; following Teotihuacan influences in Tikal and elsewhere, during the Puuc period plumed serpents, warrior figures with non-Maya profiles and other signs of this penetration appear. However, the process reached its climax during Tula's apogee – as revealed by the archaeological record and confirmed by written sources.

The arrival of Toltecs in Yucatán is specifically mentioned in the *Books of the Chilam Balam*. Chilam Balam means 'Jaguar Prophet', and these books of so-called 'prophecies' are Colonial transcriptions of earlier Mayan songs and sagas. Though called prophecies, they are a means of recording history. The Post-Classic Mayas had abandoned the Long Count, giving dates beginning in a notional year zero. Instead, they measured time in periods of approximately twenty years' duration, called *katuns*; these are numbered from one to thirteen, each accompanied by the name 'Ahau'; any given *katun* is therefore repeated every 256 years. But since their concept of time was thus cyclical, whatever had happened once in, say, *katun* 8 Ahau, was sure to recur when *katun* 8 Ahau came round again 256 years later. Accordingly, when the Chilam Balam 'prophesies' that the Quetzal, the Green Bird (i.e. Quetzalcoatl, or Kukulkan in Maya) shall come in *katun* 4 Ahau (using the future tense), this is merely a way of stating that he had arrived already in a previous *katun* 4 Ahau; the *katun* 4 Ahau in which a Quetzalcoatl really came to Chichen probably falls between A.D. 968 and 987.

The *Popol Vuh*, the great epic of the Quiche Mayas of Highland Guatemala, also stresses the Toltec ancestry of their people, and tells how they had come from 'Tulan Zuiva', or 'Tulan in the West'. The

Popol Vuh writes of Gucumatz (Quetzalcoatl in the Quiche tongue) as a wise and learned ruler who was the founder of the tribe. Such texts imply that these Mayas were at one time governed by men who came from Tula, and in particular by a leader who adopted the local version of the name Quetzalcoatl, Kukulkan or Gucumatz. Such stories are in full accord with the archaeology of Chichen and with its portrayal of so many Toltec-type figures; the people in these reliefs are clearly too important to be mere merchants, rather than warriors or conquerors.

The Maya Itzas who were living in Chichen when this Kukulkan appeared were fairly new arrivals. They also came from a westerly direction about sixty years before and managed to carve out for themselves a mini-empire in Yucatán, of which Chichen was the capital. Even the Highland Guatemalan chiefs sent envoys to the great Lord Nacxit, another name for Quetzalcoatl, who resided in Chichen.

The question still remains: how is this kinship between Chichen and Tula, with irrefutable evidence of contact, to be explained? During the closing stages of Teotihuacan, contacts had been made in the reverse direction, as we have seen, in the form of Mayan elements in Xochicalco and Cacaxtla. But no one suggests that the Mayas ruled these places, and these Maya-inspired works of art could have been the work of itinerant artists. On the contrary, one Cacaxtla mural already shows people with Mayan profiles and adornments in the clutches of other warriors typical of Central Mexico, a scene not unlike others found in Chichen, several centuries later.

The Chichen-Tula link is of a different kind, and is made even stranger by the vast territory that divides the two, and which bears few traces of a Toltec presence. The key to the riddle may lie in Nonoalco, or Tabasco, the original home of one of the two groups that founded Tula. We know that in Late Classic times the Mayas were present in coastal Tabasco, to the west of Yucatán, a presence to which the large Maya-type site of Comalcalco, north-west of Villahermosa, the modern capital of Tabasco, bears witness. Equally, we know that some five hundred years later Aztec merchants were established in a place eighty kilometres beyond Comalcalco called Xicalango, which was part Nahuatl-speaking at the time of the Conquest, but was not a tributary of the Aztec Empire. However, of any Toltec settlement in Tabasco, the gateway to Yucatán, nothing survives; the Toltecs left nothing on their route that is remotely Toltec, and yet suddenly, in far-off Chichen, we find pyramids and palaces that appear as grandiose replicas of those of Tula.

Previous investigators, including Acosta, tended to think in terms of a purely one-way traffic, and took for granted that the Toltecs had dominated the Chichen scene in every way, and created a new style, best described as Maya-Toltec. The proof lay visible for all to see, in the form of the Toltec-type warriors, chacmools, non-Maya gods, etc. But while clearly it was the Toltecs who penetrated Yucatán rather than the Mayas who established themselves in Tula, the question of where the Maya-Toltec style was invented has been argued at length. In particular, George Kubler points out that Chichen, founded long before Tula, was the centre of a new and genial flowering of Maya culture, which must have inspired the similar but cruder buildings of

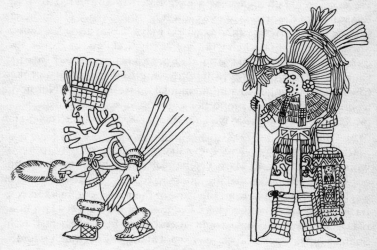

Figure 28. Warriors with Toltec features
depicted in Chichen relief

Tula. According to Kubler, the formative period of the Chichen-Tula style is to be sought only in Chichen; he merely concedes that a few common traits, including elements of the Plumed Serpent cult, originated in Tula; but he insists that in most respects Chichen was not the receptor but the creator of a new style in painting and sculpture.

Alberto Ruz Lhuiller, the discoverer of the famous Palenque tomb, argues to the contrary; he accepts the presence in Chichen of certain non-Toltec elements, but maintains that the main innovations in that centre are non-Maya. To quote one instance, Ruz insists that the distinctive serpent columns, with heads at ground level, are not a legacy from the Puuc Maya style, where they have no antecedents; he sees the dominant Plumed Serpent cult and its art forms as a Toltec import, alien to the Classic Maya.

The controversy can never be settled simply by assuming that Chichen culture is pure Toltec or vice versa. First, it needs to be stressed that certain elements of the Toltec-Maya style are neither Maya nor Toltec; for instance, the columns more probably originated in Oaxaca; other traits, such as the north-south orientation of buildings, stem from Teotihuacan and before; the ball-court reliefs in Chichen follow a pattern set by El Tajin, not Tula. None the less, aside from stylistic details, the whole spirit of Chichen betrays a Toltec presence, generally believed to have dated from about A.D. 1000. Regardless of the origins of its architecture, the essence of Chichen is Central Mexican rather than Lowland Maya. Comparing the monuments of the later Chichen with, say, the typical Puuc of Uxmal, this difference is arresting. In the florid Puuc façades, also present in early Chichen, the baroque Maya tradition survives. In contrast, Toltec Chichen, including the main ceremonial centre, is almost 'Nordic' in feeling. Its geometric proportions, its open spaces, and its stark profiles are alien to the Maya land, though typical of the cooler and barer Altiplano.

The Toltec-Maya style is the visual expression of new forms of worship. The Classic Maya ceremonial centre looks inwards, not outwards, and implies that the more sacred rites were the preserve of a select few, screened from the view of the masses. In marked contrast, the pyramids of Chichen, like those of the Plateau, face huge plazas where the people could attend the ceremonies, just as in Spanish times 'open chapels' were built at the side of churches for the benefit of the vast concourse of Indian converts.

But if the Toltecs brought a new spirit to Chichen, it does not follow that they invented the art forms which it inspired. Not only are certain Chichen buildings older than those of Tula; its art is also richer and more versatile and in this respect Tula's inferiority cannot be denied. One has only to study the two great ball-courts to see that the one flanking the Tula plaza is a pale if not pitiful reflection of its Chichen counterpart, though admittedly it was not improved by Aztec additions.

Logic suggests that the monuments of Tula were modelled on those of Chichen, rather than the reverse. If two replicas of a given structure exist, the more splendid version is presumably the original; known cases hardly exist where a building or statue made to copy another surpassed its prototype in grandeur and beauty – as those of Chichen surpass the monuments of Tula.

The Toltec-Maya epic may accordingly be reconstructed as follows. In the late tenth century A.D. bands of Toltecs, mainly belonging to the Nonoalca branch of the family, native to the Gulf Coast, went back from Tula to Tabasco, the original homeland of both the Nonoalcas and the Itzas of Chichen. From there, invited by the Itzas, they trekked onwards as far as Chichen. To judge by the pre-eminence in Chichen art of people of non-Maya profile, the newcomers came not as traders but as conquerors; the many images of the Plumed Serpent suggest that the invaders brought their god with them; they thus came armed with both the sword and the book. They cannot have been numerous, since neither the language nor the appearance of the people was altered. The Toltec incursion might therefore be compared to the temporary florescence of French culture in Egypt, implanted from afar by Napoleon, but without control of the intermediate lands and seas. Much later the Itzas were driven out of Chichen, and were not conquered by the Spaniards until 1697, at a time when they were living on various islands in the Peten Jungle of Guatemala. Their language was still pure Yucatec Maya of an archaic kind; they used few Nahuatl names and had no 'Mexican' traits.

If the Toltec invaders imposed their warlike ideology, the resulting culture was a marriage of Toltec militarism with Maya genius, dependent on Mayan artistic traditions. After burgeoning on alien soil, the main elements of the Toltec-Maya style were then retransmitted to Tula, where they were used until in the late twelfth century both centres went into a decline.

LIFE IN TULA

If Toltec power is sometimes overstated by historians, no one questions that they were indeed conquerors, who exacted tribute from their neighbours. Tula thus became a rich city, even if such riches were gained at the expense of others. Much of the tribute took the form of finery for the nobles, and brought few rewards to the masses.

Data with which to reconstruct the daily life of the average Toltec are scanty, and the temptation is inescapable to judge life in Tula by the more familiar criteria of Aztec Tenochtitlan. Comparisons between Tula and Teotihuacan may, however, be more apt, since our knowledge of both runs parallel, being based more on archaeology than on texts.

The city was not built on a clear-cut grid pattern, like Teotihuacan. Major avenues have not been found, and in this it recalls many Maya centres. But whereas in modern Mexico the rich flee to the suburbs, in Tula they lived around the city centre, where the dwellings are more opulent, though the buildings near to the Acropolis were not residential. The adjacent 'Palace' has no kitchens, and its uses were ceremonial, such as priests' robing and the storage of ritual objects, rather like the sacristy and vestry of a cathedral. This Acropolis, as the main plaza of Tula, was the successor of the earlier Little Tula, which was later almost abandoned. In this respect also Tula differed from Teotihuacan, whose planned layout survived intact.

In another respect Tula diverged from the pattern of Teotihuacan, which acted rather as a sponge, sucking into its urban perimeter almost all the people who tilled the land in the surrounding country. But within a fifteen-kilometre radius of Tula a series of villages has been found, with pottery of the Tula period, and this implies that part of the land workers lived outside the capital, amounting perhaps to half the total. Therefore, while some dwellers of Tula left the city every day to till the fields, the proportion was lower than in the case of Teotihuacan; moreover, they would have had less far to walk, given the size of the city.

The rough estimate of 60,000 for the population of Tula is based on an equally approximate figure of 5,000 inhabitants per square kilometre. This is marginally less than for Teotihuacan, since the Toltec capital was very spread out; spaces between the houses were ample, though it is far from clear to what use they were put, since the ground was ill-suited to garden plots; in this it differs radically from Aztec Tenochtitlan, with its well-watered smallholdings.

The University of Missouri project has provided useful data on individual homes, but such reports hardly convey a lifelike impression of what such houses were like to live in. Countless small mounds have been found that appear to be homes for extended families; one of these, which was excavated, contained five family units, centred upon a courtyard. This pattern of smaller dwellings is quite different from Teotihuacan's compounds, though to a certain degree it was to be repeated in Tenochtitlan. However, the proportion of the Tula perimeter given over to private dwellings as opposed to temples and palaces is much larger in Tula; its lifespan was short and its less formal layout is more to be compared with that of Teotihuacan in, say, A.D.

200, before it was fully remodelled on such a grandiose scale. Houses in Tula were built not of stone, but of adobe blocks; in certain cases their walls were made by pressing wet earth into a mould, as in modern poured-concrete construction. In the excavated dwellings the rooms are diminutive by modern standards; in a typical house the largest is about three metres square, while the four adjoining ones are little more than cubicles, whose total area equals that of the larger chamber; one house of the same group had its own pottery kiln. Such tiny quarters served mainly as a dormitory and people spent much of their time out of doors, withdrawing to rest at sunset. The monotony of the daily round was broken by feasts in honour of the Plumed Serpent and other gods.

Those who worked the fields grew the typical high-altitude crops, chiefly maize, beans and chillis; they also served as soldiers in major campaigns in the absence of full-time warriors, apart from the nobles. In the new and warlike age, the demands of military service would have been heavier than in former times, particularly in view of Tula's limited manpower.

Many obsidian workshops have been found, indicating the presence of a large class of artisans or specialists devoted to this and other industries. Indispensable both in peace and war, the importance of this material in the life of pre-Columbian peoples does not need to be restressed. By virtue of its thriving obsidian industry, Tula thereby assumed the status, in modern terms, of a 'developed' economy. Its many workshops were situated in two sectors of the city; as in Teotihuacan times, the raw material came from the great mines near Pachuca.

Weaving was another important trade, and the large numbers of spindle whorls found in domestic refuse suggest that textiles, like the everyday pottery, were made more in homes than in workshops. Evidence is scant of objects made in Tula and exported to other regions. On the other hand, many imported goods have been found in the site; these include quantities of the distinctive plumbate pottery made in the border region between Mexico and Guatemala, where fine effigy vases were produced, some perhaps specially designed for the nobles of Tula. One superb vessel, covered with plaques of mother-of-pearl, shows the face of a bearded man emerging from the jaw of a coyote dog. Plumbate was the leading trade-ware of its time and continued to be so until about A.D. 1100; it is one of the very few true glazed potteries of pre-Hispanic America.

Little trace has survived in Tula of the more exotic materials, such as turquoise and jade, reportedly used there, and only a single jade plaque has been found in the whole site. However, the dress of the warriors in the painted friezes bears ample witness to the wide use of regalia, much of which surely reached Tula in the form of tribute; even if the Toltecs did not conquer the tropical coastline which produced the gaudy feathers, their domain at least bordered on the torrid lowlands, and thus had access to such products.

Almost equal in status to the warriors were the priests. The two were closely linked, since the ruler Topiltzin Quetzalcoatl is described as both king and priest. The merchant class, which played a key role in the Aztec Empire, surely existed in the Early Post-Classic; exchange of goods took place at the time not only with people to the east, but also between Central Mexico and the distant north-west. Long-distance trade was part of the Middle American pattern of life since Olmec times and even before, and Toltec merchants undoubtedly played a part, even if theories that they themselves travelled as far as the south-western United States cannot be proven.

DECLINE AND FALL

The Toltec Empire was fairly short-lived. But as in the case of its predecessors, neither historical nor archaeological data fully explain the causes of its collapse. Tula also was in part destroyed; Acosta unearthed a building which he called the Burned Palace, adjacent to the main pyramid; its adobe blocks, turned to brick by the heat of the flames, are still visible today. Acosta, on the basis of his findings in the Acropolis, states that the city was razed by a great fire and subjected to relentless pillage. Evidence, however, from residential zones explored at a later date is less emphatic.

More data have now become available from Tula that shed light on its foundation and apogee, but archaeologists are still at a loss to explain what happened at its fall. They cannot say for sure whether or not Tula was abandoned after the great fire discovered by Acosta, before it once again became quite an important place in Aztec times. This gap in our knowledge could be filled by more excavation, and offers an example of the kind of research badly needed in the field of Mexican archaeology.

A number of written sources tell of Tula's decline. Since for the Aztecs history began with the Toltecs, many texts dealing with later times start their story with the fall of Tula, and reports of earlier events are little more than legend. These accounts tend to be jumbled and contradictory, and need careful sifting. A single happening is often assigned by different documents to quite distinct periods or cultures; only after the closest scrutiny can one hope to determine where, if at all, it really belongs in the historical record.

For the collapse of Tula the written descriptions, if confusing, are at least dramatic. Taking into account their rather conflicting material, the following pattern of events emerges. First, in about A.D. 1125, Tula entered what, in Toynbean terms, was its 'time of troubles', the preliminary stage in the process of imperial decline, in face of the enemy within and the enemy without. The two original groups who came to Tula, the Tolteca-Chichimecs and the Nonoalcas, had never fused, and a rift now opened between them. As a result, some Nonoalca-Toltecs departed eastwards, and wrested the city of Cholula from the hands of the Xicallanca Olmecs, who still held it at this time. Some six years later, however, the latter staged a comeback, turned the tables on their Toltec conquerors and made servants of their former masters.

Unable to overcome their foes, the Cholula Toltecs sent a deputation to the far-off and semi-legendary Place of Seven Caves and sought the help of the nomad Chichimecs, who by tradition lived there. The Chichimec leaders heeded their pleas, and came in force to Cholula to rescue their embattled allies. This expedition was the first of a continuous wave of migrants from the north who in the end engulfed Tula itself and then briefly dominated the scene after its fall. As told by the Tlaxcalan historian, Muñoz Camargo, one group of these Chichimecs founded Tlaxcala, the future ally of Hernán Cortés.

The story of the Chichimecs who came to the rescue of the Toltecs of Cholula is vividly described in the *Toltec-Chichimec History*. In this manuscript the Nahuatl text, transcribed in neat and flowing European handwriting, is illustrated by native-type drawings, though in a rather Europeanized style. The two leaders of the Toltecs, bearded like Spanish hidalgos and dressed in tight-fitting Spanish tunics adorned by native plumes, are shown in the act of entering the Place of Seven Caves, where the Chichimec leaders of the seven tribes await them; drawn in native style, only the heads of the latter are shown. In another folio of the manuscript, the Toltec leaders perforate the noses of six Chichimec leaders, dressed in animal skins, always used as a sign of nomadry in codex illustrations; they also carry bows and arrows, associated with Chichimecs. On the other hand, the nose-plug was a symbol of Toltec civilization, into which they were thereby initiated.

In reality the Chichimecs who came into the Valley of Mexico at this time were already semi-civilized, and to depict them as uncouth nomads is little more than a literary convention. Listed among those who went to Cholula to rescue the Toltecs of that city is a leader called Mixcoatl, named after the God of Hunting. Instead of going on to Cholula, he and his band broke off and went to Culhuacán, where he married a lady of that place, called Chimalma. A son was born to them, named Topiltzin Quetzalcoatl. Not only was Mixcoatl also the name of a god, but Chimalma was one of many names for the Mother-Goddess of the region. In this story, as in many others in Mexico that combine legend and history, the human and the divine are thus inextricably linked.

This Topiltzin, after making certain other conquests, acquired the throne of Tula in about A.D. 1150 and became the last ruler of that city before its fall. Huemac is also named in certain versions as the last ruler, and this has led to suggestions that Topiltzin was really high priest, while Huemac was temporal ruler. But such distinctions are rather unreal in Ancient Mexico, where the king also fulfilled priestly functions, and it is more likely that Topiltzin and Huemac were contemporary heads of two reigning dynasties.

A few historians, in particular Wigberto Jiménez Moreno, insist that Topiltzin was the first, not the last Toltec monarch. Quetzalcoatl, and even Topiltzin, were as much titles as names and may indeed have been applied not only to the last, but also to other kings of Tula, including the first. Undeniably, however, the majority of the surviving accounts describe the historical Topiltzin as the last, not the first, ruler and link him specifically with the fall of Tula and with Huemac, who unquestionably belongs to its end, not to its beginning. Moreover, any argument as to whether Topiltzin was the first or last ruler becomes less relevant when viewed in the light of the Mexicans' cyclical notion of history. According to their concept, if there was a Topiltzin at the beginning, then there had also to be one at the end; for Tula he was thus both the alpha and the omega.

The final episode came in 1175, or thereabouts. Topiltzin's reign had been a troubled one. Tula, first infiltrated by Chichimecs from the north, was then assailed by Huaxtecs, who lived to the east of them; Huaxtec territory then stretched much further inland than at the time of the Conquest. Reportedly 'she-devils' from the Huaxteca arrived in Tula, and introduced the practice of sacrifice by shooting arrows, though in fact the Toltecs needed no lessons in the art of human sacrifice.

Under stress of invasion from without, internal strife reached its climax, with Huemac and Topiltzin as leaders of rival factions. The rift proved fatal to both; first Topiltzin abandoned Tula, but the situation had so far deteriorated that a few years later Huemac also fled and came to a violent end. He reportedly hung himself in Chapultepec, where the famous castle now stands that overlooks Mexico City.

Before Topiltzin's flight, legend relates that a sorcerer, variously described as the Smoking Mirror God, or merely as an old man, gained admittance to the king and showed him his face in a mirror. Appalled by his ravaged mien, he was induced to take a draught of pulque, the sacred drink; in all he drank five times.

The tale is told in Book III of Sahagún's *History*. To achieve his ends, the sorcerer first asked after Topiltzin's health. He replied that he was ailing and that his body was tired, as if undone. The stranger then offered him the pulque, telling him to taste only a little.

Thereafter however he found it to his liking and drank heartily saying: 'What is this? It is very good. The sickness is now abated. Thus will my body gain strength'. But as soon as he had drunk more of it, he became besotted. Thereupon he wept, and greatly was he moved. Thus at this time was Quetzalcoatl aroused; his heart was quickened. No longer could he forget what had happened, but went on reflecting, realizing that indeed the devil had tricked him.

After this Tula was beset by evil omens and misfortunes of every kind, including drought and famine. Panic ensued when a nearby mountain burned by night:

The flames rose high. When the Toltecs saw it, they became very restless; they raised their hands to heaven; there was great anxiety. All cried out, all shouted together . . . They said 'O Toltecs, now is all in truth going from us, already the power of the Toltecs goeth. Yea, we are forsaken'.

Topiltzin himself, seeing that his city was doomed, sent for his chief feather-worker, who would prepare him for his flight. To quote another source, the *Annals of Cuauhtitlan*:

He first made him the plumed headdress of Quetzalcoatl. Then he made his green mask; he took red colouring with which he made his lips crimson; then he took yellow colouring, to make the facial stripes; then he made snakes' fangs, finally he made his beard of feathers, of the red spoonbill and the blue cotinga, which he then folded backwards.

Topiltzin again took the mirror, and at the sight of his own form so gorgeously arrayed, he again took courage. Amid the lamentations of

his people, he then set out on his long journey to the Land of the Red
and Black, often interpreted as the Maya region:

In this year I Reed, having arrived at the heavenly edge of the divine water [the
sea-coast], he stopped, wept, drew up his vestments, arranged his feather
headdress and his green mask. Then he arrayed himself, and by his own hand
set fire to his body and was consumed. For this reason the place was called the
Place of Burning. They say that when he was burned, and as his ashes
ascended, all the birds of paradise came out to see them, as they rose to
heaven, the blue cotinga, the trogan, the parrots and many other beautiful
birds . . . As far as is known, he rose to heaven and entered therein.

The account ends by telling how Topiltzin remained in the Land of the
Dead and then, on the eighth day, reappeared as the Morning Star. A
rather different version of the story, also derived from native informants, states simply that when he reached the coast, he set off into
the sea on a raft of serpents.

The self-immolation of Topiltzin Quetzalcoatl gave rise to the
legend that he would one day return from the east, not merely as the
Planet Venus, but in the flesh; this gave Cortés the chance to claim to
be the incarnation of the divinized hero.

This story, in which myth and legend are so closely intertwined, is
told on two levels, the human and the divine. Both human con-
tenders, Topiltzin and Huemac, assume divine form. Topiltzin returned as the Morning Star, while Huemac became King of the
Underworld, which he ruled from a great subterranean cave; the
luckless Moctezuma II, petrified by news of the Spanish advance on
his capital, was reduced to such a state of panic that he even begged
Huemac to give him asylum in his underground kingdom.

The surviving stories of the end of Tula are naturally Aztec versions, endlessly recited in the school of nobles and warriors, the
calmecac, and thus relayed over the centuries from one generation to
the next. By his ascent into the heavens, Topiltzin triumphed over
disaster. Notwithstanding his failings and misfortunes, he became
for the Aztecs a mighty hero, and the forbear of their own royal
dynasty.

Other historical sources give more mundane causes for Tula's fall;
some write of wars, internal and external, while others mention
drought and frost, leading to crop failure. But such stories also have to
be treated with caution. Tula depended more on water from the River
Tula than on seasonal rain, scanty at the best of times. Even in years of

low rainfall the level of this copious stream, whose waters would in those days have flowed untapped to the Tula region, could hardly have fallen so low that it could not have irrigated enough land to feed the city's population. Moreover, supplies of food could have been obtained from the central Valley of Mexico, controlled by the Toltecs and richly endowed with water and with lagoon products; it was then far less densely peopled than in Aztec times. Furthermore, since Tula traded with the well-watered Caribbean Coast, food could also have been brought from there.

The fall of Tula, like that of Teotihuacan, was surely caused by a combination of external attack and internal stresses: its class structure remained top-heavy, and for a city of its size, its scale of conquest was ambitious. Crucial to its decline was the steady erosion of the north-west frontier of civilized Middle America. The great fortress of La Quemada, situated some 480 kilometres north-west of Tula, had already been overrun by Chichimecs, forced southwards by the expansion from the twelfth century onwards of the North American arid zone in the region of the present Mexican-United States border. The withdrawal of the civilized peoples to the very gates of Tula was in process well before its fall, and at the time of the Spanish Conquest the Guanajuato region, not far from Tula, was inhabited only by Chichimecs, and the pottery found there belongs to pre-Chichimec times.

After the first cracks in the social structure appeared in 1125 with the breakaway movement to Cholula, a process of gradual decline set in, accelerated by the presence of nomads at the gate, against whom few natural defences existed. Further rifts, accompanied by economic problems, led to the fall of the main dynasty in 1175. The historical sources insist that Tula was completely abandoned; however, unlike Teotihuacan, it was still important in Aztec times; therefore even if its population was drastically reduced at the time of its fall in the twelfth century, it rose again once more, though this latter-day Tula no longer ruled an empire. Archaeology shows that the surrounding region was more thickly populated in the last century before the Conquest than ever before, and the irrigation network was more elaborate, while the population within the Tula periphery was also quite large. Not only did Acosta find that several buildings in the Acropolis were used and even modified centuries after Tula's 'fall'; in addition, Eduardo Matos was able to demonstrate that the ball-court on the east edge of this precinct reached its maximum size just before the Conquest.

7

THE RISE AND FALL
OF THE AZTECS

A POWER VACUUM

The last inhabitants of imperial Tula, later to be adopted as forbears by the Aztecs, were immortalized in painted codex and oral saga as beings cast in a heroic mould. According to tradition, the city's nemesis provoked a mass exodus in the wake of the departed ruler. But if tales of a sudden collapse match the story of Jericho's fate at the hands of Joshua, the reality was rather different. Tula did not fall in a day, though it may have declined fairly swiftly, since its glory was short-lived and its whole history spans a period scarcely longer than Byzantium's lingering death.

Like its predecessor, Teotihuacan, and its successor, Tenochtitlan, Tula had first been abandoned by its patrons. When the *tlamatinime*, the wise men, departed from Teotihuacan, legend records that they took the gods away with them; the cry of anguish 'The gods have departed' filled the air in Tenochtitlan, as the Aztec capital stood at its last gasp. Topiltzin Quetzalcoatl was both man and god, and by his fabled flight from Tula, his immolation in the east, and his rebirth as the Morning Star, he joins the ranks of the deities who leave their chosen city; shorn of their presence, it became an empty shell, and lost all claim to leadership, both spiritual and temporal.

Archaeological proof of a sudden fall in population in the Tula region is so far lacking and one doubts if the city was really abandoned to the same extent as Teotihuacan, though its empire fell apart and its greatness vanished. And if accounts of Tula's collapse are part legendary, after this event we embark on a new phase of Mexican history, for which a richer store of written accounts exists and provides more ample data on what occurred.

Two full centuries were to elapse between the decline of Tula and the rise of the Aztecs; thus, like the fall of Teotihuacan, the end of

Toltec rule left a power vacuum in Central Mexico. Archaeological surveys show that the northern part of the Valley suffered a fall in population during this interregnum, though at least six medium-sized centres have been found further to the south, around the shores of the Lake of Texcoco. Of these the most important was Culhuacán, which acted as a kind of Toltec successor state. The name Culhua derives from the Nahuatl *colli*, meaning 'grandfather'; Culhuacán is 'The Place of Those who have Grandfathers' or alternatively, 'The Place of Those who have Ancestors', and a stronghold of ancient traditions.

In the time of troubles following Tula's collapse, Culhuacán stood for Toltec legitimacy and continuity. The Aztecs later came to call themselves Culhuas to reinforce their own claim to the Toltec heritage. But from the outset of the post-Toltec period, Culhuacán's own claim to leadership was challenged as new waves of semi-nomad Chichimecs poured into the Valley of Mexico to fill the existing power vacuum; they chose as their capital Tenayuca, already an established city.

These invaders are usually known as the Chichimecs of Xolotl, after their legendary chief who bore the name of the God of the Evening Star. The dynasty of Texcoco was later to claim descent from this Chichimec Xolotl; hence the historian Alva Ixtlilxóchitl, himself a scion of the Texcocan royal house, adds to the lustre of his ancestors by making of Xolotl a kind of horseless Genghis Khan; the great nomad 'emperor' supposedly fell like a wolf upon the fold, first subdued the Valley of Mexico and then campaigned far and wide, conquering a domain that stretched for 150 kilometres to the north of Tenayuca and even further to the east, reaching nearly to the Gulf Coast.

Ixtlilxóchitl's account, based largely on another Texcocan text, the *Codex Xolotl*, affirms that this Chichimec Xolotl already had a mature grandson when he reached Tenayuca, and that he was two hundred years old when he died. Legend has stretched both the length of his life and the extent of his conquests; if indeed he made any beyond the immediate vicinity of his own capital, they were certainly more limited than his Texcocan descendants pretend. At all events, Culhuacán was a natural target for the invader, and its forces were crushed by Nopaltzin, Xolotl's son and heir. This prince then married the daughter of the King of Culhuacán, and this union once more set in motion the process by which uncouth invaders took on all the trappings of Middle American civilization.

Tenayuca was one of several rivals for the Toltec heritage. Archaeological data show that it was already settled in Classic times; its population increased in the Toltec era and rose further after the fall of Tula, when its role became more important, according to historical sources. Another contender for power was a migrant group of Otomis, who made their capital in Xaltocan to the north of Mexico City. These Otomis had their own language, still spoken in many places today; Sahagún describes them as at least semi-civilized, since they possessed priests and nobles. In contrast, the Chichimecs of Xolotl are traditionally depicted in documents as pure nomads, dressed in skins and living in caves, though in reality they were not totally uncivilized when they reached the Valley of Mexico; they already worshipped some of the older gods and took to urban life in Tenayuca far quicker than any true nomad could have done.

Figure 29. Chichimec shooting deer (Mapa Quinatzin)

During the century that followed the fall of Tula, rivalry between the various petty principalities was intense, as each one tried to dominate its neighbours and make them into tributaries. Power in the Valley of Mexico was mainly shared between Culhuacán and the leading newcomers, the Otomis of Xaltocan and Xolotl's Chichimecs of Tenayuca. The influence of Culhuacán was cultural as much as political, while the glory of its two semi-nomad rivals proved to be short-lived. More important in the longer run were two other groups who arrived in the Valley of Mexico at this time, the Tepanecs and the

Acolhuas (not to be confused with the Culhuas of Culhuacán). The former established their capital in Azcapotzalco on the western bank of the Lake of Texcoco, while the Acolhuas settled beyond its eastern shore; their first capital was Coatlichán, whose latter-day successor was Texcoco.

The Acolhua impact came to be felt about a century after the fall of Tula when they were governed by Huetzin, who reigned from approximately 1253 to 1274. This ruler made the first attempt to reconstitute a mini-empire, more concrete in form than the vast but nebulous domain of Xolotl. Huetzin also seized Culhuacán and allied himself with Tochintecuhtli (Rabbit Lord), who had inherited the throne of Tenayuca from its first Chichimec kings; these two rulers dominated the Central Valley and advanced north-eastwards as far as Tulancingo.

This ephemeral attempt to rebuild an empire did not survive its two founders. However, the second century of the post-Toltec era was to witness a much more ambitious career of conquest on the part of the Tepanecs, those other latecomers, who paved the way for the Aztecs. Until about A.D. 1300 the Tepanec part in the politics of the region had been modest. After this their capital, Azcapotzalco, gradually usurped the role of nearby Tenayuca, and by the mid-fourteenth century power was again shared by three peoples, a formula whose origins went back to Toltec times, if not before, and which, in modified form, continued until the Conquest. Culhuacán managed to survive, while the two other members of the ruling trio were now Azcapotzalco, the Tepanec capital, and Coatlichán, the leading Acolhua city.

THE COMING OF THE AZTECS

The Aztecs, the last of our four dominant peoples, first appeared upon this troubled scene in the mid-thirteenth century. Their name derives from Aztlán (Place of Cranes), the traditional home of the tribe before their southward migration. They did not, however, call themselves Aztecs, but were known as Mexicas (pronounced Mesheekas), from which Mexico derives. The etymology is uncertain: according to one theory, Mexica comes from *metztli* (moon), symbolizing its reflection on the waters of the lagoon in their former habitat, Aztlán; others, including Sahagún, prefer a derivation from *metl* (maguey cactus) and *citli* (hare). None the less, the name Aztec, hardly used at the time, has become indispensable for historians, for want of a better one. This is because, as we shall see, these Mexicas were only one of three peoples who later joined forces to conquer the 'Aztec' Empire. In particular their Texcocan partners are conventionally included within the term Aztec, but cannot possibly be described as Mexicas.

According to the official version, set out in various documents, the Mexicas were among the last of many tribes to emerge from the legendary Seven Caves, which lay far to the north-west in the vicinity of Aztlán and had been the starting point of so many migrations into Central Mexico. Accounts vary as to their route, but most relate that they spent some time in a place called Coatepec, near the already ruined Tula. At Coatepec, the Hill of the Snake, was born the Aztec patron god, Huitzilopochtli 'The Humming Bird of the Left' ('left' was often treated as the equivalent of 'south').

Figure 30. The Aztec migration from Aztlan.
The date-glyph (1 Flint) appears in the centre,
and the Curved Mountain (Culhuacán) on the right (*Codex Botunini*)

His birth, true to character, was spectacular. Like Pallas Athene, born in a coat of mail, the god emerged fully armed from his mother's womb, and immediately vanquished his 400 brothers, who sought to kill her, incited by his evil sister, Coyolxauhqui, whom he decapitated and dismembered. In the National Museum of Anthropology in Mexico City there is a carving of her severed head. The dismemberment of Coyolxauhqui is a major event in Aztec legend, recalling in some ways the fate of the Egyptian Osiris. In addition to the huge head in the Museum, the most imposing piece of sculpture unearthed in the recent excavations of the Great Temple of Tenochtitlan – to be described later – is a circular block of stone on which the dismembered goddess is carved in relief.

After wandering from place to place for over a century, and enduring endless trials and tribulations, the migrant tribe settled in Chapultepec, near the western shore of the Lake of Texcoco, some time after A.D. 1250. The long migration became the traditional version of Mexica origins, before they reached the Valley of Mexico. But while it contains a kernel of truth it is not the whole story, and clearly blends epic legend with factual history. The claim to a migratory past, beginning in or near the Seven Caves, amounted to a status symbol for the peoples of Central Mexico, and the Mexica story incorporates details borrowed from earlier intruders. For instance, Cuextecatl-Ichocayan ('Where the Huaxtec Wept') is included by several sources in the Mexica route; but this and other places also figure on the route of the first migrants to Tula centuries before; subsequently, Xolotl and his Chichimecs also stayed there.

When they first arrived, the Mexicas, like the Chichimecs of Xolotl and even the early Toltecs, were by all accounts part-civilized and part-nomad. After settling in the Valley of Mexico, they would at times proudly proclaim their Chichimec, or nomad, ancestry, while at others they laid equal stress on their descent from the city-dwelling Toltecs. More probably, like so many of their neighbours, they were a fusion of two elements, migrant and sedentary. A migration had indeed taken place, and a smallish tribe of wanderers, called Mexicas, had come to Central Mexico, where they would have mingled with peoples already settled in the well-watered lands in the vicinity of Chapultepec since Toltec times. Official Aztec historians mention intermarriage, but only with the more prestigious Culhuas at a later date. None the less, this process is likely to have begun when they first arrived; and the Mexicas, or Aztecs, of historical times seem to derive just as much from the Valley of Mexico as from the arid north; the very name of their tribal god has local associations, being derived from *huitzil* (humming bird), an ancient symbol, and *opochtli*, which literally means 'left' but is also the name of a water deity native to the lagoons of the Valley of Mexico, and closely linked to Tlaloc, one of its oldest gods.

THE HILL OF THE LOCUST

The name Chapultepec, 'The Hill of the Locust', pervades Mexican history. Here the Aztecs made their first home, on a hill where their emperors would one day have their portraits graven in the rock. Three and a half centuries later, Chapultepec became the centre of a short-lived Mexican 'empire', when Maximilian of Hapsburg chose the castle on its summit as his palace; his living quarters can still be seen today. Here also in 1847 the naval cadets had made their last heroic stand against the forces of the United States. Appropriately, Chapultepec Castle is now the National Museum of History.

Chapultepec, however, was not to be the permanent home of the Mexica tribe. Their savagery provoked their neighbours, who finally could stand them no more. In 1319 they were expelled from the hill by a coalition of city-states and taken as captives to Culhuacán. The *Codex Azcatitlan* depicts their wretched plight; the glyph of Chapultepec, the locust perched on a hill, is shown to the left of the folio and beside it we see the embattled Mexicas standing in the shallow lagoon water, surrounded by reeds. As the final episode of the same scene, they are carried off into captivity; the king and his daughter are being dragged by their hair.

The Mexican ruler at the time of this disaster was Huitzilihuitl (Humming Bird Feather). According to the historical sources, the Mexicas of the migration had been led by four priest-rulers, a traditional form of government in Ancient Mexico. The challenge which they faced in Chapultepec had forced them to choose one supreme chief and thereafter they came to be governed by a single monarch known as the *tlatoani*, literally 'He who Speaks'.

Huitzilihuitl was sacrificed in Culhuacán; while some Mexicas took refuge in other places, the main body went to Culhuacán, where they threw themselves on the mercy of the rulers of the city. Their condition was pitiful and they even lacked clothing with which to cover their backs. Owing to their fame as troublemakers, the arrival of this sorry band placed their hosts in something of a quandary. As a precautionary measure they were assigned to Tizaapán, a wasteland of volcanic rock some distance from Culhuacán, near the present site of the National University. It was taken for granted that no one could prosper in such bleak surroundings, infested with snakes and other pests. The Mexicas, however, displayed to the full their powers of survival; far from succumbing to the serpents they made a virtue out of necessity and ate them as food. They even managed to till the barren soil and used the abundant supplies of stone to build houses and temples.

Their Culhua captors put their bellicosity to good use, and engaged them as mercenaries in wars against troublesome neighbours, such as Xochimilco. They took the unorthodox step of killing Xochimilcan prisoners on the spot, instead of keeping them for sacrifice; they merely cut off their ears and presented them to their masters as proof of victory.

THE EAGLE AND THE CACTUS

A gruesome tale is told of the Mexicas' departure from captivity. Prompted by their patron deity, they went to the ruler of Culhuacán and begged him to give them his daughter as their ruler, and as the wife of their god. The request was granted, but once the princess was safely in their power they promptly flayed her and dressed a priest in her skin. With supreme effrontery they then invited her father to a feast in honour of their new goddess. In the dim light of the sanctuary he lit a censer and was aghast when he saw the priest wearing his daughter's skin. Fighting immediately broke out, but the Mexican god, unruffled by such events, told his people to leave Culhuacán calmly and cautiously. If the tale symbolized the more repugnant side of Aztec culture, it cannot be repeated too often that they were not the inventors of such rites as those of the Flayed God, whose cult goes back to Olmec times.

The Mexicas took refuge in the lagoon. After wading through its shallow waters for some distance, they reached a reed-covered plot of land, later known as San Pablo. But the god told them to press on until they found another island on which they would see a cactus with an eagle perched on its branches, in the act of devouring a serpent. They duly found the plant, and the great eagle, bowing his noble head as they approached. At last they knew that their odyssey was ended. Overcome with joy, they proceeded to found their capital and their first thought was to build a shrine to their patron god. The city was to be called Tenochtitlan, which means 'Place of the Cactus' (*tenochtli*) – or more precisely 'Place of the Fruit of the Cactus'. Modern historians tend to place the event in A.D. 1345, though the traditional date for the foundation is 1325.

The story is rich in symbol. The notion of dualism is ever-present: the eagle and the serpent stand for opposites, the sky and the earth.

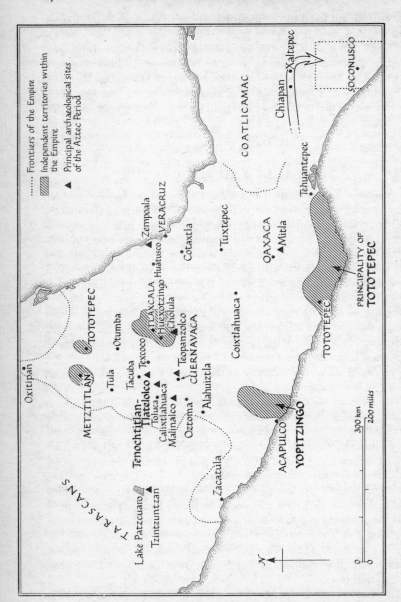

Frontiers of the Empire

Independent territories within the Empire

▲ Principal archaeological sites of the Aztec Period

MAP 4. THE APPROXIMATE BOUNDARIES OF THE AZTEC EMPIRE IN 1519

The eagle, described by the sources as devouring other brightly-coloured birds on the island, was a predator, the emblem of wars in which other peoples were to be consumed or sacrificed. The cactus fruit, both for its reddish colour and shape, represents the human hearts with which the sun had to be fed and which to that end were piled high in the 'eagle vessel'. And in Middle American iconography even the reeds that surrounded the little island had a special meaning: the place was sometimes referred to as 'Toltzallan Acatzallan', meaning 'Among the Rushes, Among the Reeds'; thus in this new city built among the rushes, Tula or Tollan, the original 'Place of Rushes', was reborn. As the resurgent Tula, re-creating its past glories, Tenochtitlan would one day claim to rule the world.

Though more immediately conscious of their chosen role as the heirs of Tula, the Mexicas at times conformed to patterns already established in Teotihuacan. We are told that after the city's foundation it was divided – like the Classic metropolis – into four quarters; these in turn contained smaller sub-districts, or wards, one for each clan; the number of these had now risen to fifteen, or twenty according to other accounts. As in Teotihuacan, certain wards were to become the homes of specific groups of artisans, such as feather-workers, and a few were settled by people from other cities. Stretching comparisons even further, one may recall that La Venta and Tenochtitlan, the seats of Ancient Mexico's first and last civilizations, were both built on small islands surrounded by marshes and shallow water.

Of the early days of Tenochtitlan few details survive. The main event was the foundation, or re-foundation, of the sister city of Tlatelolco, which took place thirteen years later. The island on which Tlatelolco was built was about the same size as that of Tenochtitlan, and the two were ringed by even smaller islets of mud, all gradually to be merged into one metropolis. Though they worked in close partnership, a rivalry, amounting at times to overt hostility, grew up between the two cities. They were to develop on rather different lines: Tenochtitlan excelled in war, whereas Tlatelolco specialized in commerce.

As often occurred in Ancient Mexico, an obsession with ritual went hand-in-hand with an eye for reality. The Mexican promised land flowed with neither milk nor honey, but the prospects were less bleak than some of the chroniclers imply. The advantages of the site outweighed the drawbacks, and the leaders' choice, ostensibly dubious, proved to be genial. The abundance of fish and birds favoured a mixed economy, based on agriculture combined with hunting and fishing of lagoon fauna. The aquatic environment was ideal for the *chinampa* system – to be explained later – that permits all-year cultivation of crops, fed by canals. Moreover, easy communications by canoe were a great asset in a country where movement by land was impeded by the lack of pack animals. And in addition to other blessings, the islands were guarded by natural water defences, unbreached until the final Spanish assault on their lagoon stronghold. The Mexicans now enjoyed many of the benefits that had paved the way, six centuries earlier, to the rise of Venice.

While the will to conquer was itself a factor, the rise of Tenochtitlan may be less hard to explain in terms of sheer economic determinism than that of, say, Tula or Teotihuacan. The absence of every kind of raw material for the making of houses, clothes, arms and utensils forced the Mexicas to look outwards rather than inwards. The *chinampas* were fertile but restricted in size and any additional food had to be obtained from other peoples, whether by trade or war. Moreover, lacking not only materials but space for seasonal cultivation, as the city grew, its people were less closely bound to the crop cycle and were therefore more readily available for military service at all times of the year. Though still poor and despised, they had found not only a home, but a base for future expansion. In this modest settlement lay the nucleus of the imperial city which, a bare two centuries later, was to astound the Spaniards as the wonder of the New World, surpassing all they had known in the Old.

This, however, lay in the future. At the outset the Mexicas were indigent, insecure, and hard pressed by greedy neighbours. By now the Tepanecs had finally emerged as the leading power of the Valley of Mexico. The Mexicas, however, at first shunned the servitude of a single neighbour, and sought to obtain building materials by selling fish and other lagoon produce in the different markets on the shore.

In its early days, Tenochtitlan was ruled by Tenoch, who had already been the Mexicas' leader during the captivity, and who seems to have been a priest-ruler of the traditional type. He died in 1370, and the two cities then decided to reinforce their status by electing rulers who were more prestigious, and who also had to be *persona grata* to the Tepanecs, to whose yoke they had meanwhile been forced to submit. The choice for Tenochtitlan fell upon Acamapichtli ('Handful of Reeds'); though his father was a Mexican nobleman, his mother was a princess from Culhuacán. The new dynasty, which was to reign until the Conquest, could therefore legitimately boast of its descent from the Culhuas, and hence from the Toltecs themselves. The Tlatelolcans opted for a member of the Tepanec royal family; in effect, however, both Mexica kings were Tepanec nominees and for the next half-century, until they turned the tables on their masters, the Mexicas were their vassals and tributaries.

A year before the establishment of the new dynasties in Tenochtitlan and Tlatelolco, Tezozomoc ascended the throne of Azcapotzalco, the leading Tepanec city. He was the virtual creator of the short-lived Tepanec Empire, which fell apart after his death. His very longevity gave him ample opportunity to expand his realm and to display his talents both in war and diplomacy. A firm believer in the principle of divide and rule, he showed a rare skill in isolating his rivals and in crushing them one by one. For this Machiavellian monarch, tomorrow's victim was his ally against today's adversary.

The two former centres of power, Culhuacán and Tenayuca, had already been overthrown shortly before Tezozomoc came to the throne. For an account of Tepanec conquests we depend on Aztec sources, which inevitably confuse the picture by claiming the main credit for such triumphs for their own rulers, though in reality, if they took part at all, they were fighting under the Tepanec aegis. Lists of places officially conquered by each Aztec monarch survive in many documents, but in effect the victories attributed to the first three Mexica rulers are Tepanec conquests in which the Mexicas, initially at least, played a lesser role.

Acamapichtli died in 1391, and by then the Tepanecs already ruled most of the Valley of Mexico. Under the next sovereign, Huitzilihuitl (1391–1416), they and their Mexican auxiliaries, following in the wake of former conquerors, pushed southwards into the warm lands of the Valley of Morelos. Their part in such conquests enhanced the status of the Mexicas, and the nobility now began to wear cotton clothing in place of the coarse maguey fibre. Other Tepanec-Mexican conquests were made in a north-easterly direction and their armies reached as far as Tulancingo. Since this was a major Toltec centre, situated near the eastern fringe of their territory, the Tepanec Empire by now controlled much of Tula's former domain; it also included the western part of the Valley of Toluca, a region with whose people the Tepanecs had certain affinities.

Tezozomoc fought his longest and most bitter war against Texcoco, erstwhile enemy but future partner of Tenochtitlan. This centre, which lay on the east side of the lagoon, had only come to the fore fairly recently, replacing Coatlichán as the leading Acolhua city.

Its previous rulers had appeased Tezozomoc, adopting a benevolent neutrality when he attacked other neighbours. In 1409, however, the situation changed overnight with the accession of Ixtlilxóchitl, a ruler of a different stamp. He openly challenged Tezozomoc, by asserting his right to be called 'Lord', or 'Emperor' of the Chichimecs (Texcoco's royal family claimed descent from Xolotl, the original Chichimec Emperor). The Tepanec ruler was quick to react; he sent for the two Mexica kings, inveighed against the upstart Ixtlilxóchitl, and said that he would be the only emperor, and would make his Mexica protégés the twin pillars of his throne. As an initial move, the Texcocan ruler was sent some cotton, with a request that he should have it woven for Tezozomoc. Though the demand was couched in diplomatic terms as if it were a routine favour, acceptance would have amounted to a token of submission to the Tepanecs. Ixtlilxóchitl refused, and flung down the gauntlet by stating that he would put the material to better use to make cotton armour for his warriors.

A ding-dong struggle ensued, lasting from 1414 to 1418, in the course of which Ixtlilxóchitl once advanced to the very gates of the Tepanec capital. The Texcocans were finally crushed by superior force; their king left his capital and was murdered as he fled. Harsh conditions were imposed on the vanquished; while Tezozomoc kept the lion's share of the spoils for himself, the city of Texcoco was forced to pay tribute not to the Tepanecs, but to Tenochtitlan. This grant to the Mexicas marks a notable advance, since they were now tribute gatherers as well as tributaries, and within the Tepanec Empire they were on the way to becoming a power in their own right. The new sovereign of Tenochtitlan, Chimalpopoca ('Smoking Shield'), who came to the throne in 1416, was Tezozomoc's grandson, since his father had married a Tepanec princess. Tezozomoc was very fond of his grandson, and reduced the tribute which he had to pay. Of comparable importance in the future dynastic struggle was the marriage of Ixtlilxóchitl of Texcoco to a daughter of the ruler of Tenochtitlan; his son and heir, Nezahualcoyotl ('Fasting Coyote Dog'), was therefore half Mexica.

Tezozomoc had crushed Texcoco, but he still had to reckon with Nezahualcoyotl, from whom he could steal lands but not the loyalty of his subjects. After seeing his father butchered before his very eyes, the young prince sought sanctuary beyond the Sierra Nevada in the Puebla Valley and spent the next ten years as a fugitive, relentlessly pursued by Tezozomoc, who was haunted by visions of a resurgent Texcoco. In one of his dreams, the tyrant was attacked by eagles, serpents and wolves, which he identified with Nezahualcoyotl's thirst for vengeance.

At one time the Texcocan prince settled in Tenochtitlan, but since the latter was still a Tepanec ally he was treated with reserve and confined within the city limits. He was later allowed to return to Texcoco, but Tezozomoc soon had second thoughts and he was once more forced to flee; during this part of his exile he had a further series of miraculous escapes from the jaws of death.

As Tezozomoc's long life ebbed, profound rifts began to divide his subjects. A major cause was the resentment at his favoured treatment of the Mexicas. Matters came to a head when, after the old king's death in 1426, the throne, instead of passing to his legitimate heir, was usurped by a younger son, Maxtla; the latter was renowned for his hatred of the Mexicas and promptly reimposed the heavy tribute of former times.

This Tepanec ruler was a man of violent disposition, with none of his father's guile, but with an unfailing talent for making enemies and losing friends. One of his first victims was the Mexica sovereign Chimalpopoca, his brother-in-law, who, together with the ruler of Tlatelolco, came to an untimely end in the first year of Maxtla's reign. Accounts, however, vary as to whether Chimalpopoca was really murdered by Maxtla or by his own subjects, resentful of his craven submission to the Tepanec usurper.

Following the death of Chimalpopoca in 1426, Itzcoatl became ruler. His accession bears the stamp of a revolution more than a routine succession, and was followed by major changes, both internal and external. Itzcoatl means 'Serpent of Obsidian'; he lived up to his name, and under his rule the Mexica policy of subservience to the Tepanecs was dramatically reversed.

Maxtla reacted to this change of course by putting his people on a war footing, and in 1428 blockaded Tenochtitlan. Itzcoatl was thus besieged in his own capital, at a time when his Texcocan nephew, Nezahualcoyotl, was still a refugee beyond the mountains of the Sierra Nevada. Both were sworn foes of Maxtla, in whose overthrow they now made common cause. An alliance was forged in which Tenochtitlan and its former enemy, Texcoco, were joined by Tlacopan (now Tacuba), a disaffected Tepanec city.

The Mexicas, backed by only token forces from Texcoco, still enemy-occupied, faced uncertain odds in any conflict with Maxtla. However Nezahualcoyotl, as much statesman as warrior, tipped the balance by gaining the support of Huexotzingo and Tlaxcala, the leading cities of the Puebla Valley, where he had been given asylum. Since the Tepanecs controlled almost the whole Valley of Mexico, these were the only worth-while allies within striking distance to whom Nezahualcoyotl could appeal. With their help he first recovered his own kingdom; the combined force then went to the aid of the beleaguered Itzcoatl. The Tepanec capital, Azcapotzalco, was in turn besieged and eventually surrendered; Maxtla himself was killed. By a revolt from within, the Mexicas had overthrown the Tepanec Empire; following this triumph, the world of Ancient Mexico lay at their feet.

ITZCOATL AND MOCTEZUMA I

The reader may well wonder from what sources such historical data on pre-Conquest Mexico can be gleaned. But whereas in the case of, say, Teotihuacan, archaeology serves as our only guide, for the last three centuries before the Conquest, following the fall of Tula, the situation changes radically, since written accounts are copious, if not always reliable. They increase in both volume and clarity as one approaches the time of the Conquest.

Broadly speaking, this material is of two kinds: to the first belong the pictorial records, or codices, painted on native paper and folding like screens. In such picture-writing most forms of action can be described: for instance, travelling is depicted by footmarks; speech is indicated by a scroll emerging from the speaker's mouth. Only abstract notions are hard to express.

The second category consists of works written in Roman script, in the century following the Conquest, using either Spanish or the Nahuatl language. For this rich post-Conquest record of information, based partly on painted codices – most of which have not survived – and partly on oral sagas relayed by informants, posterity is indebted to the early Spanish friars and to their Indian pupils. Yet notwithstanding the abundance of such works, their information is not easy to interpret, because they tend to be biased and contradictory. In particular, much of our knowledge of the Aztec past comes from two parallel histories, one written by the Spanish friar Diego Durán, and the other by a descendant of the Tenochtitlan royal family, Alvarado Tezozomoc; both are in Spanish, though Tezozomoc also wrote in Nahuatl. The two accounts are so similar that they plainly derive from a single original source.

However, a very distinct version of events survives, written from the Texcocan point of view; its foremost representative is the seventeenth-century scion of the city's dynasty, Alva Ixtlilxóchitl. A leading purpose of both the Texcocan and Tenochca historians is to magnify the achievements of their own forbears; their accounts therefore not merely differ but at times flatly contradict each other. For example, both affirm that a few years after their joint triumph over the Tepanecs, a rift between the two main allies led to armed conflict. But while Durán and Tezozomoc insist that Tenochtitlan defeated Texcoco, Ixtlilxóchitl writes of a Texcocan victory. Only by a careful sifting of the evidence and by closely comparing different versions can one get somewhere near the truth. For this purpose, certain accounts from other places are of great help. While equally partial to their own native dynasty, they at least offer a third alternative version; of these, the two most important are the *Annals of Cuauhtitlán* (a place lying to the north of Mexico City) and the *Relaciones* of Chimalpain, a seventeenth-century chronicler from Chalco, situated in the eastern part of the Valley of Mexico.

In the particular case of the Tenochtitlan-Texcoco quarrel, sheer logic suggests that if fighting took place, Tenochtitlan was the victor. Ixtlilxóchitl himself admits that Nezahualcoyotl had to depend on the help of his Mexica allies in order to regain control of his own Acolhua domains, part of which refused to accept him as sovereign even after Maxtla's defeat. Accounts which pretend that Texcoco was at any time the dominant partner in the Aztec Triple Alliance are surely exaggerated, even if their praise of the city's spiritual attainments has a more authentic ring. Moreover, archaeological studies demonstrate that while the population of the Texcoco region expanded some sevenfold in Aztec times, it rose to a maximum of about 70,000 and was therefore a mere fraction of that of Tenochtitlan.

When Itzcoatl came to the throne, he was by all accounts ably seconded by his nephew, who later ascended the throne as Moctezuma I, not to be confused with Moctezuma II, who ruled when the Spaniards arrived. According, however, to the linked histories of Durán and Tezozomoc, from the very outset of his reign Itzcoatl was overshadowed not by this Moctezuma, but by the latter's brother, Tlacaelel, who bore the title of Snake Woman (*Cihuacoatl*), an office second only in importance to that of the *tlatoani*. Itzcoatl and his successor, Moctezuma I, are generally portrayed as pusillanimous puppets, reluctantly putting on a show of bravery at the instance of the Snake Woman. According to the same version, this formidable

Mayor of the Palace dominated the scene during five successive reigns, spanning a period of sixty years. In contrast, other writers, such as the Spanish chronicler Torquemada, go out of their way to deny the very existence of Tlacaelel, stating that he and Moctezuma were the same person.

The truth must lie somewhere between these two viewpoints. A historic personage called Tlacaelel undoubtedly existed, since we possess a genealogy of his descendants, who inherited from him the office of *Cihuacoatl*. Moreover, the part played not only by Moctezuma but also by Tlacaelel in the defeat of the Tepanecs is well documented, and the latter's role as elder statesman during Moctezuma's reign and even that of his successor is described in some detail. He was, however, very young at the time of the accession of Itzcoatl, who was a well-tried leader; there is therefore no reason to doubt that he, not Tlacaelel, was the leading member of the ruling triumvirate; as *tlatoani*, Itzcoatl was the spokesman of the god, and was king in fact as well as in name.

After the triumph of 1428, Itzcoatl reigned for a further twelve years. His main task was the reconquest of city-states, both in the Valley of Mexico and beyond, who had been Tepanec vassals, but who now wished to be their own masters. This process of reconquest included the warm lands of the Cuernavaca region, who had also broken loose, and the Empire at Itzcoatl's death was roughly comparable to what the Tepanecs had formerly conquered.

This embryo empire was a state dedicated to war, ruled by a military élite. The concentration of power within the hands of this élite had begun long before Itzcoatl, and he merely furthered the process, finally completed by his successor. When Itzcoatl died in 1440, Moctezuma was chosen to succeed him; Moctezuma is a hispanicized version of Motecozuma, meaning 'Angry Lord', and he was also called 'Ilhuicamina', 'the Archer of the Skies'; both names aptly presaged his future role as conqueror. The first years of his reign were spent in subduing recalcitrant neighbours, and it was not until 1458 that he was free to embark on a series of campaigns more ambitious than any so far fought by the Aztecs or by the Tepanecs before them. The first major push was aimed at the Oaxaca region, then controlled by the Mixtecs. Moctezuma first conquered Coixtlahuaca, a Mixtec city-state that levied tribute on its neighbours. The unprecedented step was taken of killing the king, though the Aztecs normally left local rulers in charge of their domains, with the obligation to pay tribute to the Empire.

Moctezuma's campaign against the Mixtecs was crowned with the capture of Oaxaca. Many of the inhabitants were massacred, and settlers were sent from the Valley of Mexico to repopulate the city. Henceforth Oaxaca became the main bastion of Aztec power in the region, of which it is still the leading city.

The Mixtecs, now partly absorbed into the Aztec Empire, were a people of great attainments. Some of the earliest surviving codices of Mexico derive from the Mixteca, and they produced the finest gold-work and pottery, painted in patterns resembling their codex paint-ings and ceramics, similar in style to the famous Cholula ware that came to be so prized in Tenochtitlan. The best Mixtec gold can be seen in the Regional Museum of Oaxaca, and was mostly found in tombs in nearby Monte Alban.

Some of the royal genealogies given in the Mixtec codices go back at least to Toltec times. In about A.D. 1000 they had driven the Zapotecs from Monte Alban, which they used mainly as a burial ground. The leading Mixtec site is Mitla, about fifty kilometres from Oaxaca; situ-ated in country more arid than the rich Oaxaca Valley, it is best visited fairly early in the day before the dust rises. The principal group of monuments consists of three masonry halls on raised platforms; the most impressive, the Hall of Columns, is a long chamber with six great conical columns running down the middle. They originally supported the roof, though the building is now open to the sky. The walls are faced with mosaic stone decoration, cut in intricate patterns typical of Mixtec architecture.

Moctezuma subdued many Mixtec centres but his appetite for conquest was unsated. He next launched a campaign against the Totonacs, who occupied a long stretch of the coast of the Gulf of Mexico. His first objective was Zempoala, where Cortés later estab-lished a base, before turning inland to seek out the second Mocte-zuma. Complying with diplomatic usage, the Aztecs would make demands that were modest, but whose acceptance would imply submission. At first Moctezuma merely asked the Zempoalans for some sea snails and other large shells needed for religious rites; they were probably not unlike those that can be seen in many Teotihuacan murals. The Totonacs, undeceived as to the Aztecs' true aims, put up a stiff fight before yielding to superior force. Following this victory an ex-tensive region, including many prosperous towns on or near the coast, was brought under control and forced to pay tribute. Aztec terms were onerous and the Totonacs would rebel from time to time; on each occasion they were crushed and forced to pay even greater amounts.

Following these triumphs, Moctezuma campaigned against the Huaxtecs, who lived in what is now the northern part of the state of Veracruz. The haul of Huaxtec prisoners was colossal; they were dragged off to Tenochtitlan to be sacrificed in the feast of the Flayed God, which was accompanied by a peculiar rite known as the gladiatorial sacrifice, to be described later. As in the case of many such long-range conquests that were to follow, the chroniclers describe the long sad columns of prisoners, joined together with wooden yokes round their necks, dragged off to be sacrificed in the capital. At the end of their trek, far from being ill-treated, they were received with special ceremonies; as befitting men dedicated to the gods, they were called the 'children of the sun', and were fêted and feasted until they met their end upon the altar.

No single motive can be sought for Moctezuma's policy of long-range conquest, which required so many weary weeks of marching and involved endless punitive expeditions in successive reigns, in order to maintain such gains. In a land without fixed frontiers or dividing lines, one victory simply left the victors face to face with a new potential foe. Moctezuma himself summed up the situation when he voiced the unbounded Aztec will to conquer: 'Mexicans and brave knights of all my provinces. I wish you to have no illusions that our wars are at an end. We must continue to march onwards.' Incentives are obvious, particularly for the drive to the well-watered Gulf Coast. While the subtropical region of Morelos had acted as a magnet not only for the Aztecs, but for the Tepanecs and Toltecs before them, the urge to assure supplies of the tropical products of the coast was even stronger, though distance made it harder. Material and religious considerations went hand in hand. The ceremonial requirements of items such as quetzal plumes, jaguar capes, and of adornments of precious stones have already been stressed. Trophies of this kind had already become status symbols in Olmec times; and if the latter had an abundance of feathers and skins in their home territory, their move inland – as we have seen – may in part have been motivated by a quest for jade, for which their demand was insatiable. Their successors in the Altiplano depended on imported supplies of those tropical luxuries, which had come to play an essential part in Middle American civilization.

Strategic as well as economic and ceremonial reasons prompted the conquest of the Totonacs. Hostilities were by this time frequent between the Aztecs and the peoples of the Puebla Valley, of which Tlaxcala was now the leading city. Moctezuma, by conquering part of the coast, virtually encircled the Tlaxcalans, who now found themselves blockaded.

Another alleged motive for Moctezuma's push to the coast is the great famine which befell Central Mexico between 1450 and 1454; it was started by early frosts that destroyed the maize cobs in two successive years. According to certain sources, the starving people of the Altiplano sold themselves and their children to the inhabitants of the Gulf Coast in exchange for maize. The obvious course was to conquer the region, whose rains and harvests were more reliable than those of the Altiplano, and thereby to obtain supplies by force, without selling oneself into slavery.

Such stories, like many told by Mexican chroniclers, have to be treated with a certain caution. In modern times, though crops on the plateau sometimes fail, no record exists of such an occurrence in four successive years. Moreover, even if one is prepared to believe that the subjects of the great Moctezuma could so degrade themselves as to barter away their own children for food, Conquest-period tribute-lists for the coastal provinces include not a single ear of maize. Owing to problems of transport, tribute of this kind was levied only on subject peoples situated within a radius of about 200 kilometres of Tenochtitlan. The coast produced finery for the nobles rather than food for the people. For instance, the Aztec province of Cuetlaxtlan, in which the modern city of Veracruz is situated, sent an annual tribute of over 3,000 mantles of different kinds and 400 bundles of quetzal feathers, together with such special items as one string of greenstone beads, two lip plugs of crystal and twenty lip plugs of light amber. On the other hand Cuauhtochco, the province lying to the north of Cuetlaxtlan, provided luxury raw materials in the form of twenty loads of cacao and 1,600 bales of cotton, but no maize or beans.

As the result of such conquests, Tenochtitlan began, during Moctezuma's reign, to assume the form of an imperial capital. As soon as he became ruler, he proceeded to lay the plans for a sumptuous temple to the tribal god, to replace the humbler structure of earlier times. According to the chronicles, this Great Temple was finally inaugurated in 1487, an event celebrated by a sacrificial holocaust. However, notwithstanding official reports of such a once-and-for-all dedication, recent excavations of the site indicate – as we shall see – that the temple was in a constant state of renewal, and was extended in all eleven times, or more than once in each reign.

The expansion of empire completed the concentration of power and privilege in the hands of the nobility, since both the honours and the spoils of war were the perquisites of the few rather than the many. The best lands of the Tepanecs and other nearby vassals had been used to reward the nobles, not the commoners. The ruler himself assumed the trappings of an oriental potentate, to whose presence only a select entourage was admitted. Court etiquette decreed that even these privileged few should behave in humble fashion; for instance, when leading warriors appeared before the emperor, they had to wear sandals of the simplest kind, unadorned with gold. Imperial administration was centred upon the king's residence, which served as royal abode, as seat of government and as court of justice. The palace also served as a storehouse, and when the Spaniards were lodged in that of Moctezuma's immediate successor, they found a huge cache of gold objects.

THE HEIRS OF MOCTEZUMA

Moctezuma I died in 1468. The throne had now been occupied for over forty years by two august monarchs; of a modest heritage they had made a mighty kingdom. The inner council of electors now chose as their successor Axayacatl, an untried youth nineteen years old, who reigned from 1468 to 1481; he was followed on the throne by his brother, Tizoc (1481–6). Both were grandsons in the female line of Moctezuma, who died without male issue. During these two short reigns the Empire suffered defeats as well as victories. Even Aztec power had its limitations and without a strong hand at the helm its triumphs could prove fleeting. Axayacatl made certain conquests in the Valley of Toluca to the west, and thereby brought his empire face to face with the Tarascans. The power of the latter, like that of the Aztecs themselves, was based on a league of three cities, all situated on the scenic shores of Lake Patzcuaro. In Tzintzuntzan, one of their three capitals, the ruins can still be seen of a building known as a 'Yacata'; typical of the rather rudimentary Tarascan architecture, it consists of a large temple platform, surmounted by a row of five circular structures.

The Tarascans had conquered an empire centred upon the present-day state of Michoacan, but extending south-eastwards towards the limits of Aztec territory. Spurred on by the people of Toluca, whom he had conquered, Axayacatl decided to try his luck by pushing further westwards, and in the process suffered a crushing defeat at the hands of the Tarascans; of his army of 20,000, only 200 struggled back to

Tenochtitlan. Henceforth the Empire was to be exposed to a deadly foe on its flank, and no attempt was ever made to reverse the verdict of this battle; the Aztecs adopted a defensive stance, and frontier cities were fortified to guard against the Tarascan threat.

Tizoc, Axayacatl's successor, also suffered a humiliating reverse. He attacked Metztitlán, an independent principality on the northern frontier of the Aztec Empire; the army lost 300 men and took a mere forty prisoners, who were sacrificed at his coronation. Both Axayacatl and Tizoc made territorial gains in other directions, particularly in the Huaxteca on the Gulf Coast.

However, Axayacatl's most resounding victory was scored, not against distant enemies, but against Tenochtitlan's own sister city of Tlatelolco, the commercial capital of the Empire and the site of the principal market. Tlatelolco was still ruled by its own dynasty. But in 1473 a dispute arose between the two cities, and the Tlatelolcans were crushed by the superior forces of Tenochtitlan. Their ruler, accompanied by his favourite dwarf, hurled himself from the top of the main temple of his city, which can still be seen today. Allegedly this civil war was caused by a family squabble, though other pretexts are not hard to find. The Tlatelolcan merchants operated not simply as private traders, but were an integral part of the machinery of state, since they penetrated far beyond the bounds of empire, acting as spies and scouts, and thus paving the way to many a military conquest. These traders had thereby become partners in a joint enterprise, part-commerce and part-conquest, whose very scope demanded control by a single master.

Tizoc was succeeded by his brother Ahuitzotl. After an inglorious interlude, the choice now fell upon a heroic monarch, who was to extend Aztec rule to remote lands where only traders had so far penetrated. The new ruler embarked on an immediate career of conquest, starting in the Huaxteca, where he pushed his frontier farther northwards along the coast. These first campaigns yielded a rich haul of prisoners and in 1487, one year after his accession, he staged a mammoth sacrifice to inaugurate the new extension of the Great Temple. The chroniclers put the victim count at 20,000, or even at 80,000, but such figures can scarcely be accepted at their face value. It would have been physically impossible to have disposed of so many bodies in a city of some 200,000. The Aztecs counted in units of 20, and possibly a total of 4,000 victims (80,000 divided by 20) would be nearer the mark.

Ahuitzotl's main thrusts were made in two directions. The present-day Acapulco figures in his conquest-lists, and from there he advanced north-westwards for about 250 kilometres, absorbing a vast stretch of the Pacific Coast. In the opposite direction he captured Tehuantepec, situated beyond Oaxaca on the isthmus which bears its name. From there he pushed on much further, and occupied Soconusco on the Guatemalan border. In general terms Ahuitzotl was thus absorbing lands where, a thousand years before, people from Teotihuacan had already penetrated. Teotihuacan's cultural influence extended even beyond Ahuitzotl's long-range gains, since it included Guatemala, never dominated by the Aztecs, and stretched far beyond Zacatula, the limit of their conquests on the north-west Pacific Coast.

Motivations for such far-reaching conquests are harder to assess. Aztec tax gatherers already garnered vast supplies of tropical luxuries, without having to levy tribute from lands so distant that the mere conveyance of booty was a major problem. But apart from Ahuitzotl's own driving ambitions, the Aztec obsession with ceremonial created a demand for luxuries that was limitless. Repeatedly the chronicles describe the Sardanapalian displays staged after victories in the field, always accompanied by copious bloodshed. One account after another tells of the gifts heaped upon guests, both free and subject, who attended. Such festivities absorbed great quantities of tribute; for instance, a whole year's supply was given away at Ahuitzotl's coronation.

This passion for disbursing wealth invites comparison with a strange practice, known as 'potlatch', current among tribes of the north-west coast of the United States and Canada. Superhuman efforts were made to amass a temporary hoard of wealth, all destined to be lavished upon friends and enemies alike at a single feast. The Aztec Empire also might almost be described as a 'potlatch state' – a concept alien to Europeans, for whom riches were something to be saved and passed on to one's heirs. Lacking a true currency, wealth in Ancient Mexico was harder to store; what could not be worn on the owner's person was at times squandered on his guests.

Such displays, however, were not only designed to impress one's fellow men. The ever-increasing supply of gaudy feathers, precious gems and other baubles was above all dedicated to the service of the gods. The Empire was in a certain sense caught in a vicious circle of perpetual conquest. Vast wealth was expended on rites to honour the gods, who thereupon incited their subjects to further wars and rewarded them with yet more victories, which merely provided the paraphernalia for ceremonies on an ever more gigantic scale. The process was never-ending; ever wider conquests provided ever greater spoils for the gods who in return offered, not peace, but further conflict.

Soconusco, 1,000 kilometres as the crow flies from Tenochtitlan, proved to be the limit of Aztec conquest. Since their armies lived off the land, they could at least feed themselves in the remotest provinces, and subject cities on the line of march provided equipment as well as food. None the less, to cover such huge distances on foot required superhuman efforts; moreover, an army had to carry its cumbersome array of battle insignia; for fighting the enemy, these were just as indispensable as arms. And when Ahuitzotl wanted to press on beyond Soconusco, it became clear that there were limits to what even this hero-king could demand of his warriors, who protested loudly when he revealed new plans.

It was on the home front, however, that the conqueror met his Waterloo. Because his capital needed ever-increasing supplies of water, he decided to tap the sources of nearby Coyoacán. He was repeatedly warned of the dangers of his project by its ruler, whose appeal for caution cost him his life. The plan miscarried, and a torrential flow of water caused the lagoon level to rise and flood Tenochtitlan. In 1502, not long after this disaster, Ahuitzotl died; according to certain accounts he was killed by a blow on the head when escaping from the flood.

THE SPANISH INVASION

Ahuitzotl was succeeded by Moctezuma II. Because of his ill-starred involvement with the Spaniards, his fame has outlived that of his predecessors. The son of Axayacatl and nephew of Ahuitzotl, he ascended the throne at the age of thirty-four. As a prince renowned for his valour, sagacity and piety, he was the obvious choice.

Moctezuma's strategy was a radical departure from that of the previous ruler. Ahuitzotl had pushed ahead recklessly, but often his armies simply outflanked lands where they did not penetrate. Moctezuma's conquest-lists show that, instead of ranging yet further afield, he sought to consolidate his predecessor's gains by absorbing such regions that lay astride the imperial lines of communication.

The new ruler pursued this task with vigour during the first fifteen years of his reign, particularly in the Mixteca and on the Gulf Coast. Nearer home, he was determined to crush the small but defiant principalities of the Puebla Valley; his failure to achieve his aim was to have a fateful sequel. Throughout his reign, Moctezuma was plagued by hostilities with Tlaxcala, which had taken Huexotzingo's place as the leading city-state of this valley. A series of wars was fought between Tlaxcala and Huexotzingo, whose side Moctezuma took. But no decisive victory was won and in 1515, a mere four years before Cortés' arrival, the Aztecs were soundly beaten by the Tlaxcalans and most of their force was killed or captured, a disaster which caused Moctezuma to shed bitter tears. Shattered by this humiliation, he took drastic measures to stiffen the army, stripping many captains of their rank; shorn of their insignia, they were even forbidden to wear cotton clothing on pain of death.

Doubts persist as to the exact nature of these encounters. The historical sources constantly refer to 'Wars of Flowers', described as a kind of tourney arranged between the Aztecs and certain peoples of the Puebla Valley; at an appointed time and place a contest ensued, whose object was neither victory nor conquest, but the capture of prisoners for sacrifice. Such accounts suggest that the last thing that the Aztecs wanted was to conquer Tlaxcala and deny itself a rich source of sacrificial victims within easy reach of home.

These stories of mock battles contradict others that insistently tell of Moctezuma's resolve to crush Tlaxcala and of his rage when his attempts failed. Admittedly the demand for offerings was insatiable and the gods much preferred captives from nearby states to barbarians from afar. Moreover, the Empire faced a law of diminishing returns. As the radius of conquest was extended, the process of bringing prisoners alive to Tenochtitlan was complicated by sheer distance.

So pressing was the need for victims that it remains likely that on certain occasions Wars of Flowers were indeed waged against the peoples of the Puebla Valley, particularly with those that were part-vassals, such as Atlixco. But at other times bitter campaigns were clearly fought against city-states of that region; certainly in the decade before the Spaniards came, wars against Tlaxcala were no mere tourney; their aim was to conquer and it would be misleading to regard them as Wars of Flowers.

The story of the Conquest itself, in which Tlaxcala was to play an important part, has been told so often as to need no detailed repetition. The Spanish force of eleven ships and 508 men set out from Cuba on 10 February 1519. Before Hernán Cortés, its leader, ever set foot in Mexico, Moctezuma's fragile peace of mind had been shattered by evil omens. Beset by portents of comets belching fire and of eagles with mirrors in their heads, he at one time thought to flee his kingdom and take refuge with Huemac, King of the Underworld. Other omens had a more factual basis, such as the report of a peasant who spied great mountains moving in the sea; what he had really seen were the ships of a previous Spanish expedition that had sailed along the Veracruz coastline.

For several months after his first landing, Cortés dallied on the coast. During this time a bizarre exchange of messages and gifts ensued between himself and Moctezuma, whose intelligence service offered copious reports, complete with illustrations, on the strange intruders; from these Moctezuma learned to his amazement of the Spaniards' hairy white faces, the black skins of their Negroes, the ferocity of their dogs, and the swiftness of their horses; horse and rider were taken to be a single Centaur-like being. Moctezuma also sent envoys who were first struck dumb by a demonstration of cannon fire and then made drunk on Spanish wine.

Even before he left the coast, Cortés' presence was beginning to disrupt the Empire. Zempoala, the largest city which the Spaniards had so far visited, whose ruler was known as the 'Fat Chief', openly renounced its allegiance to Moctezuma. In mid-1519 Cortés headed inland and in a matter of days reached Tlaxcala, some 120 kilometres distant from the Aztec capital. After a disastrous battle, the Tlaxcalans threw in their lot with the Conquerors, now treated as liberators from the Aztec yoke. Unlike the Tlaxcalans, Moctezuma resisted the urge to chance his luck in a pitched battle and the Spaniards, after a needless massacre of Cholulans in the main court of their temple, advanced on Tenochtitlan. Deaf to the Emperor's entreaties to stay away, they reached Ixtapalapa, guarding one of the main causeways over the lagoon to Tenochtitlan.

The climax of the invasion followed, when Cortés and Moctezuma met face to face. The chronicler, Bernal Díaz, gives an eye-witness description:

When we came close to Mexico, at a place where there were other, smaller towers, Moctezuma descended from his litter while these great chiefs supported him with their arms beneath a marvellously rich canopy of green feathers, worked with gold and silver, pearls and green stones, which hung from a kind of border that was wonderful to see. He was richly dressed and wore shoes like sandals, with soles of gold covered with precious stones. The four chiefs who supported him were also richly dressed . . .
There were four other chiefs who carried the canopy and many other lords

who walked before the great Moctezuma, sweeping the ground where he would pass, and putting down mats, so that he would not have to walk on the ground. None of these lords thought of looking in his face; all of them kept their eyes down, with great reverence.

When Cortés saw the great Moctezuma approaching, he jumped from his horse and they showed great respect toward each other . . . Then Cortés gave him a necklace . . . and was going to embrace him, when the princes accompanying him caught Cortés by the arm so that he could not do so, for they thought it an indignity.

Moctezuma, addressing Cortés as the rightful successor of all the former *tlatoanis*, surrendered to him their throne and made him guardian of their people. The Spaniards then entered the capital, where they lodged in the palace of the former ruler, Axayacatl. Soon thereafter one of the most shameful episodes in human history occurred, when the undisputed master of a great empire yielded without a fight to a tiny band of adventurers and left his own palace as a craven captive. Such, however, was his control over his own people that even after this humiliation Moctezuma was able to transact the business of empire from his Spanish prison; he was not even spared the ultimate indignity, when Cortés on one occasion had him shackled.

Moctezuma may be forgiven for not giving battle to the Conquerors before they entered Tenochtitlan. Following the subversion of his coastal provinces, he was shaken by the Spaniards' easy victory over the Tlaxcalans, who had withstood the flower of his own forces. On military grounds, it was surely right to lure the invaders into the capital, and it is even surprising that Cortés accepted the obvious risks. If Moctezuma had not lost his head and capitulated, the Spaniards' situation would have been fraught with danger. Horses and cannon were of little use in narrow streets; if the invaders were invincible in the open field, in the enclosed city they could be pelted with missiles from every rooftop; Tenochtitlan was finally conquered from without, not from within.

Cortés had to hasten back to the coast with most of his force to deal with a new Spanish expedition, commanded by Pánfilo de Narváez. It was sent not to help Cortés, but to arrest him for having set out from Cuba without the Governor's permission. After defeating Narváez, Cortés returned to Tenochtitlan; his total army now numbered 1,300, partly recruited from those sent to oppose him.

The impetuous Pedro Alvarado had been left in charge in the capital, where the situation soon became critical. Provoked by Alvarado's assault on a religious procession, Moctezuma's subjects cast off their renegade master and chose a new ruler. The Emperor was killed by a stone thrown by one of his own people, when he tried to persuade them to lay down their arms.

Cortés' disastrous retreat from Tenochtitlan, where his position was now untenable, took place on the night of 10 July 1520, thereafter known as the Noche Triste, or Sad Night. Attacked from all sides as they fought their way over the canal bridges, only 440 men and 21 horses escaped alive. At this critical juncture, the Aztecs' main concern was to celebrate their victory and to sacrifice their prisoners. They not merely failed to pursue the fleeing Spaniards at the nadir of their fortunes, but even allowed themselves to be routed by this depleted force in the Battle of Otumba. The situation was then saved for Cortés by the Tlaxcalans, whose city served as his base from 21 July 1520 until 21 April 1521.

During this time the Spaniards made many sorties into the surrounding country; in a series of encounters, the ability of minute bands of Europeans to rout hordes of Indians was repeatedly proven. The final act of the drama began on 28 April 1521 with the siege of Tenochtitlan, now ruled by the intrepid Cuauhtemoc. The defenders held out for four months, and it was only after much of the city had been razed block by block that resistance ended and Cuauhtemoc was captured as he sought to flee in a canoe.

The place where he was taken can still be visited, if not by canoe. The front of the Church of La Concepción, in the Plaza of the same name, bears a plaque which reads as follows: 'Tequipeuhcan [meaning The Place where the Drudgery Began]. Here the Emperor Cuauhtemoc was made prisoner on the afternoon of 13 August 1521'.

8

THE AZTEC STATE

THE EMPIRE

To this outline of Aztec history, at least a brief account must be added not only of how they ruled their subject peoples, but also of their city, its institutions, art and architecture, daily life and above all its gods, who presided over every facet of its culture.

The wealth of data at our disposal on Tenochtitlan reveals certain aspects of society and religion about which so little is known in the case of Tula, or Teotihuacan. While close comparisons have their pitfalls, any such outline of the Aztec world may also help to convey some idea, however incomplete, of what life was like in the leading cities of former times.

Strict comparisons between the Aztec Empire and empires of the Old World can also be misleading. It had come into being as an alliance between three city-states, arising out of the war against the Tepanecs. The main objective of this Triple Alliance was not to rule other peoples, but to levy tribute. But the very word 'empire' in the Old World sense has a rather different meaning, more applicable to, say, Ancient Rome or nineteenth-century England, whose provinces were ruled by proconsuls, backed by professional garrisons, to keep internal order and to ward off external threats. The Aztec control over their domain was much looser.

It is a common fallacy to suppose that the Aztecs possessed a large standing army on the Roman model, whose task was to guard the outer marches of empire. At best, a small warrior élite stood ready at all times to obey the call to arms, but not to be uprooted from their homes for a lengthy tour of garrison duty on the sensitive Tarascan border. From all accounts, many nobles were full-time officers of state, but their duties were of a dual nature, since they also held important civil posts; only certain titles applied purely to military captains. It is also conceivable, but not certain, that the orders of knights, such as the Eagles and Ocelots, formed, like the Knights Templar, a standing corps d'élite, but no source suggests that they could be sent to man outposts in distant provinces.

Moctezuma's own bodyguard offered no resistance to the Spaniards who marched him off to their quarters. This entourage was not an imperial guard in the true sense, but merely a contingent of nobles and their sons, in attendance on the ruler on a rotating basis and performing duties that were both civil and military. The lower ranks of the army were recruited from the wards, or *calpullis*, of Tenochtitlan, Tlatelolco and other places. These were originally land-holding units, whose members were liable to be called upon to fight in specific campaigns but not for permanent duty, since they were also farmers.

The Aztec Empire, a term we use for lack of a better one, was really a mosaic of smaller principalities that had been subdued and forced to pay tribute. Government was normally left in the hands of the hereditary señores, treated by their conquerors with a certain deference. In addition, the Aztecs established in key centres their own tax gatherers, whose task was to watch over tribute payment. In the case of frontier tribes, tribute was often levied in the form not of goods but of arms and military contingents; peoples who lay on the line of march of the army also had to furnish food, weapons and manpower.

As an exception to the general tendency to retain local rulers, in a few cases far-off centres were settled by colonists sent from the Aztec capital and nearby cities. As early as the reign of Moctezuma I, a colony composed of 600 married men, with their wives and children, was sent to Oaxaca, which thereafter served as a springboard for future expansion. Another known instance of this type occurred after the Emperor Ahuitzotl had laid waste two places, Oztoma and Alahuiztla, 250 kilometres south-west of Tenochtitlan near the Tarascan border. Surpassing even his accustomed ruthlessness, he put the population to the sword, including women and children. To repopulate these key bastions, 2,000 new settlers were sent from Central Mexico; some were recruited from as far afield as Toluca, a reminder that the Aztecs and their nearest neighbours were not always eager to colonize such distant outposts of empire.

Oztoma was one of a series of strongpoints on the Tarascan frontier, mentioned in many sources. Their defence depended mainly on local levies, protected by a ring of bulwarks and barricades; only in case of emergency were these strengthened by forces sent from the imperial capital. If any frontier defences were permanently manned, such a policy did not apply to the Aztec wall on the northern border of Tlaxcalan territory, which was found deserted by Cortés.

In addition to such settlements of a mere strategic nature, certain sectors of Tuxtepec, 100 kilometres due south of Veracruz, housed people from Central Mexico. But this place was ostensibly an emporium, used as a base by merchants who penetrated from there into the farthest regions of south-east Mexico. Some of them resided at least for a time in the city, which had strong defences provided by the merchants themselves.

Historians are apt to assume that the Aztec Empire must have been held in subjection by a network of garrisons. But the crucial question then remains: supposing this was so, where on earth were all these standing forces when the Spaniards arrived? Before moving inland, they explored long stretches of Mexico's Gulf Coast; nowhere did they find one solitary imperial post, though its inhabitants were disaffected and resented forced tribute payment; the ruler of Zempoala, the 'Fat Chief', shed bitter tears on Cortés' shoulder because Moctezuma had purloined his family jewels. None the less, before the Spaniards appeared on the scene, this prince cringed before his Aztec master, restrained not by local garrisons, which did not exist, but by fears of reprisal if he rebelled. The tax collector who met the Conquerors soon after they first entered Aztec territory went unescorted by military guards; dressed in the height of fashion, he was armed with nothing more lethal than a crooked staff and a bunch of flowers. For immunity from assault he relied on the long arm of the central power and the savage punishment meted out to subjects foolish enough to molest its agents. In places not too far distant from the capital, a tighter hold could be maintained over vassals. However, the frequent risings in remoter regions show that this threat of reprisal was not always enough to exorcize the urge to revolt, and to ensure the payment of tribute; admittedly by Conquest times the Gulf Coast provinces visited by Cortés seem to have learned their lesson in this respect, and had become more submissive.

This was not always so, and a single example may serve to illustrate the limits of imperial authority. Cotaxtla, now a village, lying to the south-west of the modern Veracruz, was a fairly important centre in its time, and headed a league of Totonac cities against which Moctezuma I sent a powerful expedition in 1459. Having been duly crushed, the local chiefs were assembled at Cotaxtla; after the usual haggling, the burden of tribute was fixed, and an imperial tax collector left behind to watch over its payment. The Aztec army then marched away, but scarcely were their backs turned before the Cotaxtlans changed their minds, killed Moctezuma's henchmen and allied themselves with the Tlaxcalans. The Emperor sent more envoys who were also slaughtered; their corpses were stuffed with straw and clothed in gorgeous apparel, while piles of food were set before them. The Totonacs then mocked these effigies, addressing them as lords and asking why they declined to enjoy their feast. The irate Moctezuma now had to send a second force, and scored yet another resounding victory, leading to even heavier tribute payments. The new levy included such exotic items as richly woven mantles, robes trimmed with feathers, and labrets of crystal with blue enamel, mounted in gold.

This was far from being the end of the story of Cotaxtla. It again revolted when Moctezuma I died, and the first campaign of his successor was directed against the same Totonac cities. Their names are among the many that recur in the conquest-lists of a series of Aztec rulers as having been subdued afresh after further rebellions. After Cotaxtla's first unsuccessful bid for freedom, an unusual event had occurred: the common people denounced their rulers and declared that they themselves had done the Aztecs no harm; new ones were chosen and the deposed chiefs were taken to Tenochtitlan and flayed. Such a measure, however, was another departure from the normal practice of leaving the existing sovereign in full control, subject only to tribute payments. Only in the rarest instances did the Aztecs impose direct military rule for a limited period before choosing a new prince. A list survives of the principal local rulers at the time of the Conquest and includes most of the Empire; many such princes in turn had their own tributaries, and governed areas where Aztec rule was therefore indirect.

Thus, if the Aztec control over leading centres was loose, large tracts of land were never really conquered at all. Quite apart from independent states, such as Tlaxcala, countless hills and valleys lying off their line of march never saw an Aztec army. The Empire was more a series of strong-points than a continuous domain. And if there was more emphasis on military conquest in Aztec times than before, this pattern of a central megalopolis, surrounded by its inner metropolitan area but also extending its influence, whether military or commercial, to distant places, recurs throughout the history of Middle America.

To further their control of such a scattered realm, certain peoples were specially favoured by the Aztecs. In return, they gave every help to the Empire in the form of supplies and auxiliaries, needed for wars against hostile neighbours. Among these favoured few, Oaxaca, once colonized by Moctezuma I, was important, as well as Tehuantepec, further to the south-east, whose ruler married a daughter of Moctezuma II.

The Aztecs tended to respect conquered rulers who served their interests and upheld their power. In addition, like their own *tlatoani*, they saw these local monarchs as the living representatives of their own gods, a role which gave an aura of sanctity to their person; to have deposed them, except for special offences, would have violated the principle of monarchy, and would have slighted their gods, many of whom had their place in the Aztec pantheon. Such rulers were normally succeeded by their own heirs, who sometimes married into the royal family of Tenochtitlan; the sons of such marriages were given preference over the offspring of other wives.

The Aztecs divided this network of subject princes into thirty-eight provinces, each grouped round its provincial centre; pictures in the *Codex Mendoza* show precisely what tribute each had to deliver. The official assigned to a province to ensure these payments had his opposite number in Tenochtitlan, whose task was to make sure that the stipulated items, payable every eighty days, duly reached the capital; any robbery or fraud was punishable by death. These officials were known as *calpixques*, meaning 'guardians of the house'; this rather general term was also applied to other functionaries who were charged with public works, the upkeep of roads and the running of the royal palaces.

The provincial *calpixque* was an imperial agent rather than a governing proconsul. He relied not on soldiers but on scribes, whose duty was to keep an exact record of payments. He also sent reports to the Aztec *tlatoani* on the general state of the province. Bernal Díaz stresses the awe which these officials inspired; the Totonac chiefs were aghast when Cortés had the audacity to seize those he encountered, though they soon overcame their scruples and became so eager to sacrifice their former tax gatherers that Cortés had to take them into protective custody.

THE CITY

At the centre of this network of tribute-paying city-states lay the imperial capital, Tenochtitlan. By the time of the Conquest it had far outstripped its partners Texcoco and Tacuba, though they were still entitled to their share of tribute. The Conquistadors were bedazzled when they passed between the Great Volcanoes and saw Tenochtitlan for the first time. To quote Bernal Díaz: 'When we saw so many cities built both on the water and on dry land, and their straight, level causeways, we could not restrain our admiration. It was like the enchantments in the book of Amadis, because of the high towers, cues [temples] and other buildings, all of masonry, which rose from the water. Some of our soldiers asked if what we had seen was not a dream.'

Tenochtitlan was big as well as beautiful. Bernal Díaz did not exaggerate when he wrote of 'things never before seen or dreamed about'. For Spanish cities of the period were by comparison diminutive. Toledo, the royal capital, had only 18,000 inhabitants, and Seville about 15,000, or under a tenth of the population of Tenochtitlan. Even the largest European towns, Paris, Naples, Milan and Venice, were much smaller than the Aztec capital. Moreover it did not, like Teotihuacan, stand alone. Set in the midst of the lagoon, it was ringed by a constellation of satellite cities, situated on the shore and housing a large additional population. The public services and sanitation had no parallel in Europe: according to the chronicler Torquemada, 'there were in each street men sweeping it and sprinkling it, periodically throughout the night tending great braziers of fire, and while some of them slept others kept vigil, so that there was always someone who by night and day was accountable for the city and all that happened in it.' He further relates that in certain canals huge barges were moored for the collection of waste matter, which was carried away and used as fertilizer.

Tenochtitlan had excellent communications with the mainland, being linked to the lake shore by three causeways, wide enough to allow ten Spanish horsemen to ride abreast. In addition, its water supplies were carefully planned and two main aqueducts carried supplies to the city. The Chapultepec springs were channelled through a double pipeline, in order that one conduit could remain in use while the other was being cleaned and repaired. This aqueduct followed the western causeway, while another pipeline brought water from Coyoacán to the edge of the urban zone, from which it ran underground to the Temple Precinct. By the time of the Conquest it was evidently functioning smoothly and its disastrous teething troubles in the reign of Ahuitzotl had been overcome. Water control, in one form or another, was basic to the city's economy: the part of the lagoon in which Tenochtitlan stood had been shut off from the remainder by a dyke, built as a gift to Moctezuma I from Nezahual-coyotl of Texcoco. This dyke was sixteen kilometres long and played a decisive part in the economy, since it shut off the western area of the lagoon, fed by its own sweet-water springs, from the salty stretches to the east. The surroundings of the city were thereby made ideal for cultivation on an intensive scale.

Such man-made amenities were quite a recent creation. Had the Conquistadors come two hundred years earlier, they would have found little on the site to excite their wonder. Because the pre-Hispanic Tenochtitlan lies buried beneath the modern Mexico City, it is impossible to make an archaeological study comparable with the Teotihuacan Mapping Project; its growth, moreover, was so much more rapid than that of Teotihuacan that its development would in any case be harder to define stage by stage. The historical sources offer some data on how Tenochtitlan grew to maturity. They describe a gradual but steady expansion during the pre-imperial period, spanning the second half of the fourteenth century. By the accession of Chimalpopoca in 1415, the settlement had already become a city; according to Padre Durán, well-built houses of stone and adobe bricks then began to replace those of earlier times that were little more than huts. Growth during the next hundred years was dynamic, and by 1519 the urban zone occupied between twelve and fifteen square kilometres and housed a population of some 200,000. Much of this area had been reclaimed from the lagoon and was liable to subside. Thus all major structures had to be supported by wooden piles driven into the earth, and excavations in the area behind the cathedral have revealed thousands of these stakes. The urban core was in turn surrounded by a suburban zone in which intensive agriculture was practised; within this 'greater Tenochtitlan' lived about half a million people.

As part of this expansion, Tlatelolco, ruled by its own monarch until absorbed by Tenochtitlan in 1473, had long since merged into a single conurbation, as the swamps that divided the two original islands were drained. Tlatelolco, though it lost its independence, continued to be the main centre of commerce, where the principal market was situated. Bernal Díaz describes it vividly:

The chiefs who accompanied us showed us how each kind of merchandise was kept separate and had its place marked out. Let us start with the dealers in gold, silver and precious stones, feathers, cloth, and embroidered goods, and other merchandise in the form of men and women to be sold as slaves. There were as many here as the Negroes brought from Guinea by the Portuguese.

Some were tied to long poles with collars around their necks so they couldn't escape, and others were left free. Then there were merchants who sold homespun clothing, cotton, and thread, and others who sold cacao, so that one could see every sort of goods that is to be found in all New Spain, set out the way it's done where I come from, Medina del Campo, during fair time. There were people who sold henequen cloth, as well as rope and shoes made from the same plant, and its cooked roots, which are very sweet, all in a special section of the market set aside for them. In another section they had skins of tigers, lions, deer, and other animals, some tanned and some not.

An important part of this market was naturally devoted to food-stuffs, and the chronicler mentions stalls for turkeys, dogs, wild game and a spectacular range of unfamiliar fruit and vegetables. In conformity with the Spaniards' preconceived notions about the value of gold, he stresses the use of quills filled with gold dust as a means of exchange, though in Ancient Mexico certain other items also served as a form of currency. Both Cortés and Bernal Díaz tell of the close government control over the market. To quote Cortés:

There exists in this great square a large building like an audience hall, where ten or twelve persons are always seated and who act as judges and who give sentence on all cases and questions arising in this market, and who order punishment for those who break the law. And in the same square there are other people who continuously walk among the people, observing what is sold and the measures with which it is measured; and we saw one measure broken which was false.

Tenochtitlan was a carefully planned city, of which a walled temple precinct served as the focal point. The three causeways linking Tenochtitlan to the mainland led north, west, and south, and were joined with the heart of the city by broad avenues that converged upon a fortified gate in the wall surrounding this central precinct. To the east the city was divided from the shore by a wider stretch of open water, beyond which rose the pyramids and palaces of Texcoco.

The urban zone was laid out on a grid pattern and divided into uniform plots by its network of canals. Notwithstanding the ample causeways, the Conquerors stress that the principal means of communication were by water rather than by land, and the canoe was the only vehicle. Another eye-witness, known as the Anonymous Conqueror, describes what he saw.

The Great City has many broad streets, though among these are two or three principal ones. Of the remainder, half of each one is of hard earth like a pavement and the other half is filled in by water, so that they leave in their canoes or barks, which are of wood hollowed out, although some of them are

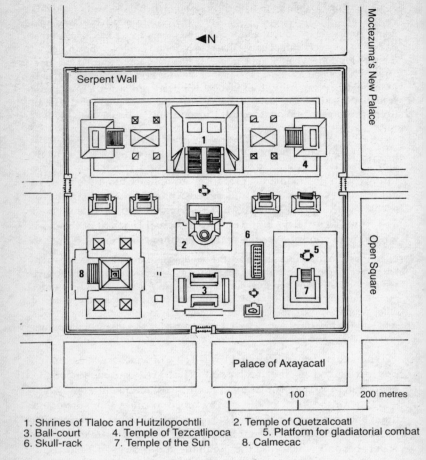

1. Shrines of Tlaloc and Huitzilopochtli   2. Temple of Quetzalcoatl
3. Ball-court   4. Temple of Tezcatlipoca   5. Platform for gladiatorial combat
6. Skull-rack   7. Temple of the Sun   8. Calmecac

Figure 31. Plan of the Great Precinct at Tenochtitlan

large enough to seat five persons in comfort. The inhabitants often go for a
stroll, some in canoes and others along the land, and hold animated conversa-
tions. Besides these are other principal thoroughfares entirely of water, and all
travel is by boats and canoes, as I have said, and without these they would
neither leave their houses nor return to them, and all the other towns on the
sweet water lake are arranged in the same way.

The pre-Hispanic city was so ravaged both during and after the
Conquest that it is even hard to determine the exact site of many of the

main monuments and of the open plazas that surrounded them.
None the less, data from excavations in certain parts of its perimeter
supplement the ample but often vague Spanish accounts. From the
latter we learn that the Great Precinct in the centre was surrounded by
a wall decorated with huge serpent heads. Inside the enclosure were
the temples of the leading gods; the principal skull-rack, on which
were displayed heads of countless victims, stood on the approximate
site of the present-day cathedral. Close to one of the precinct gates
stood a court for the ritual ball-game.

The Great Temple, dedicated jointly to the Rain God, Tlaloc, and
the tribal Humming Bird God, Huitzilopochtli, towered over this
central precinct. As illustrated by Sahagún, a double stairway ran

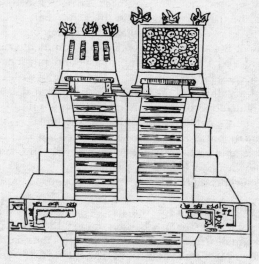

Figure 32. Tenochtitlan Great Temple
after the historian Alva Ixtlilxóchitl

down the west side of the pyramid, flanked by balustrades at whose
base stood huge serpent heads of painted stone. The shrines of the
two deities were built on a platform on the summit of the temple; they
were box-like structures, with no windows and only one door. The
lower part of the roof of Tlaloc's shrine was painted in alternating
stripes of white and blue, while that of Huitzilopochtli was decorated
with white skulls, set against a red background. On the terrace in front
of the shrines stood the stones over which victims were stretched

out for sacrifice. Two other major temples stood beside this pyramid: one was dedicated to the Smoking Mirror God, Tezcatlipoca, and the other was the round temple of the Plumed Serpent, Quetzalcoatl. Of the latter Bernal Díaz wrote:

One of its doors was in the form of a most terrible mouth, such as they paint to depict the jaws of hell. This mouth was open and contained great fangs to devour souls. By the side of the door were groups of devils and forms shaped like the bodies of serpents, and a little way off was a place of sacrifice, all blood-stained, and black with smoke and dried blood.

Sahagún lists in all seventy-eight buildings within the great compound, surrounded by the serpent wall. But in view of the limited size of this enclosure, which had long since been demolished when Sahagún wrote, he may be mistaken in this, and some at least of the buildings listed perhaps stood outside the wall in other parts of the city. A few of the structures he names are admittedly small, while others were described as housing priests and prisoners awaiting sacrifice. In a rather different account, Padre Durán writes of eight or nine temples within the precinct. He describes in detail the great statue of Huitzilopochtli and mentions various priestly dwellings grouped round a patio in front of the main temple.

Tenochtitlan, but not Tlatelolco, was divided into four administrative quarters, and each contained its own temple enclosure, though little is known of their size or character; quite possibly some of Sahagún's seventy-eight buildings really belonged to those local precincts.

Since its foundation, Tenochtitlan's Great Temple had been dedicated, at least in part, to the tribal Humming Bird God, and two early sovereigns are described in historical sources as the guardians of his temple. However, such sources unite in ascribing to Moctezuma I the grandiose project for its rebuilding on a much vaster scale, using labour and materials supplied by nearby vassals. But though Moctezuma inaugurated his version of the temple in 1455, the Emperors Tizoc and Ahuitzotl are also credited with ambitious new plans for its enlargement; a stela in the National Museum commemorates the dedication of this extended pyramid by Ahuitzotl in 1487, on the occasion of his mammoth human sacrifice.

Such accounts, however, only tell part of the story, to which a new chapter has now been added. In 1978, the Mexican Institute of Anthropology launched its Great Temple Project, directed by Eduardo Matos. A corner of the building had previously been unearthed by

Manuel Gamio, the leading Mexican archaeologist of his time. Now, however, work on a more lavish scale, involving the demolition of whole city blocks, has given a new perspective to our knowledge of the building. Perhaps the most startling find has been the identification of not merely one or two, but of a series of eleven reconstructions; each successive temple covered a larger area than the one before and therefore rose proportionately higher. Such evidence shows that single projects of renewal could hardly have stretched over several reigns, as the sources tend to imply. Compressed into Tenochtitlan's limited known lifespan, such extensions would have been made at intervals of less than twenty years and pose many problems. Repeated additions were presumably made not only to the Great Temple but to other major pyramids, such as those of the Smoking Mirror and Plumed Serpent, which were of comparable size. But these frequent additions would have left the Sacred Precinct in an almost permanent state of reconstruction, even if the work, involving the building of an identical superstructure on a smaller edifice beneath, had been carried out fairly quickly. Yet it is hard to see how space was provided for these continual enlargements without completely redesigning the general layout of the precinct, and extending its area from time to time.

A surprisingly large proportion of objects in the many offerings found underneath the Great Temple came from outside the Valley of Mexico, and in particular from Guerrero. The caches of ceremonial axes almost recall those of Olmec La Venta. Conspicuous also is the great quantity of images of the god Tlaloc, far outnumbering those of the Aztecs' own god, Huitzilopochtli, though the finest piece is the great round stone carved with the dismembered body of his sister, Coyolxauhqui. In many cases the paint which covered the pieces is excellently preserved; in contrast to these new finds, stone carvings from the centre of Tenochtitlan discovered during the past two centuries retain few traces of colouring, though their scale is often more impressive.

The monuments of Tlatelolco were second only in splendour to those of Tenochtitlan. Contrary to what is often assumed, Moctezuma took Cortés and his companions to visit, not the Great Temple of Tenochtitlan, but that of its sister city; it was on this occasion that they also saw its market, described by Bernal Díaz. The ceremonial centre of Tlatelolco was excavated in the 1960s and here also eleven temple reconstructions can be identified. The pyramid now visible corresponds to the second superposition; it is therefore a miniature replica of the eleventh version, which was vast, as one can still see from the area that it occupied; it would have risen higher than the Church of Santiago, built in early Colonial times out of its stones. These ruins stand in what is now called the Plaza de las Tres Culturas, the three cultures in question being represented by the remains of Ancient Tlatelolco, by the Colonial Church of Santiago and by the modern buildings that surround it, including the imposing Ministry of Foreign Affairs.

The palaces of the Aztec rulers stood just outside the walled precinct of Tenochtitlan. Cortés' entire force was lodged in that of Axayacatl, the father of Moctezuma, who built his own residence close to the southern wall; it occupied a rectangular site about 200 metres in length. Its dual function as royal palace and seat of government is reflected in its architecture. No description of Moctezuma's palace survives, but from a drawing in the *Codex Mendoza* it can be seen to have been built on two levels; it had three courtyards and consisted of a whole series of structures: those of the upper level housed the ruler and his retinue, while the lower storey served as an administrative centre and was mainly occupied by state officials. It was also used as a storehouse and even as a workshop for artisans; they were maintained by the ruler, along with the court officials and dignitaries. One Spanish eye-witness mentions that he walked through the building until his legs could carry him no further and yet he still had not seen all.

The historian Alva Ixtlilxóchitl gives a more detailed account of the palace of Nezahualcoyotl in Texcoco, comparable in most respects to those of Tenochtitlan. It had 300 rooms and in its council chamber stood a throne of gold, encrusted with turquoise. There were also halls of judgement, quarters for the royal guard, and counting houses for the load of tribute that fell to the share of Texcoco. The extensive gardens contained many fountains and basins, together with a labyrinth and a zoo, a feature shared by Moctezuma's residence; it housed all kinds of exotic animals, and there were painted stone statues of any beasts not present in the flesh. Texcoco was famed as a seat of learning, and one patio of the palace served as a kind of university where poets, philosophers and historians taught. Nezahualcoyotl's baths are also described by the author; built on a hill outside Texcoco, they were supplied with water by an elaborate aqueduct; vestiges of these baths still exist and can be reached from the modern Texcoco after a short drive and a climb on foot.

Apart from the rulers themselves, leading nobles were allowed to build houses of two storeys in Tenochtitlan and Texcoco; as in other

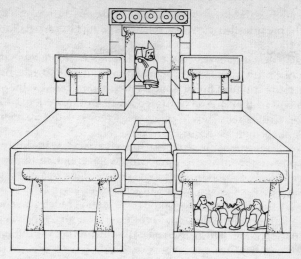

Figure 33. Moctezuma II's palace at Tenochtitlan
(*Codex Mendoza*). Moctezuma is seated in his throne room
on the top level, while councillors meet on the ground floor

Mexican cities, most of these were grouped around the centre; they often stood on raised platforms, and their stone or adobe walls were coated with lime plaster. They had flat roofs made of wooden beams, many of which were spread with earth in order to make roof gardens. The houses of the ordinary citizens were, as we shall see, very simple.

THE GOVERNMENT

From such accounts of Tenochtitlan and Texcoco, it can be seen that the ceremonial precinct and the palaces outside had distinct functions and that government was centred upon the latter. In contrast, though elaborate dwellings adjoin the main temples of Teotihuacan, they are part of a single complex grouped around the Street of the Dead and no barrier divides temple from palace.

The altered pattern in Tenochtitlan, where religious buildings are enclosed within the Wall of Serpents, reflects an apparent change in emphasis from theocratic to secular government. If the Aztec *tlatoani* retained a priestly function, as the gods' mouthpiece, he was basically a temporal ruler, governing from a palace situated outside the sacred precinct, while the day-to-day routine of religious observance was left to a full-time priesthood, whose role was distinct from that of the civil power.

Spanish accounts stress the exalted status of the *tlatoani* and the barrier of courtly ritual that screened him from his subjects; not only did the lords cringe in his presence; when he appeared in the streets, people bowed their heads or turned away, but never looked him in the face; Cortés tells how Aztec nobles rebuked the Spaniards for looking their own leader in the eye.

Absolute monarchy, in so far as it indeed existed, was a fairly recent development. According to tradition, the sovereign in former times had been freely chosen by the whole people. This was no longer the case and a new sovereign was nominated by electors, whose aim was to appoint the fittest member of the royal family. Moctezuma was the son of a former ruler, whose two brothers had both reigned before he came to the throne, which often passed from brother to brother rather than from father to son.

The choice of *tlatoani* had become the preserve of the military élite, though accounts vary as to the number of electors involved; the chroniclers concur, however, in stating that the kings of the other two members of the Triple Alliance were also consulted. In Texcoco itself, unlike Tenochtitlan, the throne did pass to the late ruler's legitimate heir, and Nezahualpilli succeeded his father, Nezahualcoyotl, when he was only seven years old. A wiser man than his colleague, Moctezuma, he died four years before the Conquest. Notwithstanding the exalted status of the ruler, he was not a total despot; upon election he was subjected to formalized speeches, stressing his duties to his subjects and reminding him that he was their servant as much as their master. The tendency of the throne to pass to a brother or nephew of the previous ruler shows that there were certain limits to his power. Like any other king, he would have felt a compelling urge to assure the succession of his own son, had he been able to.

Second in rank to the *tlatoani* came the Snake Woman (*Cihuacoatl*) whose rather ambiguous role has already been mentioned. Whereas by sheer force of character Tlacaelel had carved out for himself a role as a kind of grand vizier under Moctezuma I, the Snake Woman of Conquest times played a more limited part in the government.

Next in importance to the Snake Woman was an inner council of four, whose attendance on Moctezuma is confirmed by Spanish witnesses. Two of its members bore military titles and commanded the army when the *tlatoani* was not present in person; several rulers had held one of these two offices. The *tlatoani* himself was above all a military leader and his first act on acceding to the throne was to launch a campaign, ostensibly to obtain a good haul of prisoners to be sacrificed at his coronation, which took place later.

The select group of four dignitaries was assisted by a larger council, called the *tlatocan*. Mentioned by many sources, its functions are not well explained, and it is variously described as consisting of twelve, thirteen and twenty members. Though not incorporated into a formal body, the hereditary nobles, known as *pillis*, were in effect a ruling class, from which were recruited leading army commanders, officials and judges. The priests ranked as *pillis*, and they also were educated in the special type of school (*calmecac*) reserved for the élite.

While so much of the authority in the Empire was delegated to local rulers, its very size required a fairly complex machinery of government. The sources say little of how it functioned, apart from their mention of those officials who watched over the collection of tribute. In a warrior state, any distinction between civil and military office tends to become blurred, and many posts in the civil administration would have been filled by men who were soldiers as well as functionaries – rather as, in today's military dictatorships, colonels and generals often take charge of government departments.

Government, as in any well-ordered state, was based on smaller units; the city was divided, as we shall see, into wards, and these in turn were subdivided into groups of 100 and 10 houses.

On the judicial, as opposed to the executive, branch of government more explicit data survive. Absolute probity was demanded of judges. They were paid with funds accruing from lands set aside for this purpose and draconian penalties awaited any who took bribes or were negligent in their duties. Comparable standards were demanded of defendants and witnesses; lying in court was treated as an offence against the gods and perjury was punishable by death. As Sahagún relates in Book VIII of his work:

And likewise the ruler chose and placed in office judges who were not noblemen . . . to such as these the ruler gave office and chose as his judges – the wise, the able, the sage; who listened and spoke well; who were of good memory; who spoke not vainly nor lightly; who did not make friends without forethought nor were drunkards; who guarded their lineage with honour; who slept not overmuch, but rose early; who did nothing for friendship's or kinship's sake, nor for enmity. The ruler might condemn them to death; hence they performed their offices as judges righteously. For otherwise, these judges could find excuse for the wrongs they might do.

Like other branches of government, justice was centred upon the palace; hearings began at daybreak and food was sent from the king's kitchens at midday. Notable for its judicial system was Texcoco, where Nezahualcoyotl drew up a code of law which was copied in Tenochtitlan.

THE SOCIAL ORDER

As in medieval Europe, Aztec social structure was rigid; a man's status in life largely depended on his breeding, and chances of promotion were limited.

In this stratified warrior society costume and coiffure were the main badges of rank. Distinctions of this kind applied from early youth; boys wore a tuft of hair at the back of their head and this could only be removed when the young warrior had taken his first prisoner. To achieve this, he could call on a few comrades for help. After his initial triumph, he only gained credit for further captives if he took them unaided. Rank depended upon the taking of prisoners; those who were successful were named as leading youths, and their faces were stained with red ochre. After a fourth capture, a man became a 'seasoned warrior', a full member of the military élite.

The historical sources go out of their way to mention a few cases where commoners were raised to noble rank, and thereby imply that this was the exception rather than the rule. One even suspects that the capture of prisoners was so organized that most of the credit went to members of an officer class, manned mainly by nobles. Had this not been so, the commoners, since they were much more numerous, would logically have taken most of the captives; as a consequence, Tenochtitlan would have been full of young men of humbler origins wearing those insignia of rank that were the hallmark of nobility, an idea that ran counter to the whole spirit of a stratified society, whether in Tenochtitlan or elsewhere. Even if commoners distinguished themselves in battle, it is hard to see how they would have been allowed to don such finery except in rare instances, since the sources unite in saying that no one who was not a noble could wear a cotton garment, let alone an orange cape with a striped border, given as a reward for success in taking captives.

While the nobles were the chosen few, the commoners, who formed the bulk of the population, were known by the name of *macehualli*. Their life by comparison was frugal and their lot was to till the soil and to fight the ruler's battles. According to all accounts, the Aztecs of the migration were divided into clans, each called *calpulli*, meaning literally 'big house'; they are variously stated as having numbered from seven to twenty. The *calpulli* originally consisted of a number of related families, each of which farmed a strip of the land that it controlled. Because of this original pattern, involving blood relations, certain authors in the early twentieth century fell into the trap of supposing that Aztec Tenochtitlan was not a true state but a tribal society, regardless of all the Spanish reports of a social pyramid, at the top of which stood the monarchy, seconded by the nobility and priesthood, none of which can be fitted into this tribal mould.

A social order of a more democratic kind, mainly reliant on communal holdings, if it ever existed, belonged to the city's early days, when there were fewer people and the only land consisted of the *chinampa* plots, reclaimed from the lagoon. These were most productive, but by the time of the Conquest the situation had been transformed. The islands were tiny and the exploding population could only be fed by the use of more lands on the mainland; these were wrested from conquered cities but were then given, not to the *calpullis*, but to the state and to the nobles.

Fray Durán tells how this took place a century before the Conquest, when Azcapotzalco capitulated in 1428 and most of its land became the property of Aztec nobles. The friar tells in detail how Tlacaelel, the Snake Woman, himself received no less than ten lots, while other leading nobles were rewarded for their valour with two lots. On the other hand, each *calpulli* gained the paltry prize of a single lot, ostensibly granted for the upkeep of its temple. In the case of another conquered Tepanec city, Coyoacán, the procedure was different but the principle was the same: in this instance the Aztec ruler himself took a major share for his palace expenses; the commoners got none.

Thus, while the early Aztecs had traditionally belonged to tribes or clans, a fully-fledged state was born long before the Conquest, in which the nobles controlled a large proportion of the land. The *calpullis* never lost their collective plots and a Conquest-period map shows a small portion of the city divided by canals into *chinampa* smallholdings, each with its own dwelling.

However, the leading function of the *calpulli* as a smallholding unit had been overtaken by events, and by this time its main role was to act as an administrative sub-unit of the four quarters into which the city was divided; such sub-units were in turn split into groups of households. The *calpulli* kept its religious importance, and each had its own temple, as well as its own school. The latter establishment, known as *telpochcalli* ('house of the young'), unlike schools for the upper classes, trained the ordinary citizen for his pre-ordained role in the state. A basic grounding was given in history, religion and social behaviour, but practical skills were also taught, such as the making of adobe bricks. The principal aim, however, was to toughen the boys, to prepare them for the rigours of war, and teach them how to handle weapons. This emphasis on military training for the common people reflects the changed role of the *calpulli*, which now served as a recruiting agent for war. Moreover, the system had been modified in another respect; certain city wards were the preserve of guilds of artisans; it is not known if they also tilled the soil and provided recruits for the army.

A short description of land tenure is given by Alonso de Zurita, one of the few Spaniards to give even the briefest account of a matter so basic to status and wealth in any pre-industrial society. His remarks have convinced certain scholars that much of the land was held on a life tenure, given by the ruler as a reward for valour in the field.

Other evidence now shows that such favours were less often granted. Fresh light has been shed on the problem by studies of the social order in certain provincial centres in early Colonial times, based on data from legal documents of the period. Admittedly the situation in subject cities may not have been the same as in Tenochtitlan, about which we have less data. If anything, however, one would expect society to be even more stratified in the capital, where the nobles had been tightening their already powerful hold.

Such reports indicate that the average provincial centre had its own ruler, or *tlatoani*, subject only to the great *tlatoani* of Tenochtitlan. His principality was subdivided into fiefs, each controlled by a lord, known as *tecuhtli*, who had his official residence; they were appointed, like the *tlatoani*, for life.

But far from being a promoted commoner, as Zurita implied, the *tecuhtli* was a noble or *pilli*, chosen as their head from among his peers. Many of these *pillis* were his relations; they were the hereditary owners of most of the land in his fief and employed commoners to farm it. The rest of the land (apart from the lord's own estate) still belonged collectively to the *calpullis*, or wards, into which each place was divided, and was tilled by the commoners for their own benefit.

This basic system of communal holdings had thus, in varying degrees, been eroded by private ownership. Moreover, in some places the two systems, the collective and the private, tended to merge in favour of the latter. Records of certain provincial centres tell how lords also headed its traditional *calpullis*, whose members then became their dependants.

Accordingly, at least in nearby provinces of the Empire, a well-defined pecking order existed in the social hierarchy. At the top stood the local *tlatoani*, whose principality contained a number of fiefs, controlled by *tecuhtlis*, or lords. In these fiefs most of the land was owned by *pillis*, or nobles, but was tilled by the commoners, who, as members of the *calpulli* wards, also had the use of their collective plots within these wards.

At the base of the social pyramid slaves existed, but they were more personal servants than land workers and played a rather limited part in the economy. They could be bought in the specialized market of Azcapotzalco, where they would be paraded before the customers, dressed up for the occasion in borrowed finery; many had been acquired by the merchants in distant provinces. Citizens of Tenochtitlan could also be sold into slavery as a punishment for non-payment

Figure 34. Family of slaves with yokes
on their necks (after Sahagún)

of debts or for theft. Other slaves were people who had sold themselves of their own accord in return for shelter and food; their numbers included peasants whose crops had failed, but many are described as gamblers or drunkards, too lazy to till their own fields. Spanish accounts generally affirm that slaves were well treated by their owners. None the less, they were at times sacrificed, though this could only happen to those who had belonged to three owners, each of whom had been forced to sell them on account of misconduct.

In studying the Aztec social order, the ratio of nobles to commoners is a basic theme. In this respect also, provincial data are revealing. In Tlaxcala, for instance, seven per cent of the population in early Colonial times still belonged to the *pilli* class, while in nearby Huexotzingo the figure was fourteen per cent. While certain genealogical tables survive, no document gives the class ratio in the Aztec capital. Because the nobles alone could have several wives or concubines they are thought to have been highly prolific; however, since they were warriors, some of this surplus progeny would have met a premature end on the altars of rival cities; the taking of captives was a two-way affair.

Accounts from places outside the capital clarify another important point: while the nobles as a whole were set apart from the commoners and enjoyed many special favours, circumstances within this élite varied greatly. Some were very wealthy, and held a large share of the available land, while others were so modestly endowed that they were poorer than the richest commoners, who had enough land to be able to employ as many as twenty people.

It is likely that in Tenochtitlan also, while much of the lands on the mainland were held by a select number of nobles, there were others of their class whose holdings were too small to provide a living in keeping with their status. Since, however, such poorer gentlefolk also belonged to the hereditary élite, a place for them could have been found in the higher ranks of the civil administration and of the army. Many accounts tell of the booty given to outstanding warriors, for whom campaigns could therefore have been very profitable. The nobility clung hard to its privileges; Moctezuma at the outset of his reign made a point of bringing more nobles and their sons into his service, from which he dismissed men of baser origin, recruited by his predecessor, for whom merit counted more than breeding.

With certain marked differences, the social structure might be compared to that of medieval Europe: upward mobility was not unknown and a rich or valiant commoner might become a noble. But the number of poorer nobles equally suggests the presence of a downward mobility, seldom mentioned in the sources. This had its counterpart in medieval Europe, where the poorest knights might own nothing more than a small manor and one bony nag; they were soldiers of fortune, dependent on the higher nobility and on war booty.

But while medieval merchants and even peasants could obtain riches, the warrior nobles, as in Tenochtitlan, regarded themselves as a class apart. In both societies sumptuary laws were strict, and exact gradations of clothing and adornment were laid down for each rank.

TILLING THE SOIL

Farming techniques, whether used by noble or commoner, were primitive and had changed little in the course of hundreds if not thousands of years. The Aztecs, like their predecessors, lacked farm animals and therefore had no carts or ploughs. Instead of the Old World plough they used a digging stick, a long-handled tool ending in a blade, which served as spade and hoe. In many places this instrument could not penetrate the layer of weeds that covered the rich soil of the valleys and cultivation was then confined to the surrounding hillsides. To meet the needs of a massive build-up of population, food production was increased mainly by the use of irrigation. Rudimentary systems have been discovered that date from the early days of agriculture and by Aztec times there was much irrigated land in Mexico, since seasonal rainfall produced only a single annual crop of uncertain size, owing to the constant threat of drought, hail or frost at the moment when the maize was ripening.

Among the most sophisticated forms of artificially watered land was the *chinampa*, mentioned above as used in Tenochtitlan itself and in other places where the presence of a lagoon provided suitable conditions. By large-scale drainage and flood control, marginal swampy terrain was transformed into highly productive agricultural land. This *chinampa* system, involving a monumental exercise in hydraulics, was based on platforms, made out of layers of mud and aquatic plants, held in place by walls of basketwork to form small patches of land, such as can still be seen today in a few places. Trees were planted along the edge of these tiny islands to retain the soil, which is extraordinarily fertile. By the use of seedbeds a continuous series of crops in all stages of growth could be produced. Each of these *chinampa* plots was a narrow, rectangular strip of land; the smallest measured two by twenty metres, but the more usual size was 100 metres long by twenty metres wide. Recent studies have shown that in some places the *chinampas* could have been formed less laboriously, merely by digging a network of drainage ditches. Most of the lagoon was very shallow, and it is now known that its depth did not exceed one to two metres; therefore by this process of making deeper canals, artificial islands were automatically created and their water content reduced to a point where cultivation became possible.

Even where this intensive mode of food production was in use, maize was the main crop; next in importance, apart from chillis as seasoning, came squashes and beans. The latter helped to form nitrogen in the soil and gave added protein content to a diet that lacked dairy products and which, as far as the common people were concerned, contained little meat. Chia, used to make a kind of porridge, was another major crop. Maguey, grown on dry non-irrigated soil, was an important all-purpose plant; its spikes served as needles, while its fibre formed the basic raw material for the cloth worn by commoners, to whom cotton garments were forbidden. In addition, the juice from the heart of the plant was drawn off, stored in skins or calabashes, and fermented to make the only alcoholic beverage, pulque, which is still drunk in Mexico today. In pre-Columbian times it was a sacred potion, serving mainly for ritual intoxication; only among men and women over fifty years of age was a more indiscriminate imbibing of pulque tolerated.

TRADE AND INDUSTRY

Despite the existence of slaves, and the marked distinction between noble and commoner, it would be wrong to view Aztec society as a confrontation of two sharply defined and mutually antagonistic classes. For in addition to these, two intermediate groups, the merchants and artisans, were most important. Elaborate insignia, as already stressed, were indispensable both for religious rites and for war. The artisans who made such finery therefore played a key role in pre-Columbian society; in Tenochtitlan certain of their guilds were assigned special wards of the city. Among the most skilled of all were the feather-workers; using as their raw material the huge amounts of plumes sent to the capital as tribute, they confected the headdresses and shields used by warriors of rank; the making of feather mosaic involved complex techniques invented long before the Aztecs. Of comparable importance were the goldsmiths and the lapidaries, who worked a wide variety of imported stones. To other guilds belonged the carvers of monumental sculpture, the tailors, potters, woodcarvers and obsidian-workers. Equally, the writing or painting of manuscripts was a highly specialized trade, integral to the political and religious system. Fray Sahagún's informants offer detailed descriptions, accompanied by drawings, of how these specialists set about their tasks; on their skills, from Olmec times onwards, depended the production of those status symbols that were integral to the social fabric. In Teotihuacan, with its great export trade of luxury goods, the artisans were already numerous and in Tenochtitlan were probably in the majority.

Many of those who practised such crafts in Tenochtitlan belonged to families who had migrated from elsewhere; metal-working skills had probably been brought to the city from the Mixteca (Teotihuacan had also possessed its Oaxaca colony), while the numerous featherworkers were also known as 'Amantecas' and inhabited a city ward called Amantla; Sahagún mentions the name Amantla in connection with Tula, and the Amantecas have antecedents that go back to Teotihuacan.

Last but by no means least, the *pochtecas*, or merchants, need to be considered. As a class they were farther removed from the common people than were the artisans. A select few were even allowed to own land and their sons were educated at the schools for the élite. But the merchants' status was rather ambiguous, and their way of life presented a peculiar blend of lavish display and feigned humility. To conceal their wealth, they often preferred to avoid any triumphant homecoming after a successful expedition; instead they would sneak back to the house of a friend and unload their goods at night, pretending that they did not own them.

Figure 35. Travelling merchant and his porters
(after Sahagún)

In stark contrast with such assumed modesty on arrival, merchants would later celebrate their return by huge banquets to honour the ruler and his nobles. At these Sardanapalian feasts as many as 100 turkeys and 40 dogs might be consumed. The feast went on for several days, culminating in the sacrifice of slaves, richly dressed and fêted for the occasion.

The Aztec merchants were centred upon Tlatelolco; they had two principal chiefs and were divided, like the warriors, into well-defined categories or ranks; among their privileges was the right to be judged in their own courts. They have no precise equivalent in the Old World, where distinctions between warrior and trader were sharper. The *pochtecas* combined both functions, and at least in Aztec times were renowned as much for their military skill as for their commercial acumen. During the short lifespan of the Empire they were often used as an advance reconnaissance force, or even as a secret service; travelling at night, they would enter 'enemy' lands, whose language they had learned and whose dress they adopted as a disguise; if discovered, they were apt to be killed. Many wars of conquest were launched on the pretext of attacks against these pioneering traders. Not content with this role of imperial scouts in hostile territory, they at times fought their own campaigns and even took prisoners. In one expedition to the Pacific Coast a body of merchants was besieged for four years, and was eventually rescued by the future Moctezuma II, sent to their aid by his predecessor, Ahuitzotl.

But though they operated under the aegis of the state, they were far from acting solely as an advance guard of the army and their role as genuine traders was basic to the economy. The great numbers of artisans depended for their employment on a wide range of raw materials, many of which could only be obtained from the tropical lowlands. Not only did the ordinary needs of an expanding population have to be considered; the sumptuary requirements of the state were huge, and included not only regalia for war and religious ceremonies, but the massive gifts bestowed by the Emperor both on his own entourage and on outside visitors invited to the great feasts, who were deluged with finery.

Commerce was vital to a community whose import requirements were so great, even though part of these were met by tribute payments, not only by distant provinces, but also by the people of Tenochtitlan and neighbouring cities; only nobles and slaves were exempt. The respective roles of trade and tribute in securing supplies from other regions is far from clear. Weighty foodstuffs such as maize, beans and wood are listed in the *Codex Mendoza* tribute-lists as levied only on nearby regions. Among other bulk items was an annual total of 33,680 bunches of feathers from the low-lying provinces, while the colossal figure of 123,400 cotton mantles was brought from near and far. Such quantities could hardly have been used up in a city whose people were mostly forbidden to wear cotton. But Sahagún explains how the Emperor Ahuitzotl recycled some of this tribute; he would present the merchants with supplies of cotton mantles received by his inland revenue; these they would then trade in far-off places for other goods such as greenstones, of which the ruler was in short supply. In addition, the merchants sold their own wares in these places and thus earned a good profit both for their master and for themselves.

Tribute-lists include many kinds of mantles: 'white twisted mantles', 'rich red and white mantles, bordered in red, blue and yellow', and many others described as 'rich', 'large', or 'of the kind worn by lords'. However, the more standard types, together with cacao beans, little copper axes and quills filled with powdered gold, served at times as a kind of currency to facilitate the process of barter; probably the mantles were more widely used for this purpose than the gold quills, absent from the lists, or the copper axes, of which only 560 in all were sent as tribute.

The small amount of food levied is not surprising, since Tenochtitlan was surrounded by fertile land where such crops could be grown. It is calculated that the total amount of grain paid as tribute would have fed only about 50,000 people and quite a small area produced the basic necessities of a population that had risen from about 150,000 before the Aztecs to over a million, a total never again exceeded until the twentieth century. To import more food as tribute would in effect have amounted to importing unemployment; in contrast, to bring in raw materials for artisans was to create work. Payments in finished goods, such as turquoise masks and jade necklaces, were not great; certain exotic items such as two live eagles also figure in the total.

Certain accounts of favours granted to merchants by the last two emperors before the Conquest might suggest that they were on their way to rivalling the nobles as a power in the state. Admittedly the huge amounts of tribute, far from removing the need for merchants, added to their importance, because of the need for recycling what was surplus to requirements. Moreover, the larger the Empire grew, the greater the need for these well-travelled citizens, with their expert knowledge of foreign peoples. None the less, most of the evidence shows that at this time the nobles were still in firm control and well able to defend their status; Moctezuma II even went out of his way to reinforce their position. A prosperous merchant class, far from being a new factor, was assuredly present in Teotihuacan.

The Aztecs were therefore no more 'a nation of shopkeepers' than the British in their heyday, though so described by Napoleon. Tenochtitlan was a growing industrial centre, backed by an enterprising class of traders, and dependent on imported materials that were converted by a skilled force, the artisans, into sophisticated products; many of these were consumed at home, while others were exported mainly as gifts, or expended in war. The greatest city of the New World was an expanding society in which, if privilege was closely guarded, wealth was more widely shared.

9

THE GODS AND THEIR SERVANTS

THE PANTHEON

From the day they set foot in Mexico, the Spaniards were struck by the fanaticism of the people. Cortés, writing to the Emperor Charles V some time before he reached Tenochtitlan, described their fervour: 'If these people were to be introduced to and instructed in our very holy Catholic faith, and were to exchange the devotion, faith and hope they have in their idols for that in the divine power of God, it is certain that if they were to serve God with such faith, fervour and diligence, they would accomplish many miracles.'

Cortés hopes were to be in part fulfilled; after their own idols had been smashed the Mexicans came in their own way to adore the Christian God with equal piety. But while the friars taught the Indians only the simpler tenets of the gospel, their former religion was far from simple, and the problems it poses to the modern scholar are complex in the extreme. Documentary data on the subject are copious but conflicting. Foremost among these is the lengthy account of the gods and their ceremonies in Book II of Sahagún's *History*; some at least of his information came from people who had themselves worshipped at their altars.

But notwithstanding Sahagún's description, important gaps in our knowledge remain. He and others recount in the minutest detail the gods' adornments and the pageantry of their rites, but their comments on the beliefs that inspired such rites are brief. In this respect the Spanish legacy is like a great album of coloured prints, in which the outward trappings are vividly displayed, while the underlying principles are ill-defined. As a result, we know much about Aztec ceremonies, but less about what went on in the minds of those who attended them.

The gods were portrayed in codices and stone carvings in human and sometimes in animal form. The paintings of each god show certain diagnostic insignia such as a headdress of a special shape or an adornment of a certain kind of shell. The overall combination of such insignia was usually peculiar to one god, though individual elements are at times shared. But while most gods can therefore be recognized, to define the respective roles and relationships of this great concourse of deities is a baffling task. Unlike most of the gods of, say, Egypt or Sumer, they tend to fulfil several distinct functions and thereby defy any attempt to be pigeonholed as occupants of a single well-defined niche in the pantheon. In addition, any given human activity, such as the making and imbibing of pulque, far from being the exclusive preserve of one god, is patronized by a host of deities, whose over-lapping roles are hard to clarify.

Another facet of pre-Columbian religion puzzles the Western mind: the principle of dualism. For people trained to think in terms of modern logic, dualism amounts to sheer paradox, not unlike the notion of a tropical Eskimo or an arctic avocado. But for the Mexicans certain gods and certain themes recur in pairs, as if two opposing elements were needed to express a single idea. Descriptions of the gods and heroes are confused by this anomaly; for instance, the Plumed Serpent is both the double and the enemy of the Smoking Mirror, who occasionally wears the typical emblem of the Plumed Serpent as God of Wind, the duckbill mask. The Flayed God is to be identified with the Smoking Mirror, since he is also called the Red Tezcatlipoca; but at times he is shown with adornments more typical of the Plumed Serpent. A god is thus apt to pose as both the image and the adversary of his colleagues, in a pantheon in which a certain antithesis between Plumed Serpent and Smoking Mirror is a constant element; both are at times described as creator gods.

Henry Nicholson, a leading student of Mexican religion, sees this legion of deities as grouped around definable themes, even if the distinctions between them are hard to draw. He thereby helps to clarify this confused picture by dividing the many gods into com-plexes, each devoted to a single concept or activity, such as death and the underworld, or the growing of maize. However, he is the first to admit that such categories are perforce arbitrary, and for death and the underworld alone he identifies no less than ten gods and five goddesses. In all he lists 126 gods, divided into fourteen such complexes.

As among many peoples of the Old World, a distinction has to be made between esoteric mysteries, revealed only to the priestly hierarchy, and the simpler faith of the masses; clearly the leaders of this hierarchy could have better defined the roles of Nicholson's 126 gods than we can ever hope to do ourselves. Fundamental to the popular religion was the creation myth, learned as an oral saga in the schools. The primordial creator gods were called Two Lord and Two Lady, whose very names stress the principle of dualism. Other functions of this pair are obscure and they came to count for much less than their four sons, to whom they had entrusted the creation of all the other gods, of the world and of mankind. Each of these four gods was a manifestation of the all-powerful Tezcatlipoca, the Smoking Mirror. The first was the Red Tezcatlipoca, also known as the Flayed God, Xipe Totec: the second was the Blue Tezcatlipoca, the Aztec tribal god Huitzilopochtli: the third was the White Tezcatlipoca, the equivalent of the Plumed Serpent, Quetzalcoatl; these three gods were associated with the east, the south and the west respectively; the fourth, identified with the north, was simply known as the Black Tezcatlipoca, the Lord of the Night Sky. Before the earth even existed, to this quartet was added Tlaloc, the Rain God, and his spouse, the Water Goddess Chalchiuhtlicue.

The sequel to the birth of the major gods forms the central legend of Aztec cosmogony: the successive creation of five worlds, or suns, each named after the cataclysm that destroyed it. Different versions exist of the birth of these five worlds; in the most recurrent of these, when the first creation took place Tezcatlipoca became the sun, and the earth was inhabited by giants who lived on acorns; this age, known as the Jaguar Sun, ended when the giants were consumed by a horde of jaguars. Quetzalcoatl then took Tezcatlipoca's place in the heavens and the second age was called the Wind Sun (Quetzalcoatl was God of Wind); it was destroyed by hurricanes, after which all humans were transformed into monkeys. The Third Sun was named after the element of fire, presided over by the Rain God, Tlaloc, and it was consumed by a fiery rain; the Fourth Sun, known as the Water Sun, was identified with Chalchiuhtlicue, Goddess of Water, and it was appropriately engulfed by a flood, after which the people turned into fish.

The creation of the Fifth World, already described in Chapter 5, took place in Teotihuacan. Tonatiuh, himself the Sun God, was its sun and it was called the World of Motion, after the Nahuatl word for motion, *Ollin*, since it was to end on the day 4 *ollin*, when the world would be destroyed by earthquakes. Tonatiuh is the central figure in the famous Stone of the Sun; traditionally known as the Calendar

Stone, it today occupies a central position in the National Museum of Anthropology and has become a national symbol. It was dug up in 1790 in the main plaza of Mexico City, and was simply leaned against the west tower of the cathedral until 1885, when it was transferred to the National Museum, then situated in Calle Moneda.

Figure 36. Quetzalcoatl as God of Wind
(*Codex Magliabecchi*)

This stone is not a calendar in the true sense, though it displays the basic symbols of the Aztec cosmos. In the middle is the face of the Sun God, who is closely linked to the Aztecs' own Humming Bird God. On either side of the god's face are claws clutching human hearts, required to nourish the sun.

Surrounding the face and hands are four square panels, carved with reliefs representing the four previous worlds, named after jaguar, wind, sun and water. These are in turn surrounded by glyphs of the twenty day-signs of the sacred calendar, to be described below. The whole configuration of the central part of the stone, grouped around the Sun God's face, forms the fateful sign 4 Motion, the day on which the last of the five worlds would end.

The design of the stone, which portrays as its central motif not the sun's birth but its death, gives expression to the sense of foreboding that permeates Aztec religion. The Fifth Sun itself, which gave light and life to their world, was a fragile and fleeting concession by the gods, which they were at all times ready to destroy if not amply fed with sacrificial victims. Through travail by the gods had the world been created; through sacrifice by man it would be kept in being for a while.

The Calendar Stone has another important feature: it portrays in symbolic form the leading members of the pantheon: Smoking Mirror as creator, together with the Plumed Serpent and the Rain God, Tlaloc; the Aztecs' own patron, the Humming Bird, is represented by the Sun God, Tonatiuh. Absent only is Xipe, the Flayed God. Though intimately linked with special forms of human sacrifice, Xipe's ambivalent nature illustrates how hard it is to pinpoint the functions of Mexican gods; in effect he has few, apart from a rather limited role as patron of goldsmiths; since flaying implies not only the shedding of one skin but the growing of another, he is by implication linked to the vegetation cycle and to fertility. The human skin was a symbol of regeneration and when worn by a priest dried skin was likened to a husk enclosing a living seed.

In addition to their ill-defined functions, many gods were identified with specific regions. Xipe was also patron deity of the Yopis, a wild people living on a stretch of the Pacific Coast, south-east of Acapulco; they were never conquered by the Aztecs. The Plumed Serpent was the patron god of Tula; in this, as in certain other instances, the chief deity of a place bore the same name as its deified hero, often held to be the original founder of the tribe. The Smoking Mirror is less directly connected with a particular city or people, but was universally revered in Aztec times as the Great Lord of Everywhere (Tloque Nahuaque). If any single god ranked as head of their pantheon, it was the Lord of Everywhere rather than their own patron, the Humming Bird God. The Smoking Mirror was the all-seeing, the all-powerful, before whom all creatures were helpless. He was the capricious sorcerer, associated with darkness and with night, and also with the jaguar; no deity better represented the dark and pessimistic side of Aztec religion. An attitude of craven submission to the whims of the Smoking Mirror is a recurrent theme in Sahagún's series of prayers to the gods.

While deities representing the four aspects of the Smoking Mirror, together with the Rain God, stood at the summit of the pantheon, certain others were also important. These include a whole cluster, all of which embody the notion of Mother Goddess. Nicholson lists no less than twenty-one deities as forming part of this Earth-Mother Goddess complex; prominent among them is Coatlicue, Serpent Skirt, who was by tradition the mother of the moon, the stars, and also of the tribal Humming Bird God. In her huge image in the National Museum she wears her skirt of serpents, supported by a belt in the form of a snake; as mother of the gods, her breast is bare; her hands and feet end in claws, for she feeds on corpses; her necklace is made of alternating human hearts and hands; the head has been severed and from the neck flow streams of blood, symbolized by serpents. True to the more macabre side of Mexican religion, the Mother Goddess is thus portrayed not merely as unloving but sinister. She in some ways recalls her Hindu counterpart, Kali, who also fed on corpses and who, even today, is often represented with a necklace of human heads.

Another leading member of the same complex is called Tlazolteotl. The name means 'Filth Deity', since in addition to being Goddess of Love she is Goddess of Excrement. To her each man had to make, once only, a confession of his sins towards the end of his life, an act that could be compared with the verbal pouring out of filth, or excrement. Inseparable from the Earth-Mother was a formidable cohort of gods and goddesses who represented another aspect of the fertility theme. Because of the unique sanctity of maize, some of these bear names directly connected with the plant, including both a god of the green corn and a god of the ripe ears. One of the leading maize gods, Centeotl, meaning 'Maize Cob Lord', also presided over flowers, feasting, dancing and gaming, activities linked with the sun, and hence also with fertility.

A god whom no Mexican could afford to neglect presided over the nether world. His name, Mictlantecuhtli, means 'Lord of the Land of the Dead', a sunless region that lay in the north. Linked to the related themes of war and sacrifice, the cult of the dead is uppermost, and skulls are ubiquitous in Aztec and Toltec art. It still survives in altered form, and the sugar-candy skulls sold all over Mexico on the Day of the Dead recall the many illustrations in codices related to this theme.

A curious feature of the pantheon was a multitude of gods of the intoxicating pulque. They were known as the Four Hundred Rabbits, because this animal was supposed to have discovered the sacred drink, when he nibbled at the agave plant from whose juice it is made.

Figure 37. The goddess Tlazolteotl
(*Codex Borbonicus*)

Basic to Mexican religion were the two calendars, and in more general terms the related cult of numbers. Certain of these, such as four and seven, were held to be sacred and virtually ranked as little gods. Some deities have names that are simply numerical dates, such as 2 Rabbit, 7 Serpent, 5 Flower and 7 Flower; Nicholson also lists certain key dates, such as 4 Motion and 1 Reed, as being gods in their own right.

The annual calendar was divided into eighteen months of twenty days, to which were added five supplementary days to make up a total of 365. These extra days were regarded as most ill-omened, unpropitious for any major undertaking. Also of great significance was a second calendar, the sacred or ritual round of 260 days, divided into twenty 'weeks' of thirteen days. Illustrations of its series of 'weeks' figure prominently in a number of codices, mainly in the form of pictures of the one or two deities who presided over each of these twenty periods of thirteen days. Every day was illustrated by a sign and also had its own god or goddess; the names of these signs were as follows:

Alligator	Monkey
Wind	Grass
House	Reed
Lizard	Ocelot
Serpent	Eagle
Death	Vulture
Deer	Motion
Rabbit	Flint
Water	Rain
Dog	Flower

Each of the thirteen-day 'weeks' of the sacred 260-day calendar began with number 1, followed by one of the twenty day-signs, and ended with the number 13, coupled with another sign. Hence the first 'week' of the cycle began with 1 Alligator, since Alligator was the first day-sign; the sequence continued with 2 Wind, 3 House etc., ending in 13 Reed, Reed being the thirteenth sign. The second week then began with 1 Ocelot and ended with 13 Death; it was thus formed by

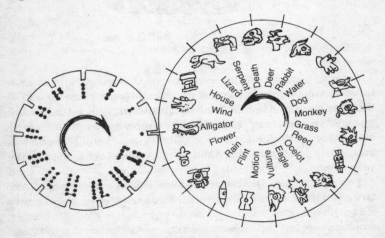

Figure 38. Diagrammatic representation of the 260-day sacred calendar. The twenty named days intermesh with the numbers 1 to 13

the last seven day-signs, to which were added the first six, repeated over a second time. Eventually after 260 days, none of which bore an identical combination of numeral and day-sign, the process was completed with 13 Flower and on the following day the cycle began once more with 1 Alligator.

This sacred almanac was all-important for purposes of divination, and a man's destiny was governed by the date of his birth. The full name of each child included the day when he was born; according to whether this was a lucky or unlucky day, his own fate would be decided. For instance, 7 Rain and 8 Flower were both propitious, but infants born on those days were quickly bathed and named, lest any part of the ceremony should fall on the next day, 9 Alligator; anyone born with that sign would be dedicated to evil; he would be a slanderer and so debase himself that he would dress in rags and tatters. Sometimes such a disastrous fate could be averted if the priest would agree to postpone the naming ceremony to a more auspicious day.

While the days were named in accordance with the 260-day almanac, the calendar of 365 days was used to count the years. Year-names bore numbers running from 1 to 13, used in combination with one of only four of the twenty day-signs: House, Rabbit, Reed and Flint. To complete every possible combination of thirteen numbers and four names took fifty-two years (13 × 4), after which the sequence began again. The use of this system of fifty-two-year cycles, known as bundles, sets many problems for the historian; with the exception of the last cycles before the Conquest, it is not always easy to tell to which fifty-two-year period a given event, simply described as happening in, say, 3 Flint or 4 House, belongs.

The fifty-two-year calendar cycle was often depicted as a bundle of fifty-two wooden sticks, and the cycle itself was often referred to as the 'year bundle'. The bundle always began with 2 Reed. In the last hours of the preceding year, 1 Rabbit, all fires were put out; household statues of the gods were cast into the water and crockery was broken. People dreaded the lighting of the New Fire, kindled as the year 2 Reed dawned; if it failed to burn the sun would be dimmed and the world would perish. Women and small children became virtually taboo: they were kept indoors and made to wear masks of agave leaves. It was believed that if the fire was not drawn, the women would become wild beasts and eat men, while the children would be turned into mice. Such a ceremony inevitably required its offering. When the crucial moment came and the New Fire was drawn on the Hill of the Star, the priests, dressed as the most important gods, operated the fire drill on the breast of a well-born captive. When the flame appeared, the captive's breast was quickly slashed open, and his heart cast into the fire. The priests then rushed forth; the first rekindled the flames in the main temples, after which it was used to relight the fires in peoples' homes.

Though the year cycle had ancient roots, nowhere was it observed with more pomp and pageantry than in Tenochtitlan; among the most important religious ceremonies were the eighteen feasts to mark the passing of each of its twenty-day months. Celebrations involved the chanting of sacred songs, accompanied by music in which drums and shell trumpets predominated, together with dancing and endless processions, in which many priests took part, dressed as gods.

Such rites almost always ended in some form of human sacrifice. The victims, mostly war captives but sometimes slaves, were first purified by ritual bathing. They were then arrayed in the gaudy insignia of the god for whom they were to die. Alternatively, their bodies would be painted in vertical red and white stripes and their faces whitened with chalk. The standard method of killing was to gash open the chest with an obsidian knife and rip out the heart, which was cast into the 'eagle vessel' of stone or wood. Other methods included decapitation (especially for female victims), shooting with arrows, hurling from a height, and drowning, to honour the Rain God. Certain captives were almost burned to death before being hauled out of the flames and then dispatched by the conventional method of cutting out the heart. The victims' heads were impaled on the skull-rack; frequently, but not invariably, the body was carried off and certain parts stewed and eaten at a ritual feast.

Figure 39. War captive adorned for sacrifice
(*Codex Telleriano-Remensis*)

One of the strangest sacrificial ceremonies marked the second of the eighteen months, the feast of the Flayed God. A prisoner, tied to a special stone and armed with a wooden club covered with feathers, was pitted against a series of knights dressed as eagles and jaguars; they also bore wooden clubs but theirs were fitted with blades of hard obsidian. After the unequal struggle had ended, the priests flayed the victim and wore his skin for the next twenty days.

No exercise is more baffling to the contemporary mind than to comprehend even remotely the Mexican approach to human sacrifice. From the time of the first contacts between Mexicans and Spaniards, the horror and disgust inspired by such offerings convinced the Conquerors that the native gods were demons, and that they were duty-bound to obliterate every trace of their worship. For the Mexicans, however, sacrifice was devoid of any notion of cruelty or hatred. The victim was no longer a foe, to be killed in an act of vengeance, as among certain Old World peoples. On the contrary, his death was a homage to the god, whose insignia he often wore, and of whom, at the moment of death, he became the living incarnation. More than anything, sacrifice was the Mexican response to life in a world that faced a constant threat of destruction and could only be kept in being, even momentarily, by the shedding of human blood.

People are too apt to think of human offering as peculiar to the Aztecs, like, say, bullfighting to the Spaniards or even cricket to the British. But not only is there ample evidence of sacrifice as an established rite in Mexico millennia before the Aztecs, in Olmec times and even before. In addition, almost all civilized peoples of the Old World, not excluding the Greeks and Romans, offered men to their gods at some stage in their history and in many lands the practice continued into modern times. By a kind of inflationary process, on the assumption that the killing of a hundred men had more effect than the death of a single victim, the Aztecs increased the tempo of mass sacrifice, though we shall never know how many were really slain, since accounts differ as to the exact number. Even in the practice of mass killing they were not alone; for instance, European travellers in the eighteenth and nineteenth centuries described in detail the mass offerings of the King of Dahomey in West Africa; the annual toll of victims in his capital, Abomey, as a ratio of the whole population, is to be compared with the numbers cited for Tenochtitlan.

In general terms, the religion of the Aztecs was an elaborate defence mechanism, born not of hope but of anxiety. Every aspect, and in particular human offering, implies a struggle to ward off disaster,

whether immediate catastrophes such as crop failure or the ultimate
doom of the Fifth, and last, Sun. While it served to placate such fears,
this faith offered few comforts and no security; favours in the afterlife,
such as they were, were not a reward for good behaviour in this world
but merely chance blessings granted to certain groups of people after
the manner of their death: in particular, to warriors sacrificed, women
who died in childbirth and protégés of the Rain God, such as those
who died by drowning.

Figure 40. Human heart offered
to the sun (after Sahagún)

Jacques Soustelle, in his classic description of their daily life, has
written of the 'imperial religion' of the Aztecs. However, little effort
was made to proselytize other peoples, who in any case worshipped
many of the same gods. War was indeed indispensable, as a means of
obtaining both prisoners for sacrifice and tribute for the gods' ceremonies. But the central theme of these rituals was not the winning of
more battles but the safeguarding of the crop cycle, and no less than
seven of the eighteen monthly feasts are concerned with Tlaloc himself or with fertility and maize deities, and surely therefore have
ancient roots.

One crucial question remains: what, if anything, can the volumi-

nous data on Aztec gods, their rites and their trappings, tell us of the
religions of Tula, Teotihuacan, and even of the Olmecs? Toltec art
forms, as we have seen, are also those of a warrior state; certain Aztec
gods, in particular Tlaloc and Quetzalcoatl, are found in Tula, though
the evidence is too scanty to tell us how many other gods of Conquest
times were present in that city. To identify the leading Aztec gods in
Teotihuacan is even harder. Certain familiar figures, such as the old
Fire God, can be recognized; Tlaloc in Teotihuacan reigns supreme,
but as we have also seen, he was probably more patron deity and
creator than mere Rain God, a function to which he was later relegated. In Teotihuacan the Flayed God is also represented, together
with others, such as the Quetzal Butterfly, unknown to the Aztec
pantheon. Moreover, the sacred calendar was almost certainly
already used.

Even though our knowledge is incomplete, it can thus be seen that
a certain thread of continuity linked the gods of one culture to those of
the next. If the Olmec jaguar changed his functions, he retains a close
link with the foremost deity, Tlaloc, of Teotihuacan and with the
Smoking Mirror of Tenochtitlan; even the Plumed Serpent of Tula
wears jaguar emblems. And though it is not always certain which
Aztec gods were already present in earlier cultures, the outward signs
of their religion were an ancient legacy: ceremonial centres with
pyramids surmounted by one or two shrines; rituals performed by
priests dressed as gods; the ball-game; human sacrifice; the use of a
sacred calendar and of codices, many of which were related to this
calendar.

ARTS AND CRAFTS

The work of the Aztec artist was dedicated to the gods' service. But
while history, social structure and daily life have been described by
modern scholars, fewer tributes have been paid to their creative
talents. To compare them once more with the Romans, they are often
lauded more for military prowess than for intellectual attainment.
Admittedly certain Aztec art forms, like those of the Romans, display
a grandiose rigidity, suggestive of a race of conquerors. None the less,
the Tenochtitlan sculpture in the National Museum is the most striking collection of pre-Hispanic art taken from any single place.
Moreover, Aztec civilization was far from reaching its prime when
destroyed by the Spaniards. While the Olmec and Teotihuacan

cultures took centuries to mature, the Aztec world was obliterated only eighty-nine years after Tenochtitlan shook off the Tepanec tutelage. It grew even faster than its immediate, but short-lived, predecessor, Tula. In literature also the contribution is impressive, though in this field comparisons are hard to draw, since the work of earlier peoples has perished.

The supreme expression of Aztec art was their huge stone statues. Fortunately many great idols were buried after the Conquest without being smashed and have been gradually unearthed. Countless others were destroyed and Cortés himself led the iconoclasts; on one occasion, in a fit of rage, he took a crowbar and hit an important statue of the Humming Bird God between the eyes, knocking off its golden mask (needless to say, no such masks have survived). The architecture itself, of which these carvings formed part, is harder to assess, since the great temples were razed to the ground, unlike those of, say, Teotihuacan or the Classic Maya, which escaped a similar fate since they were little more than grass mounds when the Spaniards came. The small number of provincial centres from Aztec times visible today convey only a limited idea of the splendours of the capital.

The Aztec pyramids follow the general Mexican pattern of a series of sloping tiers, but with one difference: the last part of a typical structure, before reaching the platform at the top, is built at a steeper angle and rises almost vertically. Another special feature is the double stairway leading to two twin shrines at the summit. Typical of Aztec and late pre-Aztec temples is Tenayuca in the north-west suburbs of Mexico City. It closely resembles that of Tlatelolco, though it is better preserved and much of the traditional Wall of Serpents that surrounds its base survives. In Tenayuca, as in nearly all pyramids of the period, the series of reconstructions, in which the existing building was simply covered by a new and larger one, can be clearly seen.

The best surviving example of an Aztec ceremonial centre, though far from rivalling Tenochtitlan, is the site of Zempoala, forty kilometres north of Veracruz. Built in a tropical and therefore untypical setting, it has the characteristic pyramids with double stairway as part of a complex of buildings, grouped around the main plaza. Bernal Díaz records that he thanked God for having brought him to such a place. Its lush vegetation and teeming population excited his wonder; he adds that their living quarters, situated in a patio lying off the main plaza, had been recently whitewashed so that they gleamed like burnished silver. Zempoala has many historical ties; not only was it the first major centre visited by Cortés, where he spent some time as

the guest of the ruler known as the Fat Chief. He was much impressed, but this did not deter him from smashing the Zempoalan idols,
described by him as horrible dragons. The city was the scene of the
battle between the forces of Cortés and those of Pánfilo Narváez, sent
to capture him. The latter set up his headquarters on the main temple;
after an artillery duel Cortés' men fought their way up the pyramid,
which they could not capture until one very tall man reached the top
and set fire to the thatched roof of one of its shrines.

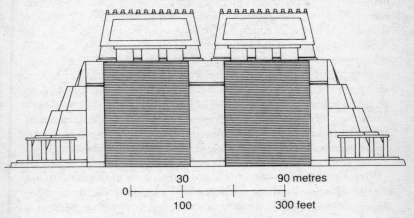

Figure 41. Reconstruction of Tenayuca Pyramid

Double Aztec temples can be seen at Teopanzolco, situated within
the modern town of Cuernavaca, and at Calixtlahuaca, near Toluca,
where a typical round building dedicated to Quetzalcoatl as God of
Wind also survives; a fine statue of the god, wearing his duckbill
mask, was dug up in front of the pyramid. A smaller, but perhaps
more dramatic example of Aztec architecture is to be found at Malinalco, set in a beautiful valley south-west of Mexico City and connected
by road to Chalma, still an important place of pilgrimage. In this site a
group of temples, some not yet finished at the time of the Conquest,
are cut into the natural rock of a terraced slope. The principal building
is a circular shrine, entered by a doorway formed by serpent heads in
profile with wide-open jaws, similar to a monument seen by the
Conquerors in Tenochtitlan. Inside the temple is a stone bench carved
with fine representations of eagle and ocelot skins; these suggest that
the structure may have been connected with the Eagle and Ocelot
orders of knights.

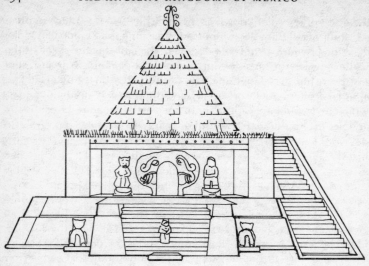

Figure 42. Reconstruction of principal temple at Malinalco

While the rich collection of stone carvings, both in relief and in the round, represents a mere fraction of the original total, their abundance contrasts with a paucity of examples from earlier periods – outside the Maya region – and any large collection of Mexican antiquities almost invariably includes some Aztec stone idols. The artistic traditions which the Aztecs inherited were basically religious and most carvings are dedicated to the gods, and adorned their temples; sculptors, however, also produced seemingly profane works in the form of vigorous and realistic images of animals and plants. Many of these, revealing a more human side of Aztec art, still exist, such as coyote dogs, birds, grasshoppers, frogs, turtles, toads, rabbits, monkeys, fish and gourds together with numerous representations of Quetzalcoatl in the form of a coiled rattlesnake, frequent in Aztec times but unknown before; the finest of these is the coiled snake that has been recovered from the Great Temple. It is outstanding for the perfect preservation of its colouring; apart from its aesthetic qualities, it tells much of techniques used in painting stone.

The precise function of these animal and plant figures in the round is not clear but it is probable that they too served a religious purpose; some, such as the coiled serpents, are known to have represented a god and are to be ranked as idols; the remainder are also more likely to have been placed in shrines or buried as offerings than to have adorned peoples' homes.

All these works, from the heaviest to the most delicate, were made with stone tools. The most widely used raw material was basalt, taken from quarries on the southern shore of the lagoon, blocks of which were hauled to the city by gangs of men using ropes, poles and wooden rollers.

Since art historians have written sparingly on Aztec sculpture, its development is poorly charted. While we are ignorant of its early history, the style had almost certainly reached maturity by the mid-fifteenth century. It drew inspiration from the Toltec tradition, though while certain Toltec forms, including the standard bearers and chacmools, were retained, others, such as the serpent columns and the giant atlantes, were discarded. The Toltec influence can be easily seen, for instance, in a relief known as the Stone of the Warriors in the National Museum, illustrating a series of Toltec-type soldiers. The Aztecs also fashioned stone masks, a tradition that stems from the Olmecs and from Teotihuacan; Toltec masks are rarer.

Characteristic of Aztec sculpture is the tendency to standardize the emblems employed; this has greatly helped modern scholars to determine meaning and function. Most of the carvings of the major gods of the pantheon can be recognized, since each wears his diagnostic symbols, which also appear in codices. In a sense these carvings, like the codices, were meant to convey meanings or ideas; as in Classic murals, their symbolic content was rich. In statues that depict gods, or men dressed as gods, their emblems such as wristbands, armbands or anklets are carved with meticulous attention to detail. Such figures represent a concept as much as a person, and ceremonial costume rather than the human form is the centre of interest, a tradition dating from Teotihuacan times. Certain nude stone figurines also exist, but they rarely show accurate anatomical detail, as portrayed, for instance, by the Olmecs. It is almost certain that such figures, like mannequins, or like Christian saints in Mexico today, were dressed up on occasion in masks, capes, skirts, jewellery and other items of ritual attire.

Two of the greatest surviving stone monuments, the statue of Coatlicue, the Mother Goddess, and the Stone of the Sun, have already been mentioned. A third, also worthy of note, is the Stone of Tizoc; on the upper surface of this huge cylindrical block is a relief of the Sun God, recalling that of the Stone of the Sun. The sides of the drum-shaped carving bear reliefs representing the victories of Tizoc

(1481–6). The Emperor is shown in a series of scenes dressed as a god, holding by the hair the captive rulers of fifteen conquered cities, whose names are given in the accompanying glyphs. The first description of Tizoc's stone was given by the English traveller William Bullock, who saw it as early as 1822 when it was still partly buried in the main plaza, about 100 metres from where the Stone of the Sun, discovered thirty years before, stood against the cathedral wall. When Bullock first viewed the monument, only the upper surface, carved with sun symbols, could be seen. At his request the earth covering the cylinder was removed, and he took casts of the fifteen scenes; this work lasted several days, during which the populace crowded round to watch his seemingly strange antics; several asked whether the English, regarded as heathen, still worshipped Aztec gods.

Sculptors at times departed from the tradition of realism, and fashioned objects that are purely symbolic. Among the more interesting of these are the models in stone of the fifty-two wooden sticks that represented the calendar cycle, and were known as the 'year bundle'. Such symbols would be buried in ritual tombs known as 'Altars of Skulls', another art form peculiar to the Aztecs, of which a good example can be seen in the National Museum.

Not only were the temples, patios and palaces of Tenochtitlan filled with painted sculpture. In addition, much of the wall space was covered with brightly coloured frescoes, which have almost totally vanished. Tenochtitlan was, like Teotihuacan, a polychrome city, ablaze with colour; only the barest notion of how the frescoes looked can be gained by fragments of a stylized warrior frieze from Malinalco or from the remains of painting on two rectangular altars at Tizatlan in Tlaxcala, that depict the Smoking Mirror and other gods in a style similar to that of certain codices. Fragments of murals have also been discovered in 1981 in the Great Temple excavations.

Even the briefest account of the Aztec achievement requires some mention of the minor arts and crafts. Artisans, such as feather-workers and goldsmiths, lived, as we have seen, in separate wards of the city and had their own craft guilds. Sahagún gives a detailed account, complete with illustrations, of what his informants told of metal-working techniques; however, few objects survived the lust for gold of the Spaniards, who promptly melted down the masterpieces that they purloined. Ornaments made of precious stone were less avidly sought, and among the finest existing specimens of craftsmanship are the turquoise mosaic masks, sacrificial knife handles and other objects displayed in the Museum of Mankind in London.

Apart from the famous headdress in the Ethnological Museum of Vienna, of which there is a copy in the Mexican National Museum, almost nothing is left of the most delicate craft of all, the making of feather adornments and mosaics. The pattern of conquest reflects the urge to acquire gaudy plumes more than gold and precious stones; these were made into headdresses, standards, tunics and capes that were the warriors' official insignia. Indispensable as badges of rank were the shields bearing mosaic designs, made of small pieces of plumage glued to a rigid backing. Unlike the stonework, in which the Aztecs developed a more distinctive style, feather-working followed traditional patterns shared by many peoples throughout Mexico; the scale of their military operations merely stimulated the demand and increased the supply, but did little to change the designs.

Among the most respected and skilled of all artists and craftsmen was the *tlacuilo*, meaning 'writer', whose task was the painting of codices. These consisted of a single long sheet of paper or animal parchment folded like a screen and bound by thin slabs of wood or skin. Colour was important, and today helps us to identify the different gods and goddesses. Unfortunately many codices were deliberately destroyed by the Spaniards as works of the devil and none that survives from Tenochtitlan and the Valley of Mexico is known to have been made before the Conquest; those that we possess are post-Hispanic copies of the originals. However, some fine codices from the neighbouring Puebla Valley exist, which were compiled at an earlier date. In this region the art of painting manuscripts was highly developed. It is surely no coincidence that much of the best pottery produced in Central Mexico in Aztec times comes not from Tenochtitlan but from Cholula, and Moctezuma dined off Cholula ware in the Spaniards' presence. The Cholulan painted vessels have designs that recall the codices from that region and from the Mixteca to the south, all of which share a distinctive style; known as Cholula-Mixteca, its significance in late pre-Hispanic times cannot be overstated, and examples of this unique mode of expressing religion and history in visual form are found in many places throughout Mexico. In these no attempt is made to portray individuals. Gods and men are shown in stylized illustrations, and are to be recognized by articles of ritual attire, some of which we can identify today; to the initiate these symbols would have almost amounted to a kind of writing. This Puebla-Mixteca mode of expression was used not only in codices and on pottery, but in mural painting and even in stone reliefs, of which those of the Stone of Tizoc are typical.

The illustration of a codex was as much an art as a mere craft. Religion was a major theme and many of the finest were dedicated to the gods more than to mundane matters. The *Codex Borbonicus*, which is one of the earliest post-Conquest copies of an earlier Aztec work, is a good example of a ritual-divinatory document. Of its two major sections, one deals with the eighteen months of twenty days, and the other is the *Book of Days*, the *Tonalamatl*, a kind of manual with painted figures showing the appropriate songs, dances and prayers for the different feasts. The most famous of the Cholula-Mixteca religious codices is the *Borgia.*

In spite of this emphasis on religion, other codices served more practical purposes, such as court proceedings, land boundaries, reports of enemy strongholds, and records of tribute or commerce. Among the most revealing is the *Codex Mendoza*, named after the first Spanish viceroy; it lists in minute detail the tribute which each province paid to the Aztecs, while another section is devoted to history and social customs. As in many native documents, Spanish annotations have been added that make it easier to interpret; other codices have similar glossaries in Nahuatl, written in Roman script. Of vital significance were those that defined land-ownership and village boundaries; a few still survive today as jealously guarded heirlooms in their village of origin. In Colonial times they were constantly cited in lawsuits by Indian claimants, seeking to establish their right to certain lands by virtue of ownership before the Conquest.

Among the painted manuscripts most closely studied by modern scholars are those that record history and tribal traditions. Some of these, such as those that tell of the Aztec migration, take the form of annals, in which the glyph for each year is accompanied by mention of any leading event, such as the death of a ruler, or the arrival of migrants at a new location. These annals served more as an aide-mémoire than as a true history and summarize the detailed oral traditions that were learned by heart in the schools. Nowadays their information supplements the more copious data recorded by the Spaniards and their pupils after the Conquest.

Aztec writing, based on techniques evolved hundreds if not thousands of years before, consisted largely of hieroglyphs in which various animals, plants and birds signify the things that they represent. Certain of these pictographs came also to possess a symbolic meaning; stylized flowers, for instance, indicated sacrificial blood, while a captive held by the hair stood for war. Verbs could even be expressed in this way, for instance by a scroll for talking, or footprints, either for travel or for dancing. Glyphs for place-names were formed by combining these conventional pictures; Coyocac, for example, is indicated by a picture of a dog (*coyotl*) together with a sandal (*cactli*). To illustrate certain names, additional conventions were used; *tzintli* means the anus and in place-glyphs serves to illustrate the Nahuatl '*tzin*', a diminutive suffix often added to such names. Hence, a picture of a wall (*tenamitl*) joined to the lower half of a human body represents Tenantzinco, the Place of the Little Wall. People as well as places had their name glyph, formed on the same principle: to cite one example, the Aztec ruler Chimalpopoca is designated by a shield (*chimalli*) surmounted by a puff of smoke (the verb *popoca* means 'to smoke').

In late pre-Conquest times this picture-writing was gradually being modified and might eventually have developed into a kind of script, based on ideograms, not unlike Chinese, whose many signs are a highly stylized version of meaningful pictures, now hard to recognize as such. Under the Aztecs, this process had not reached the point where the pictorial writing could express abstract notions and could therefore serve for recording poetry or prose sagas. However, nearly two thousand poems were written down from memory in Roman script after the Conquest; they include hymns to honour gods, epics to celebrate the deeds of heroes, and lyrical verse praising the beauty of flowers or lamenting, after the manner of the Roman Horace, the transience of our human existence.

Sahagún and others also recorded the elegant if repetitive 'Words of the Elders', consisting of speeches or sermons addressed to different categories of people, particularly the young. Nahuatl, in which these texts are written, was rapidly becoming a universal language; it possessed the qualities most needed in a civilized mode of speech, since it has a rich vocabulary and is harmonious, flexible and easy to pronounce.

THE DAILY ROUND

These 'Words of the Elders', combining a Roman *gravitas* with an almost Victorian prudery, tell much of the principles on which society was founded and of the kind of life which people led. Principle and practice had an essentially religious basis: when the father exhorts his son to be truthful, he reminds him of the constant presence of Smoking Mirror, 'who sees all that is in men's hearts and who knows all secret things'. Hence the Aztecs' daily life can, like their art, only be viewed against the background of the faith that permeated their being.

Proper conduct, as ordained in the precepts, was imposed on both noble and commoner, and taught in their respective schools. Certain speeches were intended only for the ruler, while others, such as those addressed by parents to children, were of a more general kind. A typical homily would be used by an Aztec father talking to his son:

Revere and greet your elders; console the poor and the afflicted with good works and words . . . Follow not the madmen who honour neither father nor mother; for they are like animals, for they neither take nor hear advice . . . Do not mock the old, the sick, the maimed, or one who has sinned. Do not insult or abhor them, but abase yourself before God and fear lest the same befall you . . . Do not set a bad example, or speak indiscreetly, or interrupt the speech of another. If someone does not speak well or coherently, see that you do not the same; if it is not your business to speak, be silent. If you are asked something, reply soberly and without affectation or flattery or prejudice to others, and your speech will be well regarded . . . Wherever you go, walk with a peaceful air, and do not make wry faces or improper gestures.

Like the Romans, the Aztecs impressed upon their youth the need to behave at all times with dignity and restraint. Great stress was placed on courtesy and good manners, and formal rules were laid down for every conceivable situation. For instance, a precise mode of conduct was prescribed for persons invited to dine in the house of a lord; any commoner so fortunate was enjoined to eat slowly, without smacking his lips, to take food with only three fingers of the right hand, to avoid sneezing and spitting, and above all to take care not to drop his food on the clothes of other guests.

It was even ordained how a man should behave when out in the street. He should proceed calmly, neither too fast nor too slowly. He should not walk with head lowered, nor inclined to one side; anyone who did this was to be regarded as an imbecile, ill-mannered and without discipline. Speech as well as gait had to be controlled; one should speak calmly and without getting excited; an injunction to avoid or ignore improper topics is included in this precept; bad or obscure remarks made by others were to be greeted with silence.

To enforce such impeccable conduct, precepts alone evidently did not suffice, since draconian punishments were laid down for those who failed to comply. Pulque was regarded as a sacred potion, only to be drunk on ceremonial occasions; a noble who became intoxicated for his own pleasure was to be secretly strangled; for a commoner the law was different; a first offender would be publicly disgraced and have his head shaved; if he drank again, he was to be beaten to death or strangled in the presence of all the youths of the ward where he lived.

In this outwardly puritanical society, adultery was outlawed and the many mentions in Nahuatl texts of penalties for this offence show that even the Aztec moralists found human nature hard to change. Male adulterers had their heads smashed with stones, while women were strangled. According to another account, both men and women were publicly stoned. Such penalties, none the less, could require the evidence of independent witnesses, which was hard to get, and the complaints of an aggrieved husband were not accepted as proof of guilt.

The daily life of the Aztecs has been amply described and I will therefore deal briefly with the subject. The existence of the ordinary citizen of Tenochtitlan was well-ordered but frugal. The main apparel for men was simply a loincloth, worn by night as well as by day; the women's standard dress was a skirt reaching almost to the ankles. Over this basic attire could be worn a top garment, a cloak formed of a rectangular piece of material and knotted on the right shoulder; there were no buttons. A throng of people, their garments wrapped round their bodies in this way, might have looked rather like a crowd in the Ancient Mediterranean world; the nobles would have been conspicuous for their brightly coloured clothes, made of cotton.

Diet as well as dress depended on social status. The only domestic animals, the hairless dog and the turkey, were mainly for the nobles' table, as were delicacies brought from the coast, such as shellfish and chocolate, the most highly prized drink. The daily fare of the average man was maize and beans, spiced with chilli. Most of the maize was eaten in the form of *tortillas*, flat round cakes of meal baked on clay griddles; since there was no fat, frying was unknown. *Tortillas* could be rolled up and filled in the middle with some more spicy or flavoured food, to produce what is nowadays called a *taco*. Maize was also made into a kind of porridge known as *atole*, or was eaten, as also today, in the form of *tamales*, squares of steamed maize stuffed with some vegetable or meat.

While game, such as rabbits and hares, could sometimes be obtained, ordinary people relied more on lagoon fauna to supplement their otherwise mainly vegetarian diet. These included frogs, tadpoles, sweet-water shrimps, water flies and their eggs and white worms. Aztec tastes were different from our own; reptiles such as iguanas, certain ants and even maguey worms were regarded as delicacies and eaten by nobles as well as commoners.

Information on the housing of the average citizen is rather scanty, though the subject is of special interest, since this is one aspect of Aztec life that offers scope for comparison with earlier cultures, more of whose dwellings have been excavated. A typical family lived in a one-roomed house; furniture was rudimentary, consisting of little more than reed mats that served as beds and seats, together with wooden boxes in which belongings were kept. Around the single room stood the objects of everyday use – digging sticks, hunting and fishing tackle, a simple loom, together with pots and pans and the inevitable grinding stone for maize. Even the houses of the nobles would seem to us to be sparsely furnished; like the poor they slept on reed mats, though important people are often shown in codices sitting on a kind of legless chair (*icpalli*), slightly raised from the ground and provided with a back.

Houses had no windows and pine torches provided the only lighting. Doors were without locks or bolts, and it is therefore not surprising that the laws against theft were stringent. The focal point of each dwelling was the hearth; its three stones were arranged in a triangle and supported the clay disc on which were cooked the *tortillas*. These stones were sacred, for in them resided the mysterious power of the Fire God; anyone who stepped on them was severely punished.

Such one-room units in the city were not built in isolation but formed part of a walled compound that enclosed a number of separately-entered dwellings, facing inward onto an open patio. Compounds were usually occupied by members of the same family; the grandparents might live in one room, while the others were allotted to their married children and adult grandchildren. If space was available, a new dwelling might be added to provide for a child at the time of his marriage.

These family housing structures in Tenochtitlan are more to be compared in size to subdivisions for parents and their children within the much larger Teotihuacan apartment compounds, whose total floorspace served for whole groups of workers, rather than for individual families. Each of the smaller Tenochtitlan units had its own access to streets and canals; they were usually adjacent to a cultivable *chinampa* plot. Such units are not to be confused with peasant houses in the country; each of these dwellings, of a type dating from long before the Aztecs and still used today, stood separate from its neighbours; it was usually made of wattle and daub, the traditional building material of the countryside; the roof, depicted in various codices, was gabled and made of thatch.

Spanish eye-witness accounts help us to reconstruct many aspects of daily existence in Tenochtitlan. However, when one tries to picture what it was really like to wake up in the city and go about one's daily tasks, important details are often lacking. For instance, it is far from clear how such tasks were allotted; it is unknown to what extent artisans also possessed *chinampa* plots, and how much time, if any, they spent in cultivating them, in addition to their regular work as craftsmen; however, since whole wards or *barrios* were assigned to these artisans, it is logical to suppose that they at least had some land of their own. Equally, the proportion of the life of the ordinary *macehual* dedicated to war and to farming is not clear. No source states who was available for military service and for what period of time; in such a war-orientated society the need for cannon fodder was pressing but we do not know for how long farmers had to serve and who took their place on the land when they were called away to the wars; some of the more distant campaigns could hardly have been fought between the reaping of one harvest and the sowing of the next.

The absence of any single unit of currency, of a kind used by the more sophisticated Old World cultures, must have added to the complications of life in such a large community. One doubts that the ordinary citizen kept a store of cacao beans, the commodity most often mentioned as a kind of money, but which were perishable. Farmers lived mainly off their own produce, making their own clothes and utensils; in the case of the artisans, basic pay would have included a ration of the necessities of life, such as food and clothing. However, the complications of barter to complete one's needs must have been considerable for a family who had a surplus quantity of, say, maize or maguey fibre and wanted to obtain more beans and chillis, and such a process of exchange must have been time-consuming.

None the less, time itself meant much less than it does today for people without clocks, watches, or even sun discs. Law courts simply opened at dawn, and most work, including that of artisans, also began at sunrise; no method is known to have existed of fixing alternative starting points. While midday could be determined by the course of the sun, even such notions as midnight remained rather vague, in the absence of any device for measuring time. According to Sahagún, drums and shells were sounded to mark four divisions of the day, sunrise, mid-morning, midday and sunset, while at night they served to define the end of twilight, which was when most people went to bed, the midnight hour when priests rose to pray, and a moment a little before dawn. In such a system mealtimes were not very exact. In the absence of breakfast, the first meal was taken after a few hours of work, and normally consisted of a bowl of *atole*. The main repast was taken towards sundown; it was called *cochca*, derived from the Nahuatl word for sleep, and was not therefore a midday meal, as is sometimes stated.

Rigid rules governed the raising of the young from the day they were born until they were married. The *Codex Mendoza* illustrates the formal education of children: at first the infant was given none but the simplest jobs, together with lengthy instruction on proper behaviour (indicated by blue speech signs coming from the mouths of parents). It also depicts the standard food ration for children: up to three years of age half a *tortilla*: from three to five years a single *tortilla*, rising to two for those over thirteen years old. Not until they were fifteen did the boys enter the House of Youths, to be trained as warriors; younger lads can be seen in the *Codex Mendoza* learning from their fathers how to do practical tasks, such as carrying bundles and catching fish. The education of a girl was basically a training for marriage; between the ages of five and seven she was taught to handle a spindle and make thread; in her early teens she learned to cook and at fourteen she was shown how to weave.

The *Codex* even illustrates punishments for children. Boys are shown in the act of being beaten or pricked with maguey spines; sometimes they were held over a fire of chilli peppers and made to inhale the pungent smoke. Life in general was wholly centred on the family and marriage was the most important event in the course of a person's existence. As we have seen, the bonds of wedlock were reinforced by strict laws against adultery. The rules for marriage preliminaries provide a good example of the highly formalized nature of Mexican society. Matters were arranged between the families of the prospective bride and bridegroom. The parents of the suitor would approach those of the girl and deliver a set speech, 'full of rhetoric and fine words'. Etiquette demanded that the girl's parents at first politely rejected the suit, again in formal language, saying that their daughter was unworthy of the young man and unfit for marriage, but later they accepted with a show of reluctance. The wedding, which took place in the bridegroom's home, was celebrated with elaborate rites. Tradition moreover required that the main sequel of the ceremony was worship rather than pleasure; once the newly-wedded couple reached the bridal chamber, they were supposed to pass four days in prayer before the marriage was consummated.

From such brief comments on the lives of the citizens of Tenochtitlan it can be seen that all, whether rich or poor, were governed by rigid convention that decreed how a man should eat, dress, educate his children and even walk in the street.

Notwithstanding the cosmic *angst* that underlay the Aztec world view, their society was above all orderly. It is easy to represent such a state as both over-regimented and diabolically cruel, because of the frequency of human sacrifice; it is equally possible to idealize this society, which offered its members a well-ordered, colourful and contented, if frugal, existence, until destroyed by Spanish violence. The rules, though strict, were generally accepted and the great majority of the citizens were fully prepared to follow the 'Words of the Elders'. None the less, the harsh penalties point to the presence, as in most human societies, of dissidents. These, however, posed no threat to the community, which at the time of the Spanish invasion was still in a stage of development rather than of decline.

No written source, however euphoric, can bear more cogent witness to the Aztec achievement than does the more recent research of the dirt archaeologist. William Sanders and others lay constant stress on the unprecedented population explosion in the Valley of Mexico under the Pax Azteca, in spite of all the killing that took place. Their findings make it all the more surprising that a society so ordered, so positive and so stable could succumb to such an exiguous band of adventurers.

Detailed accounts of these events hardly explain how a force originally numbering 500 could defeat an empire whose population is variously put at between 9 and 20 million. Cortés was helped by the Tlaxcalans and other allies, but the role of these auxiliaries tends to be overstated. Though much has been written of the native reaction to Aztec 'oppression' as a major factor, Cortés himself was the first to admit that most nearby cities remained loyal to the Mexican cause even when it was all but lost. In contrast, the Tlaxcalans were little more than fair-weather friends; when events took an uncertain turn during the siege, most of their force slunk away.

Any notion that Cortés was a god had been dispelled long before the final battle. Equally, the horses and cannon, originally looked on as divine weapons, were hardly decisive; at the very nadir of their fortunes, the Spaniards crushed the Aztecs at Otumba at a time when they had lost all their artillery and had only twenty-three debilitated horses.

The general absence of technical progress affected the war potential and Mexican weapons were admittedly ineffective by European standards; one is struck by the high proportion of wounded among the Conquerors, as compared with those actually killed in battle. But if they triumphed it was mainly because they were fighting a campaign of a kind unknown in Mexico, where warfare was subject to the dictates of ritual. In particular, in any fight against the Spaniards, the Aztecs were handicapped by their compulsive need to drag their enemies away alive for sacrifice, instead of killing them on the spot. So much of their strength was devoted to the laborious task of taking captives in the heat of battle; Cortés could probably have been killed several times over, if they had not been so intent upon his capture.

Indian morale was volatile, and apt to plummet at the first reverse; if things went wrong, they easily lost their nerve, and Moctezuma was no exception to this. They were persuaded that the outcome of a battle depended on the whim of the gods as much as on their own staying power. This very factor, fatal in fighting the Spaniards, had probably helped the Aztecs to make such sweeping gains in so short a time; their foes would have seen the *force majeure* deployed against them more as a divine scourge than as a feat of the enemy commander.

And if Cortés was not finally looked upon as a deity, he was in effect the instrument of the gods' will, sent to destroy the Fifth Sun. Obsessed by their dismal cosmology, the ghastly omens came as no surprise to Moctezuma and his soothsayers; the mirror fixed in the eagle's head simply reflected his own view of the universe.

No Biblical prophet of doom could have foretold more relentlessly the end of this New World Nineveh. Never have the decrees of fate been so unerringly fulfilled as were those graven on the Stone of the Sun and recorded in the sagas. The Aztecs believed that this Fifth Sun, named Motion, was to be stricken by no human agency, but by the quaking earth. And indeed, with more devastating effect than any natural upheaval, the Spanish Conquest swept away the Aztec world, and all it stood for.

10

THE SIXTH WORLD

Out of the wreckage of the Aztec Fifth Sun arose the foundations of its successor, New Spain. In many cases the temples of the new god were built from the stones of those of the old, using the same site. In a number of ways this Sixth, or Spanish, World may be compared to the Fifth, and in both empires plunder and piety went hand in hand. Among the Aztecs piety tended to come first; though tribute was the main motive for conquest, their yearning to store up riches was less intense, and many of the spoils of war were soon spent in ritual display. But if the Catholic fervour of the Conquerors was genuine, their lust for gold was no less insatiable; to this end Cortés himself did not flinch from the most un-Christian acts, such as burning the feet of his fallen rival, Cuauhtemoc, in order to extract more hidden treasure.

Cortés assumed all the powers of the Aztec *tlatoani* and lived in comparable state. However, he had to suffer mounting criticism and interference from the Mother Country, whose rulers felt a deep concern for the welfare of their new Indian subjects; many laws were passed, in a rather vain attempt to protect them. Finally, in 1535 Cortés was replaced by the first Viceroy, Don Antonio de Mendoza.

Cortés chose as his capital the site of Tenochtitlan, rebuilt as the City of Mexico. In the Colonial period and ever since, the Valley of Mexico thus retained its dominant role; owing to the concentration of population and industry in the Valley, its preponderance is as great as ever.

Though the capital was razed to the ground, for the average citizen of the Empire changes were gradual. Their new masters were merely more alien and more exacting than the old. Being ill-versed in the art of ruling Indians, they were less able to stem serious abuses, such as alcoholism. Tribute was still paid in kind, replaced only slowly by money. Tribute in the form of labour also continued to be levied; where gangs of workers, supplied in lieu of goods, formerly erected pyramids, they now built churches. The native rulers, renamed *caciques* (a Caribbean, not a Mexican word), did not at once lose all their importance. Places that had previously possessed a ruler, or *tlatoani*, of their own, now came to be called *cabeceras*, or 'leading centres'.

However, those which had formerly been ruled by several *tlatoanis* were now placed under a single *cacique*. The *cabeceras* were in turn sub-divided into *estancias*; such territorial subdivisions tended to follow the irregular pre-Hispanic pattern, whereby places that obeyed one centre were interspersed with those that belonged to another.

The *caciques* were now subject to Spanish control. But whereas they had served the Aztec ruler as their direct superior, a new authority, known as the *encomienda*, was interposed between these local princes and the supreme *tlatoani*, Cortés. In theory, the grant of *encomienda* to a Spaniard did not in itself confer land, but merely entrusted him with the Christian welfare of a large number of Indians. On these he had the right to impose an extra load of tribute, in return for a most platonic concern for their spiritual well-being.

The system was open to the grossest abuses and proved disastrous for the Indians. Even those lucky enough to avoid forced labour in the mines now had to provide, not only for their own nobles and for the central power, but also for the greedy *encomenderos*, intent upon making a fortune at their expense. From the Cuernavaca province alone, Cortés himself extracted a tribute of 4,800 cotton mantles every eighty days.

But the direst scourge for the Indians arose not from what the Spaniards took, but from what they brought with them; for they introduced diseases such as smallpox and measles, against which the natives were defenceless. This further disaster was to be a key factor in Mexican history. After a series of epidemics, the Indians were decimated. As a result, until this century the country has been thinly populated as compared with Aztec times.

To console them in their travails, the Indians were offered the solace of the Cross and the coming of the first twelve Franciscan friars impressed them deeply. At first they could not conceive how Spaniards could be poor and humble like themselves. At least they now knew that among their new masters they had friends as well as foes – men who were ready to share their hardships and to narrow the gap between conquerors and conquered.

Of all the Spanish clerics, the foremost spokesman for the Indians was Bishop Bartolomé de las Casas, whose tirades prompted the Spanish Government to pass new laws, designed, at least in theory, to protect the natives of New Spain. Meanwhile, the work of conversion went on. In this the friars faced an uphill task, since it would be wrong to assume that in the early years of the Colony the Indians were eager followers of the Cross. In reality they were obliged by force to abandon their old religion. Idols were smashed and monuments razed. The famous Bishop Zumarraga boasted that he had destroyed 500 temples and broken 20,000 idols; no one knows how many precious codices were burned on the Bishop's bonfire.

Cortés and his successors were caught between two fires: on the one hand the Government of Castile, urged on by the friars, was anxious to treat the Indians fairly; on the other hand, the settlers were out to amass riches but could not be easily thwarted, since they provided the only armed force. Bonds of affection and respect linked Cortés to his Indian subjects, but he ended by coming down on the side of their exploiters; his troubles began in earnest when he refused to obey a letter of the Emperor Charles V, ordering him to cease to impose the *encomenderos* on Indians. In reply, he drew attention to their obligation to bear arms; if they were removed, royal troops would be needed to replace them. Cortés suffered, like his predecessors on the throne of Tenochtitlan, from the lack of a standing army, and Charles V was in no position to supply one.

In spite of Cortés' opposition, the system was gradually changed and the Spanish Government began to appoint royal officials, known as *regidores*, to assume the powers of the *encomenderos*, though some of the latter retained their office, under stricter supervision, until the 1570s. By that time Mexico was merely one of Spain's many imperial provinces, the fruits of whose labours served to further her political aims and provide funds for her European wars.

Even though its ruler, the Viceroy, was sent by the Mother Country, New Spain was a land in which the Indian masses toiled for a resident élite, of which the leading members were now Spanish settlers. It therefore had much in common with the four previous 'empires'. Each of these four present many common traits: the outstanding feature of the Aztec world was its closely-knit society, in which the lives of individual members had to conform to the common good. There is, however, little reason to suppose that state control over the average citizen of Tula or Teotihuacan was less absolute. Basic to the life of all Mexicans, from Olmec to Aztec times and even

thereafter, was a devotion to the gods who presided over their formalized cosmos. And if the Toltecs and Aztecs were more warlike than
their forerunners, their battles were fought to honour the gods as
much as to win profit for the gods' servants. Any interpretation of
Aztec history in mere terms of material gain misses this essential
point.

As we have seen, the regions penetrated by the successive
'empires' coincided to an uncanny degree. Along the Pacific Coast,
Teotihuacan spread its tentacles much further north-west than the
others; in the opposite direction, both Olmec and Teotihuacan traces
are found in Guatemala, also visited by Aztec merchants, but never
conquered by their armies. Toltec expansion was on a smaller scale,
but they, unlike the other three, left their mark on the late Mayan
civilization of Yucatán. The four universalized cultures shared basic
traits, nearly all present in the time of the Olmecs, such as ceremonial
centres, human sacrifice and the ritual calendar.

While the radius of action in each case was comparable, the
methods varied. It has been stressed in this book that long-range
military conquests are much less likely to have been made in pre-
Aztec times; penetration in earlier times beyond certain limits was
more probably carried out by traders than by soldiers. All four,
however, were centred upon a metropolitan area which they controlled, and whose culture was indistinguishable from that of its parent
city.

The Olmec and Teotihuacan rulers had less need to expand by force
beyond this local hinterland to obtain raw materials; they were great
exporters of finished goods, which have been found in abundance all
over Middle America. In contrast, in only a few zones are objects
found today which can be recognized as 'made in Tula' or 'made in
Tenochtitlan'. The output of Aztec artisans was immense, but it was
largely for home consumption and for part at least of its imported
luxuries the capital relied on tribute.

No one denies that war existed in the Teotihuacan era, but in its art
there is no cult of the warrior, as in Post-Classic times. Possibly
therefore the Aztecs' use of force to subjugate distant regions – and
obtain a share of their wealth – was a new departure; the Toltec
conquests were mostly made nearer to the home base.

In this respect, population trends are a major factor. The early
centres of the Olmec heartland – one can hardly call them cities –
housed minute numbers and the rest of the people were dispersed
over a fairly wide area. The development of true cities took place in

the Altiplano. But if Teotihuacan itself was huge, fewer people lived in the surrounding countryside. Tula, with certain modifications, followed Teotihuacan in this respect. The true change is apparent only in Tenochtitlan and it has been seen that the great growth of population, not only in the city but in its metropolitan zone – amounting to about one and a quarter million – created new needs and new opportunities.

I have equally stressed that throughout Middle American history efficient transport was an unsolved problem, notwithstanding an amazing propensity for foot-slogging. The Aztecs at least made some advance by exploiting water communications in the Valley of Mexico to the full. To supply a city like Teotihuacan, which could not be reached by canoe, made heavy demands on its manpower.

In spite of such limitations on mobility, the major cultures were cosmopolitan in outlook; in the case of both Teotihuacan and Tenochtitlan, in certain wards of the city peoples of other regions made their homes; Toltecs settled in Yucatán and Cholula, and at least a few Olmecs probably lived in Guerrero.

All four 'empires' ended in total collapse. While the fall of the Aztecs was unique, the decline of the others owed much to problems which arose as the population grew and came to need more food. The likely causes of their demise need no repeating, except perhaps to re-stress that peasant revolt is the least convincing. This does not mean that, in Toynbean terms, there was no build-up of inner tensions, which, in face of the enemy without, destabilized the social fabric. Nomads on the north-western border were a constant menace to Central Mexico, though a greater threat in Aztec times was the nascent Tarascan Empire; because of their warlike qualities and their metallurgical skills, it has even been suggested that if the Spaniards had arrived a century later, they might have faced, not the Aztecs, but the Tarascans.

While each of our four cultures had much in common, differences are also to be noted. The Olmecs were a coastal people who penetrated inland, while the remainder were based on the Altiplano and spread towards the two coasts. To what extent Middle American civilization originated in central or coastal Mexico is still debated. McNeish's discovery of early farming in the Tehuacán Valley suggests that the challenge of arid conditions in parts of the Altiplano led people to till, and later to irrigate, the land. However, while this major feat probably took place inland, on the coast of southern Veracruz and Tabasco the yet more spectacular advance from small settlements to ceremonial centres and to statehood was achieved by the Olmecs.

And if the basis of Ancient Mexican religion was already established in Olmec times, changes are visible from one culture to the next. Few Olmec gods can be identified and even in the art of Teotihuacan one recognizes a mere handful of the vast concourse of deities of the Aztec pantheon. While certain principles endured, the roles of individual gods or symbols were modified: the jaguar, the universal Olmec god, came to be mainly linked with earth in later times. Tlaloc ruled supreme in Teotihuacan, but while he never ceased to be important, for the Aztecs he was simply God of Rain. Quetzalcoatl, patron of Tula, was still a leading deity in Aztec times, but ranked below Huitzilopochtli and Tezcatlipoca.

Ancient Mexican history may thus be seen as a continuum, in which basic elements endured, while certain changes took place, for which historians and archaeologists seek the causes. The question, however, still remains: in what direction, if any, was Middle America moving when the Spaniards arrived and what might have been the future course of its history if their invasion had not taken place?

The Aztecs, as Moctezuma himself implied by his efforts to consolidate former gains, were overstretched. The same centrifugal forces existed in 1519 that had caused the decline of Teotihuacan and Tula, and the very scale of Aztec conquests was a source of weakness. In terms of the only available means of transport, the human body, distances within the Empire were immense. But while nearby subjects are easier to control, it is generally less hard for remote provinces to break loose. Such a huge empire can therefore only be held together if a consensus exists among the ruled, and if it is able to offer certain benefits to subject peoples. To do this it must give as well as take. The Pax Romana and the Pax Britannica sought to confer order and justice on conquered lands; but the Aztecs did not, like the British in India, curb the absolute power of local princes over their own subjects. Stable rule must be based on more than mere pillage; even the more benevolent paternalism of British rule in India soon came to be resented, when memories of past abuses grew dim.

There is no reason to suppose that the cycle of dominance was ended in Ancient Mexico, or that Aztec power, like that of its forerunners, would not eventually have crumbled in face of internal tensions and outside pressures. Such pressures are not hard to seek. The Aztecs' only known campaign against the Tarascans on their northwestern flank ended in disaster. On the home front, the much increased population in the Valley of Mexico had so far served the Aztecs' purposes, but no end was in sight to this demographic explosion. Had it continued, Central Mexico might have faced the problems of many Third World countries today, where population soars and technology lags behind.

Nowadays technology can be imported at a price. But Ancient Mexico had access to no such sources of innovation and had to rely on its own ingenuity. In contrast, even Ancient Egypt, fairly late in its long existence, transformed its economy by the use of the horse and camel and by making iron tools and weapons, techniques introduced from outside. Middle America had evolved formulas that provided a well-ordered pattern of life for its people. But while such formulas were effective, they tended to be static: if rulers and gods changed, technical skills did not. The pyramids of Tenochtitlan were built in the same way as those of Teotihuacan over a thousand years before, and their stonework was less well finished.

Possibly therefore Mexico had reached a point where the available options had been exhausted, and where the need arose for new ideas and new skills, of a kind that European Renaissance Man was able to provide. It may have been unlucky that the more challenging ideas of contemporary Europe were slow to reach Mexico, whose pious conquerors were as priest-ridden as their old rulers. New Spain, moreover, was to suffer from the rather rapid decline of Old Spain; like that of the Toltec Empire, Spanish power was short-lived. Just as the Tlaxcalans had thwarted the armies of Moctezuma II, those of Philip II failed to crush the Dutch burghers, and a bare century after the Conquest Spain was on the decline. As a result, the lengthy Colonial period engendered stagnation and ended in confusion. It was only in the course of the present century that the Mexicans, harnessing once more their own resources and directing their own commerce, came to take their due place among the nations of the modern world.

APPENDIX
PRINCIPAL ARCHAEOLOGICAL SITES OF MEXICO*

OLMEC AND EARLY (Chapters 1 and 2)

NOTE: *The principal carvings from La Venta and San Lorenzo are not to be seen in situ, but in the museums of Villahermosa, Tabasco, and Jalapa, Veracruz. Equally, though the site is important, there is little left for the visitor to see in Tlatilco.*

SITE	STATE OR REGION
La Venta	Tabasco
San Lorenzo	Veracruz
Tres Zapotes	Veracruz
Tlatilco	Estado de México (within Mexico City)
Chalcatzingo	Morelos
Juxtlahuaca	Guerrero
Oxtotitlán	Guerrero
Monte Alban (Phase 1)	Oaxaca
Dainzu	Oaxaca
Izapa	Chiapas
El Baul	Guatemala
Cuicuilco	Distrito Federal

CLASSIC AND EARLY POST-CLASSIC
(Chapters 3, 4, 5 and 6)

SITE	STATE OR REGION
Teotihuacan	Estado de México
Cholula	Puebla
Kaminaljuyu	Guatemala
Remojadas	Veracruz
Monte Alban	Oaxaca
Yagul	Oaxaca
Xochicalco	Morelos
El Tajin	Veracruz
Tula	Hidalgo
La Quemada	Zacatecas
Castillo de Teayo	Veracruz
Teotenango	Estado de México
Cacaxtla	Tlaxcala

* Excluding Maya region

LATE POST-CLASSIC (Chapters 7, 8 and 9)

SITE	STATE OR REGION
Tenochtitlan-Tlatelolco	Distrito Federal
Tenayuca with Santa Cecilia	Estado de México
	Morelos
Teopanzolco	Morelos
Tepozteco	Estado de México
Malinalco	Estado de México
Calixtlahuaca	Oaxaca
Mitla	Oaxaca
Coixtlahuaca	Veracruz
Zempoala	Veracruz
Huatusco	Michoacan
Tzintzuntzan	Chihuahua
Casas Grandes	

SELECT BIBLIOGRAPHY

The quantity of material available for further reading has increased greatly in recent years. I merely offer a selection of those works that are more readily available and of more general interest. Many of these have extensive bibliographies. As far as possible, I have confined my choice to books, in preference to articles appearing in professional publications.

GENERAL SUMMARY

ADAMS, RICHARD E., *Prehistoric Mesoamerica* (Boston, Mass.: Little, Brown, 1977).

COE, MICHAEL D., *Mexico* (Mexico City: Ediciones Lara, 1967).

HAMMOND, NORMAN, ed., *Mesoamerican Archaeology: New Approaches* (London: Duckworth, 1974).

Handbook of Middle American Indians, Robert Wauchope, Gen. ed., 15 vols. (Austin, Tex.: University of Texas Press, 1964–75).

Historia de México, 10 vols. (Barcelona: Salvat Editores, 1974).

HUNTER, BRUCE C., *A Guide to Ancient Mexican Ruins* (Norman, Okl.: University of Oklahoma Press, 1977).

KELLEY, JOYCE, *The Complete Visitor's Guide to Mesoamerican Ruins* (Norman, Okl.: University of Oklahoma Press, 1981).

KRICKEBERG, WALTER, *Altamexikanische Kulturen* (Berlin: Satari-Verlag, 1956; Spanish ed., Mexico City: Fondo de Cultura Económica, 1961).

MARQUINA, IGNACIO, *Arquitectura Prehispánica* (Mexico City: Instituto Nacional de Antropología e Historia, 1951).

NOGUERA, EDUARDO, *La Cerámica Arqueológica de Mesoamérica* (Mexico City: Universidad Nacional, 1963).

SANDERS, WILLIAM T. and BARBARA J. PRICE, *Mesoamerica: The Evolution of a Civilization* (New York: Random House, 1968).

SELER, EDUARD, *Gesammelte Abhandlungen zur Amerikanischen Sprach- und Altertumskunde*, 5 vols. (Graz: Akademische Druckanstalt, 1960).

WOLF, ERIC R., *Sons of the Shaking Earth* (Chicago: University of Chicago Press, 1959).

WOLF, ERIC R., ed., *The Valley of Mexico. Studies in Pre-Hispanic Ecology and Society* (Albuquerque, New Mex.: University of New Mexico Press, 1972).

Most modern works tend to deal with one particular aspect or region of Middle America. However Michael Coe's *Mexico* provides a general summary of its archaeology, of which Adams's book gives a rather longer and broader account. Eric Wolf offers a short historical interpretation, ranging from Pre-Classic Mexico until modern times. Sanders and Price give an overall view of Ancient Mexican cultures that relies heavily on the principle of ecological determinism. *Mesoamerican Archaeology*, edited by Norman Hammond, has excellent articles on a wide range of subjects, together with a useful bibliography.

The *Handbook of Middle American Indians*, in fifteen volumes, offers a huge assortment of articles by specialists on every conceivable aspect of Middle American culture; supplementary volumes, the first on archaeology, are in course of preparation; Volume I appeared in 1981. The Salvat *Historia* is more handbook than history; only the first four volumes deal with Ancient Mexico. They are fairly generalized in nature, and are finely illustrated. For the archaeological sites, Marquina's weighty tome serves as an encyclopedia for everything discovered before 1950. Bruce Hunter's book is a handy and up-to-date guide to the main sites. Noguera's work is still the best summary of Mexican ceramics.

Finally, no bibliography would be complete without mention of Eduard Seler. Though he died in 1922 and began to write nearly a century ago, his five volumes on a vast range of subjects are still invaluable to scholars. No full translation from the German has ever been published.

CHAPTERS 1 AND 2: THE OLMECS AND BEFORE

BERNAL, IGNACIO, *The Olmec World* (Berkeley and Los Angeles, Calif.: University of California Press, 1969).

COE, MICHAEL D., *America's First Civilization* (New York: American Heritage Publishing Co., 1968).

COE, MICHAEL D. and RICHARD A. DIEHL, *In the Land of the Olmec*, 2 vols. (Austin, Texas, and London: Texas University Press, 1980).

Conference on the Olmec, ed. Elizabeth Benson (Washington, D.C.: Dumbarton Oaks Research Library, 1968).

COVARRUBIAS, MIGUEL and ROMÁN PIÑA CHAN, *El Pueblo del Jaguar* (Mexico City: Museo Nacional de Antropología, 1964).

FLANNERY, KENT, *The Early Mesoamerican Village* (New York: Academic Press, 1976).

MCNEISH, RICHARD, *The Prehistory of the Tehuacán Valley*, 5 vols. (Austin, Texas, and London: University of Texas Press, 1967–72).

MILBRAITH, SUSAN, *A Study of Olmec Sculptural Chronology* (Washington D.C.: Dumbarton Oaks, 1979).

Studies in Pre-Columbian Art and Archaeology, Numbers 6, 7, and 8, published in one volume (Washington, D.C.: Dumbarton Oaks, 1970).

WICKE, CHARLES R., *Olmec: An Early Art Style of Pre-Columbian Mexico* (Tucson, Ariz.: University of Arizona Press, 1971).

Ignacio Bernal's *Olmec World*, originally published in Spanish, and Michael Coe's *America's First Civilization* (which is much shorter) summarize the various aspects of Olmec civilization, as does Jacques Soustelle's recent publication in French. The Dumbarton Oaks *Conference on the Olmec* contains papers by leading specialists on a wide range of subjects. Coe's latest book, *In the Land of the Olmec*, is a finely produced study of San Lorenzo.

Charles Wicke's work deals with Olmec art in greater detail, while Susan Milbraith concentrates upon Olmec sculpture and its chronology. The murals of Guerrero are described by David C. Grove in Dumbarton Oaks' *Studies in Pre-Columbian Art and Archaeology* No. 6. Volume 3 of the *Handbook of Middle American Indians* (see General Summary) covers the Olmecs.

CHAPTERS 3 AND 4: TEOTIHUACAN AND ITS NEIGHBOURS

BLANTON, RICHARD E., *Monte Alban: Settlement Plans at the Ancient Zapotec Capital* (New York: Academic Press, 1978).

COE, MICHAEL D., *The Maya,* revised edition (London: Thames & Hudson, 1980).

JIMÉNEZ MORENO, WIGBERTO, 'Síntesis de la Historia Pretolteca de México', in *Esplendor de México Antiguo*, Vol. II (Mexico City: Centro de Investigaciones Antropológicas, 1959).

KUBLER, GEORGE, *The Iconography of the Art of Teotihuacan* (Washington D.C.: Dumbarton Oaks, 1973).

MILLER, ARTHUR, *The Mural Painting of Teotihuacani* Washington D.C.: Dumbarton Oaks, 1973).

MILLON RENÉ, ed., *Urbanization at Teotihuacan, Mexico*, Vol. I, *The Teotihuacan Map* (Austin, Tex. and London: University of Texas Press, 1973).

MILLON, RENÉ, 'Teotihuacan: City, State and Civilization', in *Supplement to the Handbook of Middle American Indians*, Vol. I (Austin, Texas, and London: University of Texas Press, 1981).

PASZTORY, ESTHER, *The Iconography of the Teotihuacan Tlaloc* (Washington, D.C.: Dumbarton Oaks, 1974).

SANDERS, WILLIAM T., *The Cultural Ecology of the Teotihuacan Valley* (Department of Anthropology, Pennsylvania State University, 1965).

Teotihuacan. Minutes of the 11th Mesa Redonda (Round Table Conference) of the Sociedad Mexicana de Antropología (Mexico City, 1966).

The Teotihuacan Valley Project, Vol. I, *The Natural Environment, Contemporary Occupation and 16th Century Population of the Valley* (Department of Anthropology, Pennsylvania State University, 1970).

THOMPSON, SIR ERIC, *The Rise and Fall of the Maya Civilization* (Norman, Okl.: Oklahoma University Press, 1954).

WHITECOTTON, JOSEPH W., *The Zapotecs* (Norman, Okl.: Oklahoma University Press, 1977).

There is no single book that adequately covers Teotihuacan as a whole. Wigberto Jiménez Moreno synthesizes its history in *Esplendor de México Antiguo*. Ignacio Bernal describes its architecture in the Salvat *Historia*, Volume I; and Volume 10 of the *Handbook of Middle American Indians* deals with various aspects of the subject (see General Summary).

George Kubler is the leading authority on the art and iconography of Teotihuacan, while Arthur Miller provides a fuller series of reproductions of its murals.

In addition to his volume on urbanization, the report of the 11th Round Table Conference of the Mexican Society of Anthropology contains three contributions by René Millon. He and William Sanders have also dealt with problems of cultural ecology and settlement plans in *The Valley of Mexico*, edited by Eric Wolf (see General Summary).

Joseph Whitecotton's *Zapotecs* gives a useful summary of Monte Alban during the Teotihuacan period. Michael Coe and the late Sir Eric Thompson describe in general terms the Classical Mayas; much has changed since Thompson's book was written, but parts of his work are now being revised and Coe's *The Maya* has been revised by its author very recently.

CHAPTERS 5 AND 6: THE TOLTEC HORIZON

CONTEMPORARY WORKS

COBEAN, ROBERT, *The Pre-Aztec Ceramics of Tula, Hidalgo* (Cambridge, Mass.: Harvard University Dissertation, 1978).

DAVIES, NIGEL, *The Toltecs: Until the Fall of Tula* (Norman, Okl.: University of Oklahoma Press, 1977).

DAVIES, NIGEL, *The Toltec Heritage: From the Fall of Tula to the Rise of*

Tenochtitlan (Norman, Okl.: University of Oklahoma Press, 1980).

DIEHL, RICHARD A., ed., *Studies of Ancient Tollan: A Report of the University of Missouri Tula Archaeological Project* (Columbia, Missouri: University of Missouri Press, 1974).

JIMÉNEZ MORENO, WIGBERTO, *Tula y los Toltecas según las Fuentes Históricas* (Mexico City: Revista Mexicana de Estudios Antropológicos, Vol. V, 1941).

MATOS, EDUARDO, ed., *Proyecto Tula*, 2 vols. (Mexico City: Instituto Nacional de Antropología e Historia, 1974).

SÉJOURNÉ, LAURETTE, *El Universo de Quetzalcoatl* (Mexico City: Fondo de Cultura Económica, 1962).

THOMPSON, SIR ERIC, *Maya History and Religion* (Norman, Okl.: University of Oklahoma Press, 1970).

PRINCIPAL HISTORICAL SOURCES

Anales de Cuauhtitlán in *Códice Chimalpopoca*, edited and translated by Primo F. Velásquez (Mexico City: Imprenta Universitaria, 1945).

Historia de los Mexicanos por sus Pinturas in *Relaciones de Texcoco y de la Nueva España* (Mexico City: Editorial Chavez Hayhoe, 1941).

Historia Tolteca – Chichimeca. Facsimile edition with translation by Luis Reyes (Mexico City: Instituto Nacional de Antropología e Historia, 1976).

IXTLILXÓCHITL, FERNANDO DE ALVA, *Obras Históricas*, 2 vols. (Mexico City: Universidad Nacional de México, 1975).

MUÑOZ CAMARGO, DIEGO, *Historia de Tlaxcala* (Mexico City: Publicaciones del Ateneo de Ciencias y Artes de México, 1947).

SAHAGÚN, FRAY BERNARDINO DE, *Florentine Codex. General History of the Things of New Spain*, 11 vols. Trans. from Nahuatl by Charles Dibble and Arthur J. O. Anderson (Santa Fe, New Mexico: The School of American Research and the University of Utah, 1950–68).

TORQUEMADA, FRAY JUAN DE, *Monarquía Indiana*, 3 vols. (Mexico City: Editorial Porrúa, 1969).

The sources listed above are those which give most data on Tula and its time, often of a rather contradictory nature. Sahagún's information occurs mainly in Book III, and also in Book X. The first part of the *Anales de Cuauhtitlán* and of Muñoz Camargo refer to Tula, also frequently mentioned in Ixtlilxóchitl's work.

Jorge Acosta, among contemporary authors, carried out the original excavations of the ceremonial centre of Tula, and published detailed reports in the *Revista Mexicana de Estudios Antropológicos*, Volume V (1941), VI (1944) and VII (1945). Data on the more recent work on the site by Diehl and Matos were published in 1974 (see list above). Cobean's thesis is a most valuable contribution to the archaeology of Tula.

The author's *Toltecs* is as much handbook as history, and seeks, where possible, to reconcile the part-legendary accounts of the various sources with the archaeological finds. Jiménez Moreno, in various publications, presents an alternative interpretation of Toltec history, and Laurette Séjourné expresses a rather personal viewpoint on the religion and culture of Tula and Teotihuacan.

Thompson's *Maya History and Religion* is the best work on Yucatec Maya history during the period, and lists the sources from which our knowledge of this derives.

CHAPTERS 7, 8 AND 9: THE AZTECS

CONTEMPORARY WORKS

ANAWALT, PATRICIA, *Indian Clothing before Cortés: Mesoamerican Costumes from the Codices* (Norman, Okl.: University of Oklahoma Press, 1981).

BRAY, WARWICK, *Everyday Life of the Aztecs* (London: Batsford; New York: Putnams, 1968).

BRUNDAGE, BURR CARTWRIGHT, *A Rain of Darts* (Austin, Texas, and London: University of Texas Press, 1972).

CASO, ALFONSO, *The People of the Sun* (Norman, Okl.: University of Oklahoma Press, 1962).

DAVIES, NIGEL, *The Aztecs* (London: Macmillan, 1973; New York: Putnam, 1974).

DAVIES, NIGEL, *The Toltec Heritage* (Norman, Okl.: University of Oklahoma Press, 1980).

DAVIES, NIGEL, *Los Señoríos Independientes del Imperió Azteca* (Mexico City: Instituto Nacional de Antropología e Historia, 1968).

GIBSON, CHARLES, *The Aztecs under Spanish Rule* (Stanford, Calif.: Stanford University Press, 1964).

HUNT, EVA, *The Transformation of the Humming Bird* (Ithaca and London: Cornell University Press, 1977).

KATZ, FRIEDRICH, *Situación Social y Económica de los Aztecas durante los Siglos XV y XVI* (Mexico City: Universidad Nacional, 1966).

LEÓN PORTILLA, MIGUEL, *Aztec Thought and Culture*, trans. Jack Emory Davis (Norman, Okl.: University of Oklahoma Press, 1963).

PORTER WEAVER, MURIEL, *The Aztecs, Maya and their Predecessors* (New York: Seminar Press, 1972).

SANDERS, WILLIAM T., JEFFREY R. PARSONS and ROBERT S. SANTLEY, *The Basin of Mexico: Ecological Processes in the Evolution of a Civilization* (New York: Academic Press, 1979).

SOUSTELLE, JACQUES, *Daily Life of the Aztecs* (London: Pelican, 1964).

SULLIVAN, THELMA D., *Compendio de la Gramática Nahuatl* (Mexico City: Universidad Nacional, 1976).

PRINCIPAL HISTORICAL SOURCES (in addition to those already listed for the Toltecs)

CHIMALPAIN, DOMINGO FRANCISCO, *Relaciones Originales de Chalco-Amequamecan,* trans. from Nahuatl into Spanish by Silvia Rendón (Mexico City; Fondo de Cultura Económica, 1965).

Codex Borbonicus, with commentary by Karl Anton Novotny (Graz: Akademische Druck und Verlagsanstalt, 1974).

Codex Borgia, with commentary by Eduard Seler, 3 vols. (Mexico City: Fondo de Cultura Económica, 1963).

Codex Mendoza, ed. James Cooper Clark, 3 vols. (London: Waterloo & Sons, 1938).

CORTÉS, HERNÁN, *Cartas y Documentos* (Mexico City: Editorial Porrúa, 1963).

Crónica Mexicayotl (Mexico City: Imprenta Universitaria, 1949).

DÍAZ DEL CASTILLO, BERNAL, *The Bernal Díaz Chronicles,* trans. and ed. Albert Idell (New York: Doubleday, 1956).

DURÁN, FRAY DIEGO, *Book of the Gods and Rites and the Ancient Calendar,* trans. and annot. Fernando Horcasitas and Doris Heyden (Norman, Okl.: University of Oklahoma Press, 1971).

MOTOLINÍA, FRAY TORIBIO DE BENAVENTE, *Historia de los Indios de Nueva España* (Mexico City: Editorial Chavez Hayhoe, 1941).

POMAR, JUAN BAUTISTA, *Relación de Texcoco,* in *Nueva Colección de Documentos para la Historia de México* (Mexico City: Editorial Chavez Hayhoe, 1941).

TEZOZÓMOC, HERNANDO ALVARADO, *Crónica Mexicana* (Mexico City: Editorial Leyenda, 1944).

VAILLANT, GEORGE C., *Aztecs of Mexico* (Harmondsworth: Penguin Books, 2nd edn 1962).

ZORITA, ALONSO, *Life and Labour in Ancient Mexico,* trans. Benjamin Keen (New Brunswick, N.J.: Rutger University Press, 1971).

On the Aztec era much has been written both in the form of ancient chronicles and modern commentaries. In addition to Bernal Díaz del Castillo's account of the Conquest, the general reader will find the best account of Aztec history in the Heyden translation of Padre Durán. One version of Sahagún's *magnum opus,* the *Florentine Codex,* has also been translated: see under The Toltec Horizon (where the historical data of Sahagún begin).

Two excellent books by Warwick Bray and Jacques Soustelle describe the daily life of the Aztecs. George Vaillant's *Aztecs of Mexico* is a classic, though much has changed since it was written. Their history is related by the author's *The Aztecs*, as well as by Brundage. The author's *Toltec Heritage* studies in detail the confused events of the period between the fall of the Toltecs and the rise of the Aztecs, and also deals with early Aztec history.

Volume 10 of the *Handbook of Middle American Indians* (see General Summary) contains excellent articles by Henry Nicholson on Aztec sculpture and religion. León Portilla's book deals with thought and ideology; those interested in the Nahuatl language should consult Thelma Sullivan's grammar. On demography and settlement plans of Tenochtitlan, a leading authority is Edward Calnek, some of whose views are expressed in an article in Wolf's *Valley of Mexico* (see General Summary). *The Basin of Mexico* by Sanders and others, listed above, also deals in detail with these questions, both in Aztec times and before, and its bibliography is ample and up-to-date.

INDEX

Page numbers in italics refer to figures

Narváez, Pánfilo de, 190, 233
National Institute of Anthropology,
    Mexican, 25, 70–71, 75, 92, 202–3
Nayarit, 91
Negritos (Philippines), 217
Negroid peoples, 26–8
nephrite, 42
New Spain, 247–50, 253
Nezahualcoyotl, 176–9, 204, 206, 208
Nezahualpilli, 206
Niches, Pyramid of, 123
Nicholson, Henry, 220, 224
Night Sky, Lord of, 221
nomads, 111, 127, 129, 166, 251
Nonoalcas, 130, 145, 152, 155, 159
Nopaltzin, 165
numbers, cult of, 225

Oaxaca, 20, 57–8, 73, 89–90, 94, 102,
    180–81, 196
obsidian, 61, 66, 87, 96–7, 100, 103,
    126, 157
Old Crow (Yukon), 13
Olmec(s), 38–9, 63, 90, 250–52
    altars, 32, 35, 57
    antiquity, 24–5, 31, 34, 55–7, 59
    creative genius, 40–46
    culture, 19–20
    decline, 117–18
    discovery of, 22–5
    engineering, 36
    jade figurines, 42, 52
    jaguar cult, 46–51, 55
    origins, 28, 41
    population, 37, 59–60
    society, 36–40
    state and empire, 58–62, 97
    territory, 29, 30–36, 55, 58–60
    ubiquity, 51–8
    works of art, 25–8, 32, 33, 35, 39–
        57, 59–60; burial of, 32, 34–5, 48;
        destruction of, 35–6, 48, 119; see
        also mural paintings; statues; ste-
        lae; stone heads; were-jaguars
    writing and date recording, 44–6
Otomis, 166–7
Otompan (Otumba), 143
Otumba, Battle of, 191, 245–6
Oxtotitlán, 43, 44–5
Oztoma, 193–4

Pachuca region, 61, 91, 96–7, 126

Payon, José García, 123, 146
peasant revolt, 118, 251
Peten Jungle, 22, 117, 119, 155
petroglyphs, 52, 54, 55, 57
physical types, medley of, 13–14
pictographs, 238–9
plumbate, 157
Plumed Serpent, 138, 220, 223
    Pyramid of, 121
    see also Quetzalcoatl
Post-Classic era, 18, 64, 115–16, 118,
    120, 140, 147
Potrero Nuevo, 34, 40–41
    altar, 35
pottery, 17–19, 42, 59–60, 65, 119,
    129, 141, 163
    Cholula, 148, 181, 237
    Teotihuacan, 70, 76, 87, 96, 103,
        108
    Toltec, 129–32, 143, 157
    see also clay figurines
Pre-Classic era, 18, 53, 55, 64
Price, B. J., 94
priests, 98–9, 111, 119, 158, 174, 205–7
Puebla, 16, 58, 92, 148–9, 182, 188,
    237
pulque, 93, 214, 224, 240–41
Puuc culture, 151–2, 154
pyramids, 92–3, 121, 123, 147, 154
    Aztec, 232, 253
    of Sun and Moon, 67, 69, 70–72, 74,
        83, 98, 106

Quetzal Butterfly, 76, 231
Quetzalcoatl, 48, 130–31, 134–5, 138,
    151–2, 221, 222, 234, 252
    Temples of, 69–70, 75–6, 98, 112,
        129, 133, 149, 202, 233
Quetzalpapalotl Palace, 76, 77, 106
Quetzaltenango, 54
Quiche Mayas, 151–2

radiocarbon dating, 25
Rattray, Evelyn, 107
Ravitz, Ronald Grennes, 53
religion, 64, 219–31, 229–30
    Olmec, 46–51, 55
    Teotihuacan, 76, 78–84, 96, 98–9,
        106, 231
    see also gods; priests; sacrifice,
        human
Remojadas, 90–91